Four Wagons West

THE STORY OF SEATTLE

By Roberta Frye Watt

Illustrations by Paul Gustin

FOUNDED · 1891

Binford & Mort Publishing
Portland, Oregon

Library of Congress Catalog Card Number: 93-070834

ISBN: 0-8323-0045-4 (Hardcover)
ISBN: 0-8323-0294-5 (Softcover)

Seventh Printing 1993

TO MY SONS—
ROBERT, JOHN, AND RICHARD

CONTENTS

Contents—Continued

INTRODUCTION

In a chimney corner of my mother's room there was a little closet that we called "the cubby-hole." When I was a girl, the door of the closet often flew open and out would come tumbling a lot of old newspaper clippings that were crumpled and torn and yellow.

I would say, "Oh, Mother, do let me burn these old papers. They are such a bother."

Always the same answer, "No, my dear, some day I am going to paste them in a scrapbook." Then I would gather up the papers, stuff them back into the cubby-hole, and jam the door tight.

That "some day" came to Mother and those crumpled, torn papers were smoothed, pieced and pasted, numbered and catalogued. Those precious scrapbooks filled with the doings in Seattle of long ago are now numbered "One, Two, Three, Four, and Five." The cubby-hole is empty now and the door stays closed.

As those clippings of the early days were sorted and pasted, I became consciously pioneer-minded. Small wonder, for pioneer stories had been my nursery rhymes told at my mother's knee—"twice-told-tales"—many-times-told-tales.

When I grew older I realized that pioneer records from word of mouth were growing fainter each day; that first-hand memory records should be caught and preserved ere it was too late.

How happy I am that I learned to value those newspaper clippings, to which I have turned many, many times in gathering the material for this book before Mother left us, not only that she might know that I valued her painstaking efforts, but also that she might supplement their content by her personal experience. She told me many interesting things of the pioneer life of that little group at Alki of which she

vii

was one. Of some I can write and of others I cannot, for as I sat listening to her as she lived o'er again the early days, I was impressed with the sacredness of her memories of those days of struggles and triumphs. I felt that some pages of her memory-book belonged to her and to others who have gone before.

But there were some loose leaves of her memory-book that fell and I have gathered them and bound them together along with material from other sources, that those who come after may read and marvel at the heroism of those who blazed the trail.

I read my notes to a friend and she said, "Yes, interesting, but why so sad?" Then I began to think that perhaps I had omitted the comedy of pioneering. I went to an old settler and asked him to tell me of the fun they had in the early days. He looked at me for a moment and then said, as he slowly shook his head, "It wasn't funny." So, if the smiles are few, remember, it wasn't funny.

In offering this book to my readers I wish to honor all pioneers. Then, too, I have an intimate reason for writing it. I want my sons, Robert, John, and Richard, to know the part their grandparents, great-grandparents, and great-great-grandparents had in the founding and building of the city of their birth.

I think I should never have undertaken this work if my sister, Mrs. Daniel Bass, had not insisted that I do it, and put at my disposal her splendid collection of Americana.

I have been fortunate in being able to turn to the priceless diary which my grandfather, Arthur A. Denny, kept while crossing the plains, and to his *Pioneer Days on Puget Sound*; to *Blazing the Way* by my cousin, E. Inez Denny; to the letters of Catherine and David Blaine, which their son, Mr. E. L. Blaine, gave me permission to use; to Clarence Bagley's comprehensive *History of Seattle*; to the unpublished manuscript of Thomas Prosch, *A Chronological*

History of Seattle from 1850 to 1897; and to the histories of Frederick Grant, Professor Edmond S. Meany, Cornelius Hanford, and Clinton A. Snowden, and to the historical collection of the University of Washington. To all of these I am sincerely grateful.

I am further indebted to Mr. Bagley for his kindly interest and approval, and for the inestimable privilege that it has been to draw from his remarkable memory for reference and verification.

Miss Almira Bailey has been untiring in assisting me, especially with the research. Her work has been invaluable, and it is a pleasure to express my gratitude to her.

I have not tried to write a formal history; that has already been done, but I have tried to write of the romance and of the heart throbs that mingle with the sterner facts. May it be an inspiration to all when life presses hard.

CHAPTER I

THE STORY of pioneer Seattle, as it was told to me by my mother, began with the journey of four covered wagons that crossed the plains in 1851. Mother's earliest recollections went back to her childhood days in her old family home in the little town of Cherry Grove, Illinois. She remembered the family gathered around the fireside on winter evenings while her father read letters from Farley Pierce, Liberty Wallace and other venturesome souls who had gone out to Oregon to seek their fortunes; she remembered when the neighbors dropped in and discussed the news from their friends. The letters told of the wonders of the Pacific; the grandeur of the mountains; the vastness of the untouched forests; but best of all they told of the mild climate and the fertile soil and of the flowers that blossom in the winter time.

Magic words and magic letters from a magic land, they seemed to her childish mind as she sat before the fire and toasted her little toes. Many times the letters were read, then folded and put away. Then came one evening colder than usual. Grandfather had plodded home through a snow storm and after supper he took out the letters and read them again. Still holding them in his hand, he went to the window, pulled the curtain aside, and looked out, then turning to Grandmother, he asked,

"Mary, will you go?"

And Grandmother answered—"Yes, Arthur."

and so was the great decision made.

When Grandfather told his father and brothers that he and Grandmother had decided to go to Oregon, it was like a final word they had been waiting to receive. Grandfather, who will be known as Arthur Denny throughout these pages, had early learned to take the initiative and to shoulder responsibility. When a boy he cared for his in-

valid mother, going to school half a day and attending
to home duties the other half. He then taught school, and
later studied surveying, which was his chosen occupation.
He became county supervisor of Knox County, Illinois.
It may have been the lure of uncharted territory that
made him so ready to heed the call of the overland trail.
He found the others as eager as he was himself to leave
the land of hard winters for the kinder climate of the
Northwest. They would go with him and so would
Grandmother's family, the Borens. And this is how it
happened that in the year 1851, the Denny and Boren
families started west.

To decide was to act. The months following were filled
with busy preparations for the journey. Hams were cured;
blankets were woven; warm comforters made; and the
household linen replenished. The women sewed far into
the night making stout garments for themselves and the
children. Even the children's little fingers were kept busy
carding wool and piecing quilts. The cobbler came and
made shoes for the whole family. New harnesses were
bought and the wagons were provided with strong, heavy
springs.

The old homes were sold. The household goods were
scattered among friends and relatives, for only the things
that were absolutely necessary and those that could be
packed conveniently into the covered wagons were kept.
Most of the provisions were crammed into sacks to save
the weight of boxes.

It was a saying in those days that nothing must be
taken on the trail that was not worth a dollar a pound.
I doubt that Louisa Boren was particular about the value
per pound of the wall mirror that she wanted to take.
Her elders objected on account of the extra weight and
the risk of breakage. However, Louisa would have her
way; when no one was looking, she tucked it in.

The women were glad to be busy. It kept them from thinking too much of the moment that was coming when they must part from old friends and associations at Cherry Grove. One day shortly before the emigrants started, Louisa and her dearest girlhood friend, Pamelia Dunlap, visited for the last time. As they stood together in the sweet, old-fashioned garden of Edmond Dunlap, two quaint girls of the Fifties—Louisa, dark and vivacious; Pamelia, fair-haired and quiet—there came over them the realization that they might never see each other again in this world. For a little while their grief overwhelmed them. Louisa was the first to recover. She would take the sweetbriar seeds that she had gathered in this very garden, she said, and plant them at her new home. It was like a tryst that they were to keep, and somehow it comforted them.

I have been told how, when the travelers were ready to start, my grandmother walked through the empty, echoing rooms of her home for the last time with a strange feeling of unreality. For months all had worked and planned for this time of departure, which was always in the future. But now the hour, the very minute had come when she must turn her back upon her old home, old scenes, old friends—and she was unprepared. She went from room to room—out into the kitchen where she had spent so many busy hours. But there was no time to linger. She gave one tear-blurred look about the old, familiar, homely room and then passed out into the April sunshine. The barnyard was empty; the chickens were gone; even the dog was perched up in the wagon. All that was left was her flower garden, neglected of late. The very air was filled with suppressed emotion and sadness.

The children were excitedly calling her. The men were ready; so she gave one last look at the old home, one last glance at her brave flower garden, and then resolutely climbed into the wagon and took her seat beside her husband—facing west.

The men took the reins, cracked the whips, and drove through the gates for the last time. The women choked back the tears, and the men swallowed the lumps in their throats. Friends hurried to their gates to wave a last farewell, for the whole town was astir to see the Dennys and the Borens start for the West. The departing children had not been allowed to tell certain of their playmates good-bye because the latter had the whooping cough; but before anyone could stop them, they jumped from the wagons and ran and kissed their little friends through the picket fence. The procession moved slowly down the village street, wagons creaking and rumbling, with grease pots swinging at the ends.

Soon the last good-bye was called, the last handkerchief waved, the last house in town passed. Then the farm houses, one by one, were left behind. And then it was The Overland Trail to Oregon.

The party comprised Arthur Denny, his wife, Mary, and their two little girls, Louisa Catherine (my mother) and Margaret Lenora; his parents, Mr. and Mrs. John Denny with their six-weeks-old babe, Loretta; his four unmarried brothers, James, Samuel, Wiley and David; Carson Boren, his wife and small daughter, Gertrude; and Louisa Boren. These families were closely connected for John Denny, Arthur's father, having been left some years before a widower with a large family, had married Sarah Latimer Boren, the mother of Carson and Louisa Boren and of Arthur's wife, Mary. Later, in what was to be the first romance in Seattle, David Denny married Louisa Boren.

This group is known in Seattle history as the Denny party. There were other overland trains that wound their way into the settlement; the story of each belongs to

Seattle. I record the overland story of this family not because it is the story of my kith and kin, but because it is the one with which I am most familiar and is more or less typical of the experience of all the founders.

There were four wagons in this overland train: one for each family and a fourth for the four unmarried sons of John Denny, along with the provisions. Three of the wagons were drawn by four-horse teams and the other by a single span. There were also a few saddle horses, two faithful watchdogs, and a few head of cattle. Such was the caravan that took its departure one April afternoon in 1851 from the little town of Cherry Grove and began the long, weary march across the plains.

My grandfather's diary was begun on that day. The first entry reads: "Journal of the route to Oregon kept by A. A. Denny. April 10th, 1851, left home at 3 o'clock P. M."

Seven men, four women, and four children setting out alone on the great adventure that would take them through hostile Indian territory, over barren plains, and across rugged mountains! A little train of four wagons.

How did they do it? Why did they do it? I once thought that perhaps the Dennys did it because they had so little to leave behind; but after visiting some of the old homes, I knew it was not that. Something greater than themselves was urging them on; they were part of a great movement that had been going on since history began. The great army of emigrants may have thought they were seeking a new climate—new lands to conquer—or gold —but they were really the vanguards of progress.

"It would seem that manifest destiny was leading them on."

FROM ILLINOIS TO FORT LARAMIE

The four wagons crossed the Mississippi River at Burlington and continued across sparsely settled Iowa. Arthur Denny made no comments in his diary while crossing the state other than, "proceeded to Kanesville by the way of Burlington, New London, Mt. Pleasant, Fairfield Agency, Ottumwa, & Eddyville on the Des Moines River."

On the 31st of April the travelers reached the Mormon town of Kanesville (Council Bluffs) on the Missouri River. On the 5th of May, a small steamboat ferry took them across the river and they then set out on the old emigrant road that led along the north side of the Platte.

To the children it was one long holiday of camping; to the women it was heartache for what they were leaving; to the men it meant anxiety and responsibility. During the first weeks they tried to live, as nearly as possible, as they had been accustomed. They spread a white cloth at meal time; at night they undressed and put on white nightgowns, and lay down between linen sheets in neatly made beds. But one night after they had crossed the Missouri River, a terrific thunderstorm came up, blew down their tents, and tore the tops off the wagons. Everything and everybody was drenched. It took several days to make repairs, dry out their provisions, and repack. Thereafter, they generally tumbled into bed in the easiest way.

Arthur Denny frequently mentions the weather in his diary while crossing the present state of Nebraska. He had reason to be weather-minded, it seems, for he wrote. "This Platte country is the most remarkable country for sudden storms I ever knew." The emigrant was at the mercy of the weather. In the record of May 10th, we find, "Had the most disagreeable night I ever experienced, it being my turn to stand guard, & it rained heavily with a strong gale of wind."

In the entry of the following day, just two words— "Water bound"—tell the story. Later we find this comment:

Road good & weather fine until about 3 o'clock when we had a hail storm which lasted but for a few minutes during which time there was the greatest confusion & everyone had enough to do to look to his own team & but little time to look at others; at one time I had almost given up my 2 horse team containing the family & nearly all the other valuables I possessed.

However, despite discomfort and disillusionment, those first weeks in May on the westward trail were weeks of novelty and adventure, especially to young David Denny and his unmarried brothers. On May 7th, the diary reads. "This evening we had the first stampede caused by the horses taking fright at Indians while feeding . . . . . Indians camped in two hundred yards." Many times the keen sense of smell of the horses and cattle caused them to give warning that Indians were near long before their drivers were aware. On May 23rd, "the boys brought in a fine young deer," and three days later, David and Carson Boren supplied the travelers with their first buffalo meat.

The travelers "passed numerous dog towns & saw plenty of antelope." The little dogs perched upon their mounds and the rattlesnakes about were one of Mother's most distinct memories. In Joel Palmer's *Journal of Travels Across the Rocky Mountains* [1847], long since out of print, the author speaks of a dog town along the banks of the Platte that occupied nearly three hundred acres. Then, as now, the little creatures chose strange bedfellows, for he writes: "It is singular but true that the little screech owl and the rattlesnake keep them company in their burrows."

What a friend and what a guide the Platte River was to the little band, like the pillars of cloud and of fire to the Israelites in their journey to the Promised Land. Sometimes the travelers even drove in the river bed and once, for six miles, they drove along an island in its midst. The river furnished water, which was muddy but safe to drink. They drank it, dirt and all, when there was no time to let it settle. The river furnished fuel, willow and cottonwood, that grew on its banks; it gave them a camping place; it was a guide, a roadbed, a water and fuel supply, and a resting place. Arthur Denny writes again and again, "camped on the river"—"drove on the river bottom"—"waded for willows for fuel." And finally on Friday, June 13th, he records, "camped on the river perhaps for the last time." Another friend to be left behind.

The Platte, known among the emigrants as "the river that was a mile wide and a foot deep," was not a difficult river to ford provided they kept moving after they had once started, because the river bed was full of quicksand. One precaution was to water the horses well before starting, so that they would not be tempted to stop to drink while crossing. The men waded across pushing and guiding the wagons as they went. I remember hearing Mother tell how Uncle Dobbins—as they called my great uncle. Carson Boren—stopped in midstream for some reason and was starting to sink with his load when the others yelled frantically at him to keep moving.

A great event in the monotonous journey across the treeless miles was the first glimpse of the Rocky Mountains. These prairie-dwellers had never seen mountains and thought that they would be immense hills which could easily be climbed on one side and as easily descended on the other, after which they would be in Oregon and could see the Pacific Ocean. At last they saw them; almost a month before they were to cross the summit.

For days and then weeks the emigrants strained toward them—dream mountains, sometimes lost in drifting clouds. They caught the flame of sunset, held the blue of twilight, beautiful beyond all the travelers' dreams. Nor was the beauty destroyed as the little band began to climb, for the grade was gradual and easy at first.

What unsung heroes were the faithful animals that strained and pulled the heavy, creaking emigrant wagons day after day! They, too, were valiant pioneers. Providing them with water and forage became almost the first consideration, for the overlanders were helpless without them.

Grass and water and roads to travel, the care of the stock, the responsibility of the very lives of his loved ones; that was what the journey meant to Arthur Denny and what he recorded day by day. Picture a tall, sandy-haired man sitting on the wagon seat, always looking ahead, facing the same old questions each new day. Water? Grass? Fuel? Camp? And at night crouched on the ground writing in his diary in the flickering light of the camp fire, too tired to write much, but recording the supply, or its lack—that was his brief story of the journey.

But the long, weary hours between the stops for grass and water and camp, when jolting along, are the unrecorded ones that were felt more keenly by the women. For hours at a time there was the sound of the crack of the whip; the creak of the wagons; the thud of the hoofs; the cry of a fretful child, perhaps; and the crooning of a tired mother. The women were relieved, no doubt, when the train halted to camp; but then the back-aching and discouraging work of cooking and washing without conveniences, and the many other duties that fell to their lot devolved upon them.

For days they went without sufficient water of any kind; often what they had was so alkaline that it could not be used. Hands and faces became rough and grimy with dirt; tongues and throats were parched, and lips cracked.

The women became experts in quick cooking. They learned how to mix biscuits in the top of a sack of flour by wetting just enough flour for immediate use, and then tying the sack up again for the next hurried stop. According to Arthur Denny's journal, on May the 26th, they "moved 4 miles to a willow island in order to bake bread and prepare for our journey over the plains." That sounds as if it was real bread they baked. One can fancy the tiny loaves that were unquestionably baked for the children, and their high glee when that incomparable smell of fresh bread floated out over the prairie.

On the whole, the travelers were well provided with food, with the exception of fresh vegetables and fruits. The dried fruit gave out and the fate of the last pailful of peaches was vivid in the memory of one of the little girls. The peaches had been saved as a special treat. When it seemed that the dry food could be endured no longer, the peaches were cooked. The children stood around and sniffed and wrinkled their little noses as they watched while the fruit was cooking. It smelled so good they could hardly wait for supper. When the peaches were done, the pan was carefully set on a wagon tongue to cool but, alas, someone spilled them over into the sand. The women scooped them up and tried to save them, but the sand could not be washed off. The loss to the hungry children was a real tragedy. Mary Denny's heart ached when she saw her little girls' sober faces, and her thoughts turned back to the home they had left where there had been plenty. Such incidents made it hard for her to turn her thoughts resolutely from the past and look straight ahead.

The spirit of adventure was not so strong in the women. They had been contented in the old homes; they had taken pride in their household affairs—their quilting, their spinning and weaving, their rows of pickles, jellies, jams and apple butter. They did not long for new worlds to conquer. They came West because their men came. These were the times of unshed tears, of brave smiles in spite of homesick hearts. It was the old, old story of the woman following her man.

So the prairie schooners ploughed their way, day after day, first across the long unsheltered miles of trackless prairie, which gave place to the seemingly endless stretches of sands. The monotonous days lengthened into weeks. The sun beat down upon them with its relentless heat; the flowers and grass withered; the earth became hard and parched; the horses jogged along with heads hanging. Sometimes when the heat became unbearable the train rested during the day and traveled at night. On moonlit nights, weird and lonely were the shadows the four wagons cast as they crept along in the silence and mystery of the night.

Beside the road, worn by many wheels that had gone before, stretched the footpath of the ox drivers, a path that told its mute story of footsore travelers who had walked while urging on their teams. Household goods that other trains had abandoned in order to lighten their loads were scattered along the way. Crockery, some favorite family bureau, feather beds, mirrors. Often there were signs attached—"Help yourself." Along the roadside lay the whitening bones of stock that had died. On either side of the trail were newly made graves—graves of travelers whose hopes had been perhaps as high as theirs. At one time the Dennys came to the grave of some lone pilgrim where they sang that plaintive old song:

I came to the place,
Where the white pilgrim lay,
And pensively stood by his tomb,
When in a low whisper I heard something say,
"How sweetly I sleep here alone."

This must have been at some place where they made camp for the night, for they had little time to stop, even for a tribute to the dead.

One pioneer woman of Seattle, of another train, tells of passing a tiny mound with a little pink sunbonnet hanging on a stick at the head of the grave. Even after the passing of so many years, our eyes are dimmed at the thought of that mother, sitting in the back of the covered wagon, watching the tiny bonnet grow smaller and smaller—like a pink anemone waving in the breeze—until at last it passed out of her sight forever.

Fortunately our little band escaped without a single casualty. They were spared the horrors of the cholera which swept through the trains the following years and claimed many victims.

They were not entirely free from sickness, however. To add to the worry and discomfort of Mary Denny, who was expecting her third child in a few months, Lenora and Catherine developed whooping cough as a result of the kisses stolen through the picket fence.

The four wagons sometimes passed other trains—longer trains perhaps—and sometimes other trains passed them. They met none. One that passed them was the John Low Company which they overtook and joined forces with later on.

On June the 6th, thirty-two days after crossing the Missouri River, the Denny party reached Fort Laramie, five hundred and thirty miles distant.

ON TO OREGON

Further incidents of the trail of the four wagons, recorded on the precious leaves of Mother's memory-book, come to my mind. Some are faded and obscure; but they are bits—scraps, if you will, that tell the story of that journey, or better, soften the story with its stark outline of breaking camp—the morning start—the pushing ahead through the day—the halt—the making camp—the night watch—the same thing the next day, only a little harder, a little wearier.

Before starting out in the morning these west-bound emigrants of '51 consulted their guidebook as the ardent motorist does today. Mother remembered distinctly Grandfather's frequently consulting one. I am not certain which he used. We have a transcript of a quaint one printed in 1846: "Route and Distances to Oregon and California, with a description of watering places, crossings, dangerous Indians, etc., etc." by J. M. Shively.

Let me quote one bit from it, which is not unlike the motor vernacular of today: "When you start over these wide plains, let no one leave dependent on his best friend for anything; for, if you do, you will have a blowout before you get far."

At the end of a long day, how the children welcomed their only romping-time, the halt at night. Tired of riding or trotting along in the dust beside the wagons, they could hardly wait for evening to come. But even the children had their tasks; they sometimes had to pick up buffalo chips for fuel when there was no other to be had along the barren prairies.

One evening when the travelers had stopped for the night, my mother and her sister spied a sand pile and were starting toward it when they were called back and told not to go away from the wagon. But the temptation was too great. The sand was in such a nice pile and they had had no fun all day; so while supper was being prepared, away they went. No sooner had they dug their fingers and toes into the sand, than they were covered with big, black ants—the kind that bite. Their screams brought their elders running and supper was forgotten while everybody picked ants off the screaming children.

The friendly camphor bottle was brought out and both smarting bodies rubbed with camphor, and the whimpering little girls put to bed. They learned their lesson well, for after that, no matter how tempting the sand pile or pretty the flower, they never wandered from the wagons without permission.

We still have the old crooked-necked camphor bottle. I can remember Mother showing it to me and telling me "a true story" about two little girls who "did not mind" and what happened.

I wish I could remember more about the travelers' stop at the famous Independence Rock—that huge rock on the Sweetwater River in Wyoming, 660 feet long, 100 feet wide, and 60 to 70 feet above the plain. It was the pioneers' directory—the "Great Register of the Desert"— indeed a "rock in a weary land," whereon each pilgrim searched for messages from dear ones or for the name of someone they knew who had passed that way. It was the place where they chiseled or painted their names or left messages for those who followed, sometimes using for paint, tar from the old tar bucket. What joy and happiness that rock has given! What disappointment and sorrow! On its face the weary wayfarer has read pathos, romance and tragedy. It was more than a directory; it was history carved in enduring stone.

When our pioneers stopped at Independence Rock, the children, of course, wanted to have their names inscribed thereon. There is a faded memory-picture of Louisa Boren's helping them; but how she did it no one is left to remember. It is a dear picture to me—the little sunbonneted group marking their names somehow on the face of the great rock.

The travelers followed the Sweetwater River toward its source. On June 21st they reached the mountain summit at South Pass. At that time, it will be remembered, the Rocky Mountains formed the eastern boundary of Oregon Territory; so when they reached the summit, they were facing Oregon. How happy they were! They swung their hats and sunbonnets and shouted, "This is Oregon! Hurrah for Oregon!"

Poor, weary little band! They were not at the end of the journey yet; there were still weeks of painful and toilsome climbing ahead.

The nights were cold and snow still lingered in places; but the days were warm and the first mountain flowers were beginning to bloom.

Another milestone of the journey was Soda Springs on the Great Bear River. What a welcome diversion it was! The older members of the party had little time for the wonders but the younger ones were fascinated. To their amazement the springs threw up boiling hot water in one place and cold in another. My mother remembered distinctly the intermittent "puff, puff" of Steamboat Springs. She also remembered that one of the group burned her mouth by drinking from a hot spring, thinking it was cold. The Daniel Bagley party, which came a year later, drove their tired horses in to water them and were surprised to see the animals snort and rear. They had driven them into a hot spring.

At this stop David Denny and Louisa went fishing in the river. The trout they caught and the wonderful meal they had were outstanding incidents of the journey.

A few miles beyond Soda Springs, the trail divided, one branch turning toward California, the other toward Oregon. Here the emigrants were met by guides from California urging them to the south and its gold fields. Our party paused at the crossroads. In which direction did fortune await them? Which way? South to the gold of California or north to the green of Oregon?

They did not hesitate long. Remembering the wonderful tales of the great, rolling Oregon Territory; the mild climate; the forests; the rivers; the green grass and flowers—all of which seemed to them like the Promised Land

—they turned their faces to the north and west and kept on on the Oregon Trail. They were pioneers, not adventurers, not gold-seekers.

The train was now approaching Fort Hall in Southern Idaho. None of us today can quite appreciate what a haven Fort Hall was to the emigrants crossing the plains. It was a Hudson's Bay station surrounded by a heavy wall and marked the end of the definite and traveled trail. At Fort Hall, most of the emigrants stopped for a day or so and reorganized their trains and, warned of the greater difficulties ahead, discarded every nonessential bit of their goods. There were acres of abandoned household goods, wagons, and parts of wagons. If a traveler saw a better wagon than his own, he exchanged or perhaps reinforced his with a different wheel. Provisions for the remainder of the trip could be bought and, if desired, guides procured.

It was a fitting coincidence that the four wagons reached this important stop on the Fourth of July. But the Dennys did not linger. So economically had they packed that it was not necessary to discard anything, not even Louisa's mirror. The superintendent of the fort gave them valuable advice as to camping places and water supply. He advised them on no account to stop at the call of Indians, as unfriendly Shoshones were on the trail.

A few days after leaving Fort Hall the party almost had an unwelcome gift of some ponies. One evening while they were making camp for the night a lone Indian made his appearance and hung about the camp until dark and then disappeared. That night a close watch was kept by the one on guard. Nothing unusual happened; but early in the morning while the women were preparing breakfast an Indian rode up with a string of ponies which he wanted to trade for Louisa Boren. He was so angry and persistent on being refused that Louisa became frightened for fear he would snatch her and run away. She hid herself in one of the covered wagons while young David Denny stood guard. Camp was quickly broken that morning and the travelers drove away at a good smart pace with the Indian and ponies following. Finally he gave up the chase and turned back.

The overlanders traveled all that day along the south side of the Snake River and camped that night at American Falls. The next morning they made an early start. It was a peaceful summer Sunday morning. Across the river they could see an encampment of Indians but felt no uneasiness. The falls were extremely beautiful. They were enjoying the sight, when below them in the river, they saw what they had supposed were ducks suddenly turn into Indians, who rushed up the river bank toward them, pretending that they wanted to trade.

The leader, who must have been lying in wait for them behind some rocks, approached. He was a tall Indian, wearing a silk hat and a long, swallow-tailed coat—nothing else. His costume would have been ludicrous had one not wondered as to the fate of the original owner of the hat and coat.

"How-de-do! How-de-do! Stop! Stop!" he called to the pioneers.

But they had been warned. They whipped up their horses and hurried on. Indians from behind rocks and sagebrush opened fire. The travelers could hear the bullets and arrows whistle past, see the smoke puffs, see the dust fly where the bullets hit the ground; but fortunately none of our party or their horses were struck. The frightened women and children huddled in the bottom of the wagons. Mother remembered looking out—a curious little girl of six who wanted to see what was happening—and being pulled back just in time to be saved from an arrow.

Great-grandfather, John Denny, a veteran of the War

of 1812, objected very seriously to running away from the
Indians. He had never run away from anything or anybody in his life and his sons had a lively time persuading
him that it was the wise thing to do at this time.

The drivers could see ahead and realized that other
Indians were crossing and running down the river toward
the mouth of a ravine which they were approaching. The
trail ahead led down one bank of this ravine and up another. They realized that there was just one thing to do
—to get down the bank and up on the other side before
the Indians reached it.

They whipped up the horses, which snorted and
plunged ahead over the rough trail. Down the steep bank
they rushed, the great wagons rocking crazily without
locks or brakes, while the terrified children clung to their
mothers. If an axle had broken or a linchpin loosened, the
founding of Seattle would read different, for the little
band of seven men would have been no match for what
proved to be a band of armed Indians.

The travelers reached the bottom of the ravine and
with desperate energy hurried up the opposite bank. My
great-grandmother, Sarah Denny, took the reins and laid
on the lash so that the men in that wagon could be ready
with their rifles. At the top, when they had gained an
advantageous position, they halted to open fire, but the
Indians were careful to keep out of range. They then gave
up the chase. All that day the pioneers did not slacken
their speed to the usual pace.

A few weeks after this, a family by the name of Clark
was ambushed and massacred in this same ravine and, no
doubt, by the same band that had so nearly intercepted
our four wagons.

After traveling until late that night, the pioneers saw
before them what was undoubtedly one of the happiest
sights on their whole journey—the friendly, welcome

light of a camp fire. It was that of the John M. Low Company, who, it will be remembered, had passed the Denny train some time previously. There on the banks of the Snake River they made camp for the night. Guards were posted and the women prepared the delayed evening meal.

The women of the two parties evidently did not meet until the following morning, for Mrs. Low said afterward that the first time she saw the women of the Denny party they were frying cakes over the camp fire for breakfast. When the two companies compared notes they found that the Lows had crossed the Missouri just two days ahead of the Dennys and had traveled along the south bank of the Platte while the latter were on the north.

The two parties joined forces at this time and traveled together to the journey's end. There were six men and two women in the Low train, besides some stock; so the caravan was now of considerable length. Fortunately, too, for the hardest part of the journey lay ahead.

We are indebted to Ezra Meeker, grand old pioneer, who crossed the plains westward for the first time in 1852 at the age of twenty-two, for reminding us of what that trip across the continent once was. In 1906, he retraced this old Oregon trail by covered wagon for the purpose of arousing interest in permanently marking the emigrant road. Ready response to his efforts resulted in the placing of the markers that one may see today along the course of "America's Greatest Trail," which is paralleled much of the distance by a railroad and by an automobile highway known as "The Old Oregon Trail."

When I have made the trip East in Pullman comfort, I have tried to picture that little train of four wagons that crept so slowly across the sands. I have tried to realize some of the hardships endured by those brave men and women who crossed the continent and helped found a city on Puget Sound.

I have thought of two little girls who made that trip long ago. One of them lost her shoes; so they took turns wearing the remaining pair. To relieve the tedium of the journey, they frequently got out and walked. One would run barefoot in the hot sand as long as she could and then stand with her feet in the shade of sagebrush until her sister came up with the shoes. Then she would take the shoes and the other little girl would literally hotfoot it over the sands until she, too, had to cool her feet. One of these girls was my mother. I asked her why they did not sit down and rest, and she said, "Why, my dear, it was too hot."

ARRIVING AT PORTLAND

On went the pioneers through what is now southern Idaho and eastern Oregon. Progress was hazardous. Fording swift mountain streams was very different from fording the quieter rivers of the plains. It was very difficult. Their usual procedure was to calk the wagon beds with tar and tallow, and push or pull them across as if they were scows. Frequently men and animals had to swim.

I have heard the men tell of one experience that provoked laughter years afterwards, but not then. One of the wagon bodies was not loaded heavily enough and went floating off. By quick work and tremendous effort it was replaced, and the wagon guided to the opposite shore.

The Blue Mountains were decidedly more difficult to cross than the Rockies. Beautiful in the distance, they soon became stern realities. Soft contours vanished; huge crags and steep walls—rough, rugged, and cruel—exacted every ounce of the travelers' strength and endurance. Even today the trees along the old trail bear mute scars made by the chains that were passed around the trunks to act as brakes for the heavy wagons of pioneer trains.

If only these emigrants could have had the most difficult traveling when their spirits and bodies were fresh.

But not so. Furthermore, they were seized with the dread mountain fever. Exhausted, grimy, ill. Was it they who had started out so blithely, resolving to sleep between sheets every night?

We get very little of all of this hardship from Arthur Denny's diary. There are few comments, only brief, hurriedly written notations that in themselves look tired and anxious.

"Thursday (July) 24th. Camped on Burnt River," is all he wrote of that momentous stop at that time; but in later years he wrote:

On leaving home for what we called the Pacific Coast, we had no other purpose than to settle in the Willamette Valley. But we met a man on Burnt River by the name of Brock who lived in Oregon City and had come out expecting to meet some friends, failing in which he turned and came back to The Dalles. He gave us information in regard to Puget Sound and called attention to the fact that it was about as near to the Sound from where we first struck the Columbia River, now known as Umatilla Landing, as it was to Portland, but as yet there was no road over the mountains by which it could be reached. My attention was thus turned to the Sound and I formed the purpose of looking in that direction.

So while they "camped on Burnt River" the course of the destiny of the four-wagon pioneers veered, and seeds of desire for exploring the Puget Sound country were planted in Arthur Denny's mind. I like to picture those two men about the camp fire, one eagerly telling of the inland sea and forested land to the north waiting to be claimed, while the other as eagerly listened. The claims in the rich Willamette Valley were at this time well taken up; but to the north there were new worlds to conquer, no farther from Umatilla Landing than was the Willamette Valley, but separated from the Landing by the Cascade Mountains. But mountains could be conquered.

At Burnt River the travelers met a train of Indians moving their families. With grim Indian humor, one of them remarked, "Heap sleep now. We good Indians."

Perhaps he had heard of the attack at American Falls, or, perhaps, he saw the look of fear on the white men's faces.

On July the 30th, the tired travelers were refreshed by the fragrance of the evergreens—that inimitable fragrance that spells home in the Northwest to many of us. Grandfather's comment on that day reads, "Over mountains and through a heavy pine forest which is delightful after traveling so long over barren deserts."

On August the 1st they "Camped on the Umatilla bottom about 5 miles after striking it." Here were Indians who had been taught by the white man how to grow vegetables, and one of the pioneer women gladly exchanged a calico apron for a mess of green peas.

Friendly Indians with fresh salmon to sell frequently went out to meet the incoming pioneer trains as they neared the Columbia River. The Denny party had bought dried salmon at the Snake River, but Mr. Low wanted some fresh fish. He was afraid to stop and trade; so without stopping he pulled his shirt off over his head, threw it at an Indian, and snatched the fish. The trade proved to be satisfactory, for our party found their first taste of fresh salmon delicious. They were amazed at its enormous size. Mother remembered that the only receptacle large enough to hold the fish was the washtub.

Another week of hurried notations records their progress along the Columbia, often in sight of the river but high above it. It was an extremely wearisome journey. Frequently, it was necessary for every one to get out and walk while the wagons were lifted and dragged over the boulders in the trail.

At last on August 11th they reached The Dalles, which was as much of a milestone as Fort Hall had been. In *Pioneer Days on Puget Sound*, Arthur Denny wrote years afterward, "The estimated distance from the Missouri River to The Dalles is 1765 miles—eighty days' travel,

entire time 97 days, and to Portland 108 days." An
average of eighteen miles a day—very good time, according to covered-wagon standards.

The pioneers made a decided change in plans at The
Dalles. Low, Boren, and Arthur Denny chartered two
boats to take their families and part of their "plunder"—
the emigrant name for baggage—down the river. One of
their reasons was to spare Mary Denny the rough journey
over the mountain pass. The teams and stock were to be
sent over the Cascade Mountains by way of Barlow's
Pass in charge of the other men.

All was activity; unpacking, separating, and repacking;
some for the wagons, some for the boats. Of that day,
Mr. Denny wrote: "Monday 11th. To Dalles on the
Columbia and prepared for the water route. Started just
at dark. At about 4 miles we had to land and lie on the
shore till morning in consequence of the boat leaking."
What volumes in one short paragraph!

The travelers stumbled up the river bank in the dark,
dragging the sleepy children, and then somehow made a
bed. During the night, little Gertrude Boren, a child of
three, rolled down the sloping bank almost into the water
before her mother caught her. In the morning they saw a
rattlesnake neatly coiled near where they had lain in the
night; so, although it was a dreadful night, it might have
been worse.

The diary continues: "Tuesday 12th. Stopped the leak
and set sail and had to turn in at the mouth of a creek in
about half an hour in consequence of wind. Laid up until
sunset. Started and ran until 12 o'clock.

"Wednesday 13th. Ran down to the Narrows at Wind
mountain and stopped for wind to lay.

"Thursday 14th. Started at daylight; ran 2 or 3 miles
and stopped in consequence of wind; started again about
3 o'clock, stopped at 4 miles.

"Friday 15th. Laid up the principal part of day."
So near their goal and then to be obliged to wait a whole
day on the river bank.

However, someone in the party used this enforced wait
to go hunting for they needed a change of diet, since by
this time they were tired of salmon. The hunter's bag—a
sage hen—was never to be forgotten. They had had sage
hens before but never one like this one. It also had eaten
too much salmon and was so fishy they could not eat it.

The emigrants were now nearing the Cascades. We
read that on "Sat. 16" they "Started in the middle of the
night and ran down to the landing and took the handcar
on the portage 2 miles to the next point for shipping."

The details of that midnight ride in one of the boats
were supplied in later years by Louisa Boren. She and the
other women and children were in the larger of the boats.
Wearied, most of them were asleep curled up as best they
could on top of their plunder; but Louisa was wakeful
and uneasy.

From the time they started the boatmen had been passing a bottle among themselves which they called "Blue
Ruin." A good name it was, for it nearly proved the ruin
of all of them. "Keep 'er goin'," they kept singing fool-
ishly.

It was nearing midnight and the river was lighted by
a waning moon. The solitary watcher noticed foam out in
midstream and a distant hum caught her ears. The boatman continued to pass the bottle and sing, "Keep 'er
goin'." The hum grew louder. Soon the waters began to
roar, and Louisa realized all at once that they were nearing the rapids.

She called to the crew to stop. They paid no heed. She
frantically called her sister, "Mary, Mary, wake up. We
are nearing the falls. I hear them roar, and the men don't
know what they are doing."

She climbed over the luggage, tugged at the boatmen, and begged them to pull for the shore.

They answered, "What's all the fuss about? There ain't no danger, Miss. Keep 'er goin'."

Her strong, young arms grasped one of the men by the shoulder and shook him. "Oh, man," she cried, "Don't you hear the falls? Look! Turn the boat to shore! Hurry or it will be too late."

Apparently not so drunk as the others, he awoke at last to the danger and said, "My God, men, the gal is right. Make for the shore quick, none of us want to be drowned." They pulled for the shore, and landed safely some distance below the usual landing place. All were drenched. They built a fire, hung their wet clothing and blankets on the bushes to dry, and camped there the rest of the night. In the morning they had a thrilling story to tell the men, who had had no such eventful trip in their boat.

Here at the Cascades were the first real houses that the travelers had seen since crossing the Missouri River. There had been only traders' tents at The Dalles.

F. A. Chenoweth—later a judge in Washington Territory—had had the enterprise to begin building a tramroad for the transfer of freight and passengers around the rapids. The baggage of our party "was the first freight to pass over the tramroad and was taken over on a car by hand." There was no accommodation for passengers at this time, so the emigrants had to walk to the lower end of the rapids. Here they camped for the night ready to board the *Henry* in the morning.

The *Henry* was an old brig—"no longer fit to go to sea"—which Chenoweth was running between Portland and the Cascades. She had been a carrier of salt, salmon, and other freight, and had no accommodations for passengers. The children were tied to the mast to keep them from falling overboard, for there were no bulwarks. Beds were made below on barrels of fish. The travelers lay down but not to sleep, for the mosquitoes were thick and hungry and the beds like a corduroy road. One woman complained a little at the hardness of her bed, and her husband said, after investigating, "It's nothing but the tea kettle wedged in between the barrels."

Another woman lost her moccasins overboard and, having worn out her shoes on the way, had to continue in stockinged feet.

The trip on the *Henry* was not a pleasure trip. We can feel the tediousness of it from the following entries:

"Tuesday 19th. Wind unfavorable but made some progress."

"Wednesday 20th. Reached Fort Vancouver and lay aground all day. Cleared and anchored in the mouth of the Willamette. Rain tonight."

The next day the emigrants grew tired of lying aground so near to Portland and we read, "Thursday 21st. Lay aground 3 miles below Portland. Left the brig. Lodged at Mr. Guiles."

"Friday (August) 22nd. Footed it up to Portland." Thus ends the diary.

On August 22, 1851, the weary travelers reached Portland, then a town of two thousand people. In one hundred and thirty-four days—almost four months—they had traveled a distance now covered easily in sixty hours by train, or in nineteen hours by airplace. Their journey's end, one would think, considering that when they started out they had expected to settle in the Willamette Valley.

But their joy on reaching Oregon was short-lived, for most of the party were stricken with ague, shaking with chills one day, and burning with fever the next. It came so closely upon their attack of mountain fever that they were laid low in both spirit and body.

This malady, added to their restlessness after the long journey, made their stay in Portland a time of discontent and longing for the trail. They had been gypsies so long that they wished themselves back in the covered wagons bumping and grinding along. They had traveled weary days and nights; they had borne both heat and cold; they had faced hunger and even death; but there had always been the hope of better times—of better places—of another day—another camp. Over the plains—over the mountains—Oregon and rest! Instead, this—malaria, homesickness, and the urge to move on—but where?

Then Arthur Denny remembered with renewed interest what the man at Burnt River had told him concerning the wonderful country and inland sea to the north. He also heard from Hudson's Bay men and prospectors glowing accounts of the same region. His attention was thus again directed toward Puget Sound, and he determined to look in that direction, for the more he heard, the more he felt that that was their destination, and he was eager to push on. But he was doomed to disappointment and delay, for the ague held him prisoner until late in the fall and defeated all his plans for immediate exploration of the north country.

An amusing story with a note of pathos is told of that trying time. Arthur Denny and his wife shook from ague on alternate days. On his free day Mr. Denny would supply his wife with wood and water and food enough to last over his sick day. Thus they took turns caring for each other and for their family. Miserable as they were, they saw the humor of the situation and smilingly said they were always glad to share with each other, even the ague.

CHAPTER II

ALKI

WHILE THE OTHERS suffering from the ague remained in
Portland, John Low and David Denny, on September 10.
1851, started north on an exploring trip. Their immediate
object was to find winter range for Low's cattle. Later they
intended to go on to the Puget Sound country, which they
had heard so much about.

They drove the stock over to Ford's Prairie on the Chehalis River and then struck out for Olympia, which was a
little settlement of about a dozen cabins, a post office, and
customhouse, Olympia at that time being the port of entry.

Over two hundred miles of winding trail! From Portland
to Olympia by foot! How easily we say it! Carrying their
blankets and provisions upon their backs, along the Indian
and trappers' trail they walked, over logs, under logs, not
knowing what a crack of a twig might portend or what lay
beyond yonder trees.

In Olympia the explorers met Lee Terry, a New Yorker.
who was also anxious to see the country. The three made
arrangements to take an exploring trip about the Sound with
Captain Robert C. Fay, who was just starting out in his
open boat to buy salmon from the Indians to salt for the
San Francisco market.

On the afternoon of September 25th, they landed at
Skwudux, on the eastern side of the peninsula of West Seattle, where the ferry used to land. Here they found a number of Indians camped, fishing for salmon, among them
Chief Sealth—later called Seattle—chief of the Duwamish
and Suquamish Indian tribes. It is significant that he was
standing on that shore to welcome his strange white brothers, who afterward took his name into their keeping and
wrote it on the pages of history. The old chief and his
braves seemed friendly; so the travelers spent the night
there under a large cedar tree.

The next morning, Terry, Low, and David Denny hired two of Sealth's young Indians to take them up the Duwamish in a little, tippy, dugout canoe, leaving Captain Fay to cruise around the Bay to see what he could do about buying salmon.

The morning was clear and beautiful with the tang of fall in the air. The dark firs encircled the Bay to the water's edge; the sky line was the silhouette of the forest; over the tops of the trees, just ahead of them. Mount Rainier towered majestic and aloof, while back of them was the panorama of the Olympics. The water was smooth, the paddles dipped, and the canoe sped along in the stillness and beauty. Soon it entered the mouth of the Duwamish and ascended the river between age-old firs and cedars, which crowded the banks and made the water dark and shadowy. A few miles upstream brought the party to the edge of a prairie where Low and Terry landed and then set out on an Indian trail through the woods to look at the country. David Denny waited in the canoe with the Indians.

An hour passed and the explorers did not return, then two and three and still they did not come. The sun went down and the air was chill. David became more and more alarmed; he shouted himself hoarse and then fired his gun, but there was no answering shout or shot. Slowly he and the Indians returned down the river, now gloomy and sinister between the walls of trees. It had grown dark; so they landed and camped at what was afterward known as Maple Prairie. There was no sleep for David that night, for it was an anxious time for this young boy, not knowing the fate of his friends and uncertain of his own.

At daybreak the Indians took him up the river again in search of his friends whom, to David's great joy, they met coming down in a canoe. The two men had had their troubles too, for they had been lost in the woods until they came to an Indian camp at the junction of the Black and

Duwamish Rivers, where they spent the night. The next morning these Indians had piloted them back to meet the anxious David. Happily reunited they all returned to Skwu-dux, the starting point, where they found Captain Fay awaiting them, and where they again prepared to spend the night under the cedar tree near Chief Sealth's camp.

That evening as they sat in the afterglow of the sunset. the sound of voices came from the water—white men's voices, and white women's voices, too. Could it be true? Or was it their imagination? Going down to the water's edge they saw a scow being poled along around Duwamish Head. Seeing white men on the beach, the men on the scow stopped offshore for a visit.

He gave his name as Luther Collins and told them that he was on his way up the Duwamish to the claims which he and three other men had located. He had just been down to Olympia for his family and household goods. His wife and daughter had learned some Chinook and laughingly conversed in the jargon with Captain Fay. Collins spoke glowingly of the Duwamish Valley as a fine location for settlers.

But it was growing dark and all too soon the scow moved on, entered the river, and disappeared from view, leaving our four explorers standing on the beach. They then rolled up in their blankets and spent a second night under the big cedar tree.

The three men who had taken up claims with Collins were Henry Van Asselt, Jacob Maple and his son, Samuel. Collins had been in "Northern Oregon"—as that part of the Oregon Territory north of the Columbia River was called—before coming to the Duwamish Valley and had taken a section of land at Nisqually. He then went to the California gold fields and on his return he fell in with these other men on their way to the Willamette Valley from the gold fields. An old account tells of their meeting thus:

"Collins being a frank, open-hearted man, fond of talk, frequently told stories of the grand country on the Sound, the clams and oysters of the bay, the delightful climate, and the wild fruit and fowl and fish." Since his description was so glowing, he prevailed upon the others to investigate Puget Sound before settling in the Willamette Valley.

Van Asselt, a thrifty Hollander who had been in this country only four years, was not impressed with the Puget Sound country along the Nisqually River, and intended to return to the Willamette Valley when Collins told him and the others of a river valley "forty miles down the Sound among the Duwamish Indians," and suggested their investigating it. This they did in June. And, according to Frederick Grant in *The History of Seattle*, "on reaching the river, the party found it to be a full stream with extensive meadow lands or bottoms of the most fertile soil having certain grassy prairies." All of them liked the place and returned and staked their claims September 14, 1851. Van Asselt and the Maples then returned to the Willamette Valley to make preparations to move, and Collins went back to the Nisqually River to sell his claim. It was after selling his claim, and while on his way back to the Duwamish with his wife and daughter that he was hailed by David Denny and the others as he was passing Skwudux. His wife and their daughter, Lucinda, described as "a bright girl of fourteen," were thus the first white women in King County.

Collins chose for his claim the land that is today Georgetown. He had no way of knowing at the time that the year before this same land had been tentatively chosen by John Holgate, a boy of nineteen. Jacob Maple chose his claim south of Collins; beyond his came Samuel Maple's; and farthest up the river, Van Asselt's. Each claim had a good river frontage and extended up the hill to the east. The river has been straightened since then, and their exact water front cannot now be defined. The present municipal airport includes part of the Maple claims.

The settlement on the Duwamish was the first in King County. The boundaries of the City of Seattle have been extended until now they include these claims; but, for years. they were miles from the city. I doubt that the most visionary pioneer dreamed that Seattle would ever include the Duwamish farms.

The next morning after their meeting with Collins, our little party moved camp to what the Indians called "Smaquamox," known today as Alki. Low and Terry liked the place so well that they decided to locate permanently and lay off a townsite.

It is easy to understand why they were attracted to Alki; the land sloped gradually to the water with a sandy, gravelly beach. It seems to have been the only open and level space in the dense forest where they could build homes, and at the same time be close to where any sailing craft might pass.

Captain Fay was returning at once to Olympia; and Low. who left with him to go back for his family, hired David Denny and Lee Terry to build him a cabin.

Low went as far as Olympia with Captain Fay and then walked alone through the wilderness to Portland. In his pocket he carried this letter from David Denny to his brother Arthur:

We have examined the valley of the Duwamish River and find it a fine country. There is plenty of room for one thousand settlers. Come on at once.

Just a little note from David Denny to the others saying that it was a good country with plenty of room and advising them to come. Just a note, but how important! A forbear of those letters sent out from Seattle today, saying to the world, "Come!"

Left alone on the beach, Lee Terry and David Denny

started work on the cabin. Felling the trees and working
with only an axe, a hammer, and their bare hands was slow
hard work. Finding the logs too heavy to lift into place
alone, they hired Indians to help, paying them with ship's
bread. Besides helping with the cabin, David did the cooking.

While they were building they again saw their neighbor
Collins, who, with an Indian known as "Nisqually Jim,"
passed along the beach driving cattle, which he was bringing from Nisqually to the Duwamish Valley. He had a
difficult time getting them to the valley. He started out
with them on a scow, but the craft sank and the cattle swam
ashore. He then drove them along the beach as far as Duwamish Head where the mud flats were so soft that he was
obliged to again use a scow, which in the quiet river waters
proved successful.

By the latter part of October, Terry and David had Low's
cabin built as far as the roof. They found themselves in need
of a frow to split cedar shakes for the roof. Opportunely.
Mr. Collins again passed on his scow on his way back to
Nisqually and Lee Terry went with him to get the much-
needed tool. David was left to do what he could by himself. For three weeks he was alone.

Those lonely three weeks were a vital part of the bravery
and pioneering that made Seattle history. David had worked
alone only a few days when he cut his foot; and then, exposed as he was to the wet and cold, he came down with the
fever and ague and a severe case of neuralgia. There he was
under a shelter of cedar boughs with Indians camped about
him and wild animals lurking in the woods. The ceaseless
lapping of the water, the sighing and moaning of the wind.
the hooting of owls, and the weird chanting of some brave
on a distant shore only added to his loneliness. Surely this
boy of nineteen needed all of his pioneer spirit.

THE LANDING AT ALKI

When Mr. Low reached Portland he found that a new

pioneer had joined the party. On September 2nd a baby boy had come to Mr. and Mrs. Arthur Denny. However, on receiving the letter from David and hearing Mr. Low's report, the intrepid little band, with the exception of Mr. and Mrs. John Denny, their daughter Loretta and sons, James Samuel, and Wiley, began to make preparations to move.

During their stay in Portland, the Dennys had become acquainted with William N. Bell and his family, and Lee Terry's brother Charles. When Mr. Bell and Charles Terry heard what Mr. Low had to say about Puget Sound they too decided to go north.

The extent to which this land north of the Columbia River was settled at that time is described thus by Thomas Prosch in an unpublished manuscript, *A Chronological History of Seattle from 1850 to 1897:*

At the beginning of the 2nd half of the 19th century, there were but three places north of the Columbia River that by any stretch of the imagination could be called towns. These were Vancouver, Tumwater, and Olympia.

These with the Hudson's Bay posts, trading houses, and farms constituted. with the religious missions, two military garrisons and individual settlements, all of Northern Oregon, now Washington.

The overlanders of the four wagons who decided to go north, together with the Bell and Low families, took passage on the little schooner *Exact,* which was sailing on November 5th with gold prospectors for the Queen Charlotte Islands and with other emigrants for Puget Sound. The *Exact,* the Mayflower of Seattle's history, is described as a "two-masted craft of about 60 or 70 tons burden." The master was Isaiah Folger from Nantucket, Massachusetts.

According to Arthur Denny, the *Exact* sailed from Portland on November 5, 1851; and, as shown by the custom-house records, the ship cleared at Astoria on the 7th.

The preparations which the pioneer women of Seattle had made for the trip north were described by one of the passengers on the *Exact,* Mrs. Alexander, who with her husband was bound for Olympia. Perhaps nothing illustrates better the high courage of those pioneer women in trying to keep up their personal appearance than this story of their washing and starching their trusty sunbonnets good and stiff so that they might be clean and neat for the trip. Having no ironing board, they laid them on a cloth on the short grass to iron. Such was their brave departure for the Promised Land; such was the morale of these people.

A number of years later, Mrs. Alexander—or "Grandma Fav," as she is known in Seattle history after her subsequent marriage to Captain Fay—told of the morning of the departure from Portland in an interview that appeared in a Seattle paper.

The morning we came on board the schooner to come to the Sound some Indians came along with some salmon, and we all bought some. The stove was small and so I let the others cook their breakfast first. We couldn't all cook at once and so I fixed up my two little boys and attended to some other work. Well, the rest all got through and I was just going to cook my salmon when I began to feel sick. I didn't any more than have to look around before I see that I wasn't alone. Everybody was sick together. The Dennys had their bunk on one side of the stove and I had mine on the other. I guess I never will forget Mr. Denny lying there, and every time he'd get so he could speak he'd look across at me with a kind of a twinkle in his eye and say: "What are you lying there for, Mrs. Alexander? Why don't you get up and cook your fish?"

Them that stayed on top didn't get sick, and Mr. Terry was among them. I don't know whether he thought he'd celebrate having got over the plains safe or not, but anyway he told the men that he had some good cigars down in his chest and he'd go down and get them. So down Mr. Terry comes, and he hadn't any more than stooped over and unlocked his chest than he got sick, and instead of taking his cigars up to the boys he crawled into his bunk, about as sick as any of us. The men on top, not being sick, could afford to have a little fun, so they all kept looking down at Terry and calling out: "Hurry up with them cigars you went after, Terry. What are you doing down there, Terry?"

Among those who stayed above were the young miners. all jolly good fellows, spending the greater part of the time singing and playing cards. Their favorite ditty was the round

"Three Blind Mice." Over and over, and round and round
they sang it, until their voices seemed to rise and fall with
the swell of the sea. To the people below the recurrent blind
mice were almost as much an affliction as seasickness.

For what the ship lacked in size and seaworthiness she
made up in the number of masters, for there were two old
skippers on board besides Captain Folger. Not one was familiar with Puget Sound, and each wanted to command.

The *Exact* sailed down the Columbia River, up the coast
and entered the Straits as far as Dungeness, where she was
becalmed for one day and a night. Suddenly a strong wind
sprang up at three o'clock in the morning. Immediately
there was great commotion on board. All of the masters
were giving orders at once. Some of the passengers lent a
hand to help them get under way. They finally succeeded in
hoisting the anchor without mishap, and "just came a flying
up the Sound."

The wind was fair and strong, so strong that they arrived
at Alki at eight o'clock that morning of the 13th of November, 1851—eight days out from Portland. No one on board
but Mr. Low had ever been on the Sound before, and no
one else had the slightest idea where to stop; so all the way
he was on the lookout to see if he could recognize the place
where he had left Lee Terry and David Denny. In some
way or other he did. I marvel at it when I think of the con-
tinuously wooded shoreline and of his not having approached
the place from this direction before.

Captain Folger decided that it was better to anchor well
out in the Sound, and put his passengers ashore by rowboat
at low tide; and so he did. There they were, these founders
of a great city, dumped on the beach in the rain! Men
women, children, and baggage!

The night before they landed, David, crippled and feverish, had made himself some hot tea and crawled into hi
blankets under his shelter and gone to sleep, to be awakened

THE LANDING AT ALKI

next morning by the rattling of the anchor chain of the *Exact.* He looked out and saw the little ship. They had taken his advice and come! Overjoyed he crawled out from the cedar boughs and limped down the beach to await them.

They were delighted to see him, but the sight of him limping, with his head wrapped in cloths, was not encouraging. He tried to greet them cheerily and said, "I'm glad to see you for the skunks have gotten in and eaten all my provisions."

The men took little time to contemplate their surroundings but set to work immediately to get their precious household goods and provisions up the bank before the tide returned. While they were hurrying to save their plunder the women, chilled through and wet to the skin, looked for some shelter for themselves and their little ones. They found one log cabin without a roof! With heavy hearts and longing eyes they stood on that lonely shore and watched the little ship with the three skippers sail away. So this was the end of their long pilgrimage! This was the Promised Land!

Concerning the landing at Alki I quote Grandma Fay:

I can't never forget when the folks landed at Alki Point. I was sorry for Mrs. Denny with her baby and the rest of the women. You see, it was this way. Mr. Alexander and me went on to Olympia, but the rest stopped there. I remember it rained awful hard that last day —and the starch got took out of our bonnets and the wind blew, and when the women got into the rowboat to go ashore they were crying every one of 'em, and their sun bonnets with the starch took out of them went flip flap, flip flap, as they rowed off for shore, and the last glimpse I had of them was the women standing under the trees with their wet bonnets all lopping down over their faces and their aprons to their eyes.

Curious Indians, who were camped near, went hurrying down to the beach, some of them naked, others scantily clad with pieces of blankets or skins. Chief Sealth was ahead, but to the pioneers at that time he was just another Indian. These natives made a fitting audience standing there watching the landing of the Seattle Pilgrims.

I always think of the landing of the Pilgrim Fathers when I think of that little band landing at Alki Point on that cold, rainy morning of the 13th of November, 1851. Little did those of the Mayflower dream that, in years to come, some of their descendants would make a pilgrimage and land, as they had landed, on a strange shore. Perhaps it was the blood of those Pilgrim forefathers coursing through their veins that gave them the fortitude for the task before them.

Fortunately there was the shelter of the kindly trees under which they were standing when "Grandma Fay" last saw them. What they did next is described for us in an interview which Frederick Grant had with Arthur Denny years later. Mr. Denny said:

> We were landed in the ship's boat when the tide was well out, and while the men of the party were all actively engaged in removing our goods to a point above high tide, the women and children had crawled into the brush, made a fire, and spread a cloth to shelter them from the rain. When the goods were secured I went to look after the women, and found on my approach, that their faces were concealed. On a closer inspection I found that they were in tears, having already discovered the gravity of the situation. But I did not, for some time, discover that I had gone a step too far; in fact it was not until I became aware that my wife and helpless children were exposed to the murderous attacks of hostile savages that it dawned upon me that I had made a desperate venture. My motto in life was never to go backward and in fact if I had wished to retrace my steps it was about as nearly impossible as if I had taken up my bridge behind me. I had brought my family from a good home, surrounded by comforts and luxuries and landed them in a wilderness, and I did not think it at all strange that a woman who had, without complaint, endured all the dangers and hardships of a trip across the great plains, should be found shedding tears when contemplating the hard prospects then so plainly in view.

No wonder that Arthur Denny found his wife weeping as she sat on a water-soaked log in the pouring rain, holding her baby in her arms. By her side her two little girls clung in open-eyed wonder to her wet skirts. It all seemed to her like a series of terrible dreams. An anguish of homesickness swept over her; she longed for the security of the old home. She was so tired and weak. She longed for comfort and warmth and for a place where she could lie down with her baby and rest. It was a gloomy outlook for all the women as they huddled together with their aprons to their eyes. At their feet were the wet sands; before them lapped the cold, gray waves of strange waters; back of them stood the dark and forbidding forest; and in the shadow of that forest stood a cabin—a cabin without a roof. Half-naked redskins gathered about them and peered at their children, filling their hearts with fear and nameless dread. Is it any wonder they wept? Professor Edmond Meany has truly said: *"The foundation of Seattle was laid in a mother's tears."

The women's tears on that occasion have become historic. They have accented for us, all through the years, what pioneering meant to women.

Neither men nor women of this group of pioneers were robust when they landed. Although they were young—Mr Low and Mr. Bell being the only two over thirty—they were worn by the trip across the plains, and weakened by ague and the recent trying experience of seasickness. Mary Denny and Sarah Bell were especially frail. Truly they were a brave little band landing that day and forming the nucleus of a great modern city.

It is only right that we should include here the list of names as they appear on the monument erected on the site of their landing.

Adults

Arthur A. Denny and wife	Louisa Boren
John N. Low and wife	David T. Denny
Carson D. Boren and wife	Charles C. Terry
William N. Bell and wife	Lee Terry

*From *History of the State of Washington* by Edmond S. Meany. By permission of Macmillan Company, publishers.

Children

Louisa C. Denny	Minerva Low
Lenora Denny	Gertrude Boren
Rolland H. Denny	Laura Bell
Alonzo Low	Olive Bell
Mary Low	Virginia Bell
John Low	Lavinia Bell

To fully realize what that landing meant, we must remember that three of the children were babes in arms while several were only toddlers. Mary Low and Laura Bell, the oldest, were only nine. Alonzo Low leading his four-year-old brother John by the hand, was seven. My mother, Louisa Catherine, was seven, and her sister Lenora four, and their brother Rolland was a tiny, two-months-old babe held close to his mother's breast for warmth. Mrs. Low's little Minerva was only two years old. Mrs. Bell and Mrs. Boren each carried a baby girl in her arms. Olive Bell, a child of five, and her four-year-old sister Virginia, were so wet and cold that not even the knowledge that they would be immortalized side by side in the two streets, Olive and Virginia, would have comforted them. All that these women and children wanted just then was a place of shelter from the rain. Only one rift in the day's dark clouds was remembered and told of afterward by Louisa. Just once the clouds were pierced by a sudden sunbeam which lighted an old Indian hut across the Bay. It was a good omen.

LIFE AT ALKI

Arthur Denny tried to comfort his wife, but when he saw her in tears—she who had never faltered before—his courage all but failed him. But it was only for a moment. Squaring his young shoulders resolutely, he exclaimed, "This is no way to begin pioneering."

Then turning to the other men he said, with that humor which is the very acme of courage, "They say white women are scarce out here. The best thing we can do is to go to work to provide shelter for those we have."

Though her sister wept, Louisa Boren's heart sang, for David, her friend and companion across the plains, was safe. Danger might surround her, but care dropped from her young shoulders like a garment. David was safe! And what must that meeting have meant to the lonely boy! In that little group, at least two were happy. The rain was forgotten. History was repeating itself—that other landing—those other Pilgrims—John Alden and Priscilla—David and Louisa!

But David's joy was mingled with apprehension. As he looked at the helpless children, at Mary Denny with her tiny baby, at Louisa, radiant with youth and happiness, and then at the swarms of Indians about, he was suddenly conscious of the seriousness of their position. Turning to his brother he said, "I wish you hadn't come."

"Why, what do you mean?"

Seeing his brother's concern and realizing there was no turning back now, David answered quickly to allay the other's fear, "Why, there's no place for the women and children because the cabin isn't finished yet."

The men set about speedily to finish the cabin. They worked all that day splitting cedar for shakes for the roof. but night found them still without one. Meagre protection was provided with Indian mats and a piece of tent, and here they slept as well as they could that first night. Even though Mother was a child, she never forgot how cold and wet and stiff she felt when she awoke next morning. She formed a distaste then and there for camping that lasted all her life.

As soon as possible the little cabin was finished and all twenty-four people, twelve of whom were children, moved in. Until they could build a second cabin, those twenty-four people lived peaceably in that one room. Mary Denny owned the only cookstove, which was set up in the centre of the room and used by all. The other cabins were built with mud fireplaces for heating and cooking.

Only a few days after the pioneers landed, the little cabin sheltered two guests over night—F. W. Pettygrove and L. B. Hastings—who were on their way from Portland to Port Townsend. In spite of the fact that they were obliged to sleep on the floor, they survived to become prominent pioneers of that settlement.

The Indians came and crowded around the first lone cabin. They crowded into the cabin. They were especially curious about Mary Denny's little white-faced baby. They marveled at his curly hair. Never before had they seen a child with a face like snow and hair like the sun. They shook their heads and said as they touched his hair and cheeks. "Acha-da! Acha-da! memaloose — memaloose!" which means, "Too bad! Too bad! He die! He die!"

They were false prophets, however, for this curly-headed babe is living today, eighty years after the prophecy was made, the last of the twenty-four who landed.

As soon as the second log cabin was completed, Arthur Denny's family, including David and Louisa, moved into it, thus relieving the first cabin of four adults and three children. After that, to quote Mr. Denny:

We had now used up all the timber suitable for log houses which we ~ould get without a team, so we split cedar and built houses for Bell and Boren. These we considered quite fancy but not so substantial as the log houses.

According to Clinton Snowden in *The Rise and Progress of an American State*, the pioneers "had learned either from their own experience or from the Indians that the long. straight-grained cedar trees in the vicinity could be easily split into very tolerable boards."

They made good progress in their building, for they did not mind the rain. By the first week in December four cabins were nearly finished.

Just about this time the brig *Leonesa*, Captain Daniel S.

Howard, appeared off the Point as if sent by a wise Providence. Seeing that the place was inhabited by white people. the master came ashore. He was looking for piles, he told them, with which to build wharves in San Francisco. He and his men were full of news of the gold excitement in California, which was resulting in a great building boom.

Sailing vessels by this time had learned that they could expect to find lumber around Puget Sound, but apparently they had been very uncertain at first as to what this region was like, for, during the first year of the gold boom, a ship had been sent to what was thought to be the "frozen north" for a cargo of ice. She returned disappointed in the search for ice but happy to have discovered a rich supply of timber.

With characteristic enterprise the young pioneers readily agreed to load the *Leonesa,* and signed a contract to that effect. Just what the terms of the contract were, is not known. One account states that it was drawn up between Low and Captain Howard. Charles Terry acted as timekeeper and his old notebook, faded and worn, now in possession of the University of Washington, has given us valuable information of the transaction.

On December 10th, they went to work at the timber nearest the shore, for much of it had to be rolled and hauled by hand, since they had only one pair of oxen. Low had brought back this pair from the Chehalis River when he returned for his stock shortly after the landing at Alki. In order to speed up the work, Lee Terry bought another pair from settlers on the Puyallup River. He drove them home along the beach and returned in time to work nine days with his cattle before the contract was filled on January 1st, the others having already worked ten days. The amount of timber cut varied from "4 sticks—205 feet" cut on December 11th to "26 sticks—1348 feet" cut on December 22nd. the first day that Terry's oxen worked. On Christmas Day the pioneers worked half a day and cut 11 sticks, 561 feet.

In sixteen working days they had ready for shipment 13,-458 feet of lumber. By their enterprise they had solved their own economic problem, and had established trade relations with San Francisco.

Regretfully, they watched the *Leonesa* set sail leaving them there among the Indians. Frederick Grant says: "Many of the navigators of that time were intelligent and entertaining men and the officers of the *Leonesa* were no exception. Their visit was a most agreeable break in the monotony of woods life."

As for Captain Howard, he sailed away with as many orders for merchandise as a modern Santa Claus. He took the money earned by the settlers back to San Francisco to convert into food and clothing. Their most pressing need was for flour, for as the ship sailed, the flour supply was nearly gone.

Arthur Denny gave the skipper $43.00 with which he was to buy a barrel of pork, flour and batting. Evidently Mary and Louisa were planning to do some quilting.

C. D. Boren also ordered a barrel of pork and the remainder in flour.

William Bell did not put in an order; either he was well provisioned when he came, or intended to buy from Low or Terry.

J. N. Low, however, put in a larger order, for in addition to the barrel of pork and the flour, he ordered "1 stove." No Santa Claus was ever commissioned with an order as eagerly awaited and longed for as that "1 stove." All during those trying months when Lydia Low's eyes smarted from the smoke as she cooked over her mud fireplace, she knew that relief would come some day when the good ship *Leonesa* came sailing in from San Francisco with her new stove.

As we read that list of stern necessities, we cannot accuse the city founders of frivolous buying—unless it be for an

item of "pepper sauce"; but remembering that they had no
modern salads, they may be granted this simple relish as a
necessity. The ship master's shopping list read as follows:

25 bbls. pork	1 doz. window sash
3500 lbs. flour	1 box glass 8x10
150 gals. molasses	1 doz. grind stones
800 lbs. hard bread	½ doz. cross-cut saws
1 case boots	½ doz. files cross-cut
1 case Brogan shoes	1 case mustard
1 bale Domestic	1 case pepper sauce
1 doz. pieces prints (calico)	400 lbs. sugar
1 cask whiskey	400 lbs. soap
6 doz. hickory shirts (dyed with hickory bark)	

The pioneers' first Christmas in the new land was not
cheerless. While the men were loading the *Leonesa* the women were busy in their cabins making preparations. Not
since they left Illinois the spring before, had they had the
opportunity as now to mend and sew. They had no new
material, but made over and freshened up what they had.
In spare moments, the men turned shoe-makers and soled
and patched the well-worn shoes. On Christmas Day every
one appeared bright and gay in clothes that were clean and
whole.

And they had presents too. With the same foresight with
which she had insisted upon bringing a looking-glass along,
Louisa Boren had tucked in some shell boxes and other
trinkets for the children. How beautiful these little gifts
looked to them in this wilderness! What a joy this blithe.
young girl must have been, not only to the children and
David but to all of them!

They all celebrated Christmas dinner together with wild
goose as the main dish. The memory records are faint here
but I am sure that I heard Mother say that they had "company for dinner from the Collins settlement." The guests
were probably Samuel Maple and Henry Van Asselt who
were bachelors at that time.

The fare of the newcomers was meager that winter but

no one went hungry. The lack of milk worked the greatest
hardship. Not only Mary Denny's tiny baby but the other
young children had only clam broth for milk substitute all
that year. A barrel of dried apples which they had brought
on the *Exact* supplied fruit. They bought salmon, clams
and venison from the Indians. Before the *Leonesa* could return with more, the flour gave out and they had to use hard-
tack, which was not such a hardship as long as the potatoes
lasted.

In March they bought one hundred bushels of potatoes
from Dr. William F. Tolmie of the Hudson's Bay Company at Nisqually for $1.00 a bushel. Dr. Tolmie got an
immense war canoe from the Indians and the order was
delivered by Edward Huggins, who landed in a storm.
which nearly wrecked his canoe. Mother remembered that
"the man who brought the potatoes" slept on their cabin
floor that night.

Of that winter at Alki, Grant writes:

> It will not be inferred that life was carried on here in great splen-
> dor, neither must it be thought that it was passed in misery or with-
> out refinement. These were all men and women of intelligence and
> native and acquired culture. Much in the way of romance was woven
> in with the duller threads of life here, as among cultivated people
> everywhere.

The great problem that first winter was to adjust themselves to living among Indians. After the arrival of the
pioneers, increasing numbers of Indians continued to come.
Arthur Denny says:

> Alki Point had not been a general camping ground for the Indians
> but soon after we landed and began clearing the ground for our
> buildings, they began to congregate and continued coming until we
> had over a thousand in our midst. Most of them remained all winter.
> Some of them built their homes very near to ours, even on the
> ground we had cleared. Although they seemed very friendly toward
> us, we did not feel safe in objecting to their building thus near to
> us for fear of offending them, and it was very noticeable that they
> regarded their proximity to us as a protection against other Indians.

These "other Indians" were the fierce, warlike tribes from the North of whom the Indians in this vicinity were afraid. It is said that when they heard canoes coming around the Point, the squaws and children would run and hide while the men prepared to fight in case the visitors were not friendly.

Where the popular Alki bathing beach today swarms with thousands of gay summer people, those first little cabins stood surrounded by the primitive huts of over a thousand Indians. The beach was lined with canoes. There were the pioneers, a small group of seven men, five women, and twelve children, among hundreds of Indians. The newcomers dared not offend the natives, yet how trying it was to have half-naked, ill-smelling savages always around! It took infinite patience and forbearance to get on with them for they were intensely curious about everything that the white people did and were constantly hanging about in the way. This is why the cabins were built with doors in two parts; the lower half could be closed and fastened with a wooden button near the floor out of the Indians' reach while the upper half was left open for light and air. However, this precaution did not prevent their crowding around the door and leaning over the lower half, shutting out both air and light. In a short time they learned to take a stick and slide the button, and then there was no keeping them out.

One day Mrs. Denny lost patience and struck an Indian across the knuckles just as he was reaching into the frying pan for a fish she was cooking. With a howl he ran out of the house. Then there was consternation in the cabin for fear the Indians might be angry and attack them; but after a great powwow, they settled down.

Another time an old Indian kept annoying Mrs. Low by following her around the cabin while she was doing her work. When she was stirring a big pot of corn meal mush

with a wooden paddle, she turned around just in time to see
the Indian, who was wearing nothing but a shirt, reach up
for a ham that was hanging on the wall. That was the only
ham for miles around and Mrs. Low was not going to give
it up without a struggle. Quick as thought she took the paddle dripping with hot mush and gave him a smart spanking.
The astonished Indian, swearing and sputtering in Chinook
and English, ran out of the cabin. Frightened at what she
had done, Mrs. Low sat down and cried. When her husband
came home he took his gun and went out and chased the Indian away from the cabin. He told him to stay away or he
would kill him. Mrs. Low was not annoyed again.

So the settlers lived amidst fear and annoyance, afraid
to order the Indians out lest they take offense, and many
times, after they did go voluntarily, finding it necessary to
burn a bit of precious sugar to dispel the odor.

The Indians picked up everything they could lay their
hands on; consequently the clothesline had to be watched
carefully since they had a great liking for the children's
clothes, especially the baby's. Once when one of the women
missed a garment, they asked Chief Sealth about it as tactfully as they could. Not only was the missing garment returned but others that they had not yet missed.

More than one brave looked with favor upon Louisa
Boren. One day several brought poles and leaned them
against the cabin near the door, and then went off a little
distance, squatted down among the bushes and watched
the house. This performance made the pioneers uneasy.
They asked an old Indian woman, who had learned some
English from the Hudson's Bay people, what the poles
meant and she told them that each of the young Indians
wanted the white girl for his "klootchman." This was their
way of courting. The young buck whose pole she chose
would be the lucky suitor. The settlers diplomatically pretended they did not understand, and Louisa was careful

not to touch any of the poles. After several days of patient and stoic watching the Indians took their poles and went away, to the great relief of everyone, especially Louisa.

One incident that must have caused quite a ripple in the quiet life of the settlement is described by Arthur Denny:

On one occasion during the winter, Nelson (Chief Pialse) came with a party of Green River and Muckleshoot Indians, and got into an altercation with John Ka-nim and the Snoqualmies. They met, and the opposing forces, amounting to thirty or forty on a side, drew up directly in front of Low's house, armed with Hudson's Bay muskets, the two parties near enough together to have powder-burnt each other. They were apparently in the act of opening fire, when we interposed and restored peace without bloodshed, by my taking John Ka-nim aside until Nelson and his men left.

This account was supplemented by the memories of the two frightened little daughters of Arthur Denny, my mother and her sister Lenora. One of them remembered that in the consultation between her father and John Ka-nim, held behind their cabin, the Indian chief proposed that he would slip out around behind the enemy and stab the other chief in the back. This their father dissuaded him from doing, never dreaming that Nelson, the chief whose life was thus spared, would four years later become the leader in the most brutal massacre of whites that the Northwest was to experience.

Another incident that was a combination of tragedy and comedy occurred when Chief Sealth's wife died. All that winter the chief and his family and followers made the white settlement their headquarters, going to Olympia occasionally in their canoes. When the chief's wife died, William Bell and Arthur Denny made a coffin. They did a creditable piece of work, but when they tried to place the body therein, they found that the coffin was too small. The two kindly intentioned whites looked on in dismay, but the Indians were equal to the emergency; they removed some of the many blankets that had been wrapped about the body until it fitted into the casket.

Among the mourners on this occasion was the daughter of Chief Sealth, Kick-is-om-lo, the widow of Dokub Cud, sincerely grieving for her mother. In after years she became famous as Princess Angeline.

Notwithstanding the constant annoyance of having the natives about, these experiences were valuable. The whites were learning how to get along with them and were establishing some friendships that were to stand them in good stead four years later. They also learned to speak some Chinook that first winter and the Indians learned some English.

The weather in the Promised Land continued to delight and surprise the newcomers by being as open and mild as it had been painted in those enthusiastic letters that had helped Arthur and Mary Denny decide to come west. My mother remembered distinctly hearing her father and mother rejoice in the wonderful weather. Whether that first winter was an unusually mild one for Puget Sound or whether it was mild in comparison with Illinois winters is not known, but in all accounts it is described as "unusually mild."

Remember that during those first winter months all lived on claims located by Low and Terry, who named the settlement "New York" after their native state, believing even then that it would become a great city some day.

The name "Alki," meaning "bye and bye" in Chinook was added in a spirit of fun and the place was actually known for a long time as "New York-Alki." Eventually "New York" was dropped, and "Alki" retained. It is pronounced with the "i" given the sound of "i" in "ill" not as in "ice."

Just how and when this humorous addition of "Alki" came about, we are not certain. One story is that whenever Terry spoke of the little row of cabins as "New York," Low would laugh and say, "Alki."

A grandson of Lydia and John Low tells this story: One day a sailing vessel was passing around the Point and the master, seeing a man standing by a camp fire, called out. "What town is this?"

"New York!" shouted the nimble-witted Terry.

"Ha, ha!" they could hear the skipper laugh, as he called over the water, "Yes, New York Alki, I reckon."

But, hopeful as the Terrys were of a great future for their tiny "New York," Boren, Bell, and the Dennys did not share their belief that it was a good location for a future city, because the water was too shallow at that point.

In January, 1852, these men set out to look for a better location for the claims they intended to take in the spring. They paddled down to the mouth of the Puyallup but did not like the prospects, so returned to look somewhere else.

They realized that getting out piles and squared timber would be their immediate means of support and that the two essentials for this industry would be available timber and a good harbor. They had been looking across the bay at the heavily wooded shore of what is now the City of Seattle, and after their return from this scouting trip up the Sound, decided to go across and explore.

This determination was strengthened when Arthur Denny learned from the Indians that there was a trail near this point that led over the mountains. The historian, Herbert Howe Bancroft, gives this as Mr. Denny's main reason for choosing the present site. It was not his main reason, but it did influence him, for ever since he had talked with Mr Brock at Burnt River, he had realized the advantages of a pass through the Cascade Mountains.

While he and the others were looking for claims, Low and the Terrys were preparing to develop "New York." But Lee Terry's enthusiasm must have waned for in his brother's old timekeeper's book, which was also somewhat of a diary, we find this item: "Leander Terry left this place, New York, for the States, April 18, 1852; quit work on the 17th." So Lee left his claim and his dreams of a great city to his brother, Charles, who was to be the energetic town builder of "New York" and who was to become later actively identified with the history of Seattle.

Charles Terry had come west to California with the Forty-niners and knew pioneer ways and needs. Even when he set sail on the *Exact* he had had the enterprise and foresight to take with him a stock of goods which he considered essential to pioneer life. His list included: "1 box tinware, 1 box axes, 1 box tobacco, 1 keg brandy, 1 keg whiskey, 1 box raisins."

With this supply he was prepared to do some trading and in an old memorandum book he records what was probably his first sale. It was made to Collins and included: "6" pans, 1 large and 2 small pails, 6 pint basins, 1 coffee pot, 2 frying pans, 2 candlesticks, and 1 dipper." In another place Collins was credited with twelve salmon, which may have paid for the tinware.

In this same old notebook we find this memorandum showing that some of the refinements of life came high:

1 bottle ink	$1.00
½ quire blotting paper	.50
Coffee mill	2.50
2 table cloths	2.50

Tucked in close is an extremely practical notation—not entirely irrelevant, perhaps, for the coffee mill and tablecloths might thus have been paid for:

Set hens
April 21 on 11 eggs
" 25 on 12 eggs

When the *Leonesa* returned to "New York" in April, she brought further supplies which enabled Terry to set up a store in his cabin, the first store in King County. Some of the merchandise brought to him either on this trip or on a later one included flour, ammunition, calico, a barrel of molasses, and one of Sandwich Island sugar.

Much of Terry's trade was with the Indians, who dearly

loved molasses, sugar, and tea. In exchange for these commodities, and for bread, calico, beads, and trinkets, they would barter things useful to the settlers—fish, game, and wild goose and duck feathers, for instance.

That was the day of feather beds and the pioneers were glad to get feathers for that purpose. Some of them, however, had carried their precious feather beds at great pains across the prairies, only to find that feathers were one of the easiest things to obtain in the new country.

Terry's location at Alki Point, which extended out into the Sound in sight of all passing craft, was an excellent one for a trading post for both Indians and pioneers. In October of '52, in the first issue of the *Columbian*—Washington's first newspaper published at Olympia—we read this prosperous-sounding advertisement:

Charles C. Terry, thankful for past favors, takes this opportunity to inform their numerous friends and customers that they still continue at their well-known stand in the Town of New York on Puget Sound where they keep constantly on hand and for sale at the lowest prices all kinds of merchandise usually required in a new country. N. B. Vessels furnished with cargoes of piles, square timber, shingles etc.

The *Leonesa* continued to make regular trips between "New York" and San Francisco, loading with lumber on Puget Sound and returning with supplies. Low and Terry. with the help of Indians and transient immigrant arrivals. were able to furnish her each time with a cargo. The supply of timber was soon exhausted at "New York," and they were then obliged to get it from across the Sound at Port Orchard.

For months after Bell, Boren, and the Dennys had moved to the east side of Elliott Bay, "New York" continued to be the leading settlement. Low and Terry went into partnership and opened a store as "C. C. Terry & Co., the New York Markook House"—Markook being the Indian word for trading. But interesting as it would be to linger on the beach at "New York" with Low and Terry and their little store, and anxious as we are to go on to the serious task of exploring the forested shore line across the Bay and bring the little band of four wagons to the end of its quest, let us first take time to learn more of the Indians, for they are to play a big part in the Seattle drama.

THE PUGET SOUND INDIANS

The Puget Sound Indians in whose midst the Seattle pioneers established their settlement were the Duwamish and Suquamish tribes, who lived, respectively, around Lake Duwamish—now called Lake Washington—and around Elliott Bay and on Vashon Island. The names were pronounced "Duwampsh" and "Suquampsh" in a guttural way which the whites found difficult to imitate. Being fishing tribes, they were contemptuously called "fish eaters" by the Indian horsemen east of the mountains.

These Indians were not specimens of noble red men— tall, straight, and handsome as the plains Indians were; they were short, squat, and pigeon-toed, because of spending so much time paddling canoes, fishing, and digging clams. Their sloping foreheads, which resulted from the practice of head-flattening, were considered signs of great beauty. however.

This beauty treatment was begun in infancy. The papoose was lashed to a smooth board which served as a cradle, and another board was fastened across his forehead. The "cradle" with the baby attached could be hung anywhere or the mother could carry it on her back, and after weeks and months the forehead board shaped the child's head to the mother's liking.

When the little colony of inland white people landed at Alki, they knew little about forest and beach life. They learned much from the Indians; what herbs, greens, and berries were good to eat and what to avoid, how to dig clams, and how to paddle a canoe. Paddling a tippy dugout canoe required skill and the settlers at first hired Indians to paddle for them. The Indian and his canoe were to the pioneers what our taxicabs are to us today. Picturesque and romantic was the red man as he sent his dark canoe swiftly and silently along with the dip, dip of his paddle.

The Sound Indians did not use the little round tepee. Their huts were made of split cedar boards, skins, and mats with grooved boards for roofs. When moving day came they put the mats and the roof-boards in canoes and paddled away. Their canoes were hollowed out of cedar logs by means of an adze and fire. Some were small, holding one or two; others were the great war canoes, large enough to hold thirty or more braves.

The chief and his principal warriors had Hudson's Bay muskets, but the others of the tribe were still armed with bows and arrows, knives and hatchets. They would trade almost anything they had for a bit of iron to hammer into knives. The masters of the sailing vessels obtained many fine furs by trading scrap iron and old files for them.

The native children were well disciplined. Mother told me of seeing an Indian father take a sputtering little papoose by the hair and souse him in the sound. Unlike the mother of Achilles he left no vulnerable spot. Then he brought him up and scolded him; when the little fellow sputtered the more and shook his head angrily, down he went again; when he came up he still shook his head, but not so vigorously; after he had gone down the third time he came up meek and amenable, and his father was satisfied. for this time the boy nodded his head.

The Indian ordeal of becoming a medicine man was one that only the strongest could stand. The candidate was laid on a plank and deprived of both food and sleep. A crowd of Indian men gathered around him, beat their drums. chanted their incantations, danced, and howled. If there were any signs of sleep or exhaustion they made him crawl around, or tied a cord around his waist, wove a wreath for his head of thorny branches, and then chased him through the forest. This torture was kept up for nine days. If the candidate lived, he might get well or he might be ruined in health or mind, as was the case with Indian Sampson, who had gone through the ordeal. Perhaps that was the reason Indian doctors were few among the Sound Indians. None were very old, for they did not live long to practice their art. If a patient died, by the Indian law the doctor's life was forfeited and some relative of the patient put the medicine man to death. It is no wonder that the Indian doctor worked over his patient in such a frenzy, for two lives were always at stake.

In times of sickness the Indians often took primitive Turkish baths. Their bathhouses or "sweat-houses," as they were called, were located on the beach below First Avenue. This bath was a strenuous treatment and always proved effective one way or the other; it either killed or cured. A hole was dug in the sand on the beach and around it a wall two or three feet high was made of stones. Upon this structure boards were laid for a roof, the side next to the water being left open. Red-hot stones were dropped into the house and water poured over them; then a layer of green boughs laid on the stones and more water poured on. Into the clouds of steam went the patient and the opening was closed. When the heat became unbearable the sufferer made a rush for the Bay and plunged in. This treatment was given in both summer and winter. If the patient was not very ill he recovered; if seriously ill he died. Measles, which the Indians never had until the white man came, were always fatal, for this harsh treatment drove the rash in. The white people tried to make the Indians see how dangerous these baths were in cases of serious illness but their warnings went unheeded.

The Indian burying grounds were along the bluff above

the beach, one at the foot of Seneca Street. All of the graves had more or less of the personal belongings of the deceased on them. They were shallow, and as time passed bodies were frequently exposed. A number of graves had roofs of cedar slabs built over them with posts driven at the four corners which were hung with clothing, tinware, beads, or anything else that the Indian had prized. Some of the bodies were wrapped in rush mats and laid on the ground with canoes turned over them. Infants were generally entombed in hollow trunks of cedar trees. If the banks caved away during a thaw after a hard freeze, one would find exposed bones. stone implements, and quantities of blue Hudson's Bay Company beads. These beads were the size of a robin's egg and are very scarce at the present day.

Indian camps were not so sweet as clover beds. The hundreds of drying fish that were hung on poles over small fires and inside the mat houses, and the strings of clams were very offensive in odor. White children who played with Indian children could be easily detected by the smell. Furthermore, it was not an unusual thing for the pioneer mother to find it necessary to soak the children's heads in coal oil and to give other vigorous treatment after they had played with the little Indians.

When the pioneers first came, the Indians wore very few clothes; sometimes none at all. At one time, they had dressed in the hides and furs of animals but after the Hudson's Bay Company came, they sold the furs and went without much covering besides blankets. The children went naked. When the Indians could get hickory shirts and other items of white man's wear, they adopted them, but they were not neat to look upon in any stage of their development.

Their ethics were naturally not like the white man's, but the "Bostons" (the Indian name for the American settlers) often outwitted them. An amusing story is told of one of the first potato patches on Puget Sound on Whidby Island. The Hudson's Bay people had taught the Indians how to raise potatoes. When planting time came, the settlers bought seed potatoes from the Indians and planted them. They also obtained their daily supply from the natives. One day one of the pioneers went to see how the potatoes were doing and much to his surprise found that someone had been digging them. It then dawned upon him that the Indians had been stealing the potatoes and selling them to the settlers for the second time. Not wanting to anger the natives by accusing them, the pioneers sprinkled the patch with flour and told the Indians that some wild animals had been digging the potatoes, and that they were sprinkling poison over the ground in order to kill the animals. After that the potato patch was undisturbed, and the Indians had no more potatoes to sell.

The "Siwash," as the white men called the Indians, were most superstitious. There was an old squaw who came to the houses and always begged for a cup of tea. For some reason or other, which no one was ever able to find out, she would never finish her cup of tea without throwing her tea leaves at the table leg. No matter how tidy the pioneer woman's cabin might be or how she might remonstrate, this performance was never omitted—and sure and accurate was the squaw's aim.

One day the Indians saw some of the pioneer white children in great glee driving snakes into a brush fire. In much excitement and alarm they went to the children's fathers and told them to stop the children from killing the snakes or it would bring a flood. Sure enough, immediately after that the heavens seemed to open and the rain poured down in what became almost a flood, just as if the snakes had had something to do with it.

The jargon the Sound Indians spoke was not a pure Indian language, but Chinook, which Judge Cornelius Hanford, in his *History of Seattle and Environs*, describes as:

A language of convenience that grew gradually from the necessity for intercommunication between white people and the natives of the Pacific Northwest. Although its vocabulary is not extensive it substitutes words for the sign language which had to be depended upon when the first white people came to the Pacific Coast. In the time of the Lewis and Clark Expedition at the beginning of the nineteenth century, only a few words were used, these were added to by the Hudson's Bay people and American trappers, explorers and missionaires, so that when the American emigration to the Coast began, there was enough of it to serve the purpose. It had become extensively used by the Indians themselves in their intercourse with different tribes, and by white people in their communications with the Indians. It is derived from French and English names of things and places, and from Indian words. Knowledge of it was easily acquired, and children learned it easily.

Most of the pioneers learned to speak Chinook, some fluently. Many words became so common that they eventually seeped into the vernacular of the Northwest and, while they are not pretty or musical, they are very expressive to the old-timer. It is not an unusual thing to hear the pioneers at their reunions sprinkle their conversation with Chinook words.

There is something in the way that an old settler affectionately says that this one, or that one is his "tillicum" that makes you know that the word means friend; when he squares his shoulders and exclaims "hiyu kopa nika," you may know that he thinks well of himself. Then there is "skookum" for good, and "cultus" for bad. If one has "hi-u-chik-a-mon" he has plenty of money. "Illahee," often used for the name of a country home, is the word for country, land, or home. "Ko-pet" means stop, "nan-itch" is look see; "now-it-kah" is yes, while "wake" is no, never. Heart or mind is "tum-tum" and "wah-wah" is much talk or speech. "Wap-a-to" is our potato. "Klaw-how-yah" is to pass the time of day, meaning "How do you do"; and "klat-a-wah," when spoken by an old Indian, made the children scamper, for it means "Go away!"

Some of the Indian expressions for the white man's strange belongings were English words used with a child-like simplicity. A newspaper or letter was a "talk paper," sailing vessels were "bird boats," and later when the steamship came they called it a "fire boat."

But Chinook was scorned by the greatest Indian of them all, Chief Sealth, who always used his tribal tongue. This warrior was a staunch friend of the whites. From the time of their landing at Alki the settlers found him friendly and helpful. He was a wise old chief who read the signs of the times and realized that it was useless for the Indians to struggle against the encroachment of the whites, and that soon their hunting grounds would be under the Great Chief at Washington. For he said, "Our pale-face brothers are like the grass that covers the vast prairie, while my people are few and resemble the scattering of a storm-swept plain."

At the time of the landing at Alki, Sealth must have been sixty-five years old. He was taller than most of the Sound Indians, dignified and solemn. He walked with a staff. A blanket was his only garment, which he held in place with one hand. When rising to speak he raised his free hand, and the words rolled from him in deep tones in his native Duwamish tongue. So great was the carrying power of his voice that he was heard at great distances. At his first word there was silence, and all turned their heads and listened. At his last words they nodded their heads in approval. His great influence was no doubt largely due to his eloquence.

A very typical story both of Sealth and the Indians comes to us from Grandma Fay:

I never can forget how old Seattle scared me once. He and his tribe were camped that winter where Olympia is now and our little log house stood right on the edge of their camp, but they were quiet and peaceable and I wasn't afraid. One day I put up a new clothes-line, and the next morning it was gone. Mr. Alexander said he knew the Indians had it and I'd better go and see Seattle about it. So I went over to his tent and there he sat in his skin mending his pants. I told him I thought some of his Indians had stolen my clothesline. He just grunted and got up and walked to the door. He just drew in one big long breath and then I never in my life heard anything like the screech he gave. I was scared almost to death and almost fainted for once in my life as every Indian in the tribe came running to where we stood, for I had followed him outside the tent to get my clothesline. Then they came, old and young, old men just crawling and young men running like horses, and old women and young women carrying babies, and little children and the dogs and everything the camp held that was alive. I did not know but I'd made him mad and they were going to kill me then and there; but no, that wasn't it. Old Seattle said something to them that I couldn't understand, and every Indian disappeared as quickly as they had come. As soon as the way was clear, I got into my own house in a hurry but I'd no sooner stepped over the sill than an Indian came and handed me my clothesline. And that was the last thing I ever had stolen.

The headquarters for Sealth and his tribes were in the famous Oleman House on the present Port Madison Reservation. Oleman — accented on the first syllable — is the Chinook for "old man." It was the custom of the Puget Sound Indians to have in addition to their temporary homes large tribal headquarters which became a fort in time of war. Oleman House covered an acre and a quarter and was divided into forty apartments. Its roof was supported by seventy-four posts ornamented with drawings and carvings of the "thunderbird" and other designs. To students of Indian lore, this was one of the most interesting structures known; to the people of Seattle it was the birthplace and the death-place of the old chief who was to leave his name for their heritage.

But at the very best the Puget Sound Indians were not so romantic as were the Indians of some other localities. As Frederick Grant says, "There was much in them to love and respect and there is an unlimited pathos about their attempts to be good and their futile attempts to imitate the white man . . . . . nevertheless they were not pleasant neighbors."

CHAPTER III

IN FEBRUARY of '52, Bell, Boren, and the Dennys carried out their plan to explore the eastern side of Elliott Bay and take soundings offshore in their combined search for locations for claims and for a good harbor. At daylight on a cold gray morning these four men pushed their canoe off the beach at "New York" and paddled across the Bay. They then glided along in the shadow of the shore line. The dip of the paddles and their voices were the only sounds that broke the stillness. Tiny and frail their bark; and in the shadow of the towering trees how puny the men!

As they neared what we now know as Smith's Cove they rested their paddles; then cast overboard the sounding line and plummet — a clothesline with horseshoes attached.* More and more line was let out; and then drawn in and notations made. Again and again, all the way from Smith's Cove to Yesler Way, the horseshoes were lowered and raised — sometimes Arthur Denny heaving the line, sometimes David — while Bell and Boren paddled the canoe. One might say that those four men christened Seattle with drops of water falling from horseshoes. Auspicious it was too, for good luck has been with the city ever since.

They found the water near shore very deep and when they saw that the timber on the bluff above was heavy and thick, they decided that this was the place to locate. By noon, they had sounded down as far as the present Spring Street where they stopped to eat their lunch on a pebbly beach where a spring came trickling down. Looking up. Arthur Denny could see a little farther south a break in the timber where the sky showed through the dense evergreens. He climbed the bluff to investigate and found that

---

*When the canoe left Alki, Mary Denny cautioned her husband to take care of her clothesline, and the Terrys called out, "Don't lose the horseshoes."

a fire had thinned the trees. It was here a little later that he built his cabin home.

In the afternoon as they paddled south, the explorers discovered that the high bluff gradually dropped from a height of forty feet to the level of a little tide stream with meadow grass on its banks, which we know as Yesler Way. North of this was a knoll at the foot of Cherry Street. South of the stream was a low wooded section, and half hidden therein were the ruins of an Indian hut. The distinct shore line ended rather abruptly and merged into tide flats at what is now the foot of King Street, making a point at low tide and an island at high tide.

At nightfall, the men paddled back to "New York" highly enthusiastic over what they had discovered, and satisfied that the east side of the Bay was the best for a town site. What is now downtown Seattle they decided to divide equally among themselves. It had been a good day's work.

A few days later they returned to stake their claims under the new donation law that had just been enacted, which gave a man and his wife the right to three hundred and twenty acres. The law originally read six hundred and forty acres, but was changed when it was seen that with such large claims the land in the Willamette Valley would soon be taken and held by a few.

On February 15, 1852, the canoe crossed the Bay again and the explorers staked their claims. This was the actual founding of Seattle. On that day was created a second memorable date, which parallels the date of "The Landing at Alki," November 13, 1851.

Without ceremony, the pioneers drove the north stake at what is now the foot of Denny Way, where the shore line came to a point; and the south stake on the other "Point," now First Avenue and King Street. Two stakes! The beginning of a city!

The three friends agreed that between these two points

Bell should have the north section, Arthur Denny the middle, and Boren the south. David was only twenty, and so could not take a claim then in his own name. It is quite probable that he took up the claim north of Bell's either in the name of his father, or jointly with him, for in '69 the first plat of David's claim is filed by John and David Denny jointly.

How far back their claims would reach, or what was beyond those wooded slopes, they did not bother about just then. As long as each obtained a water front, they were satisfied for the time being. The land had not been surveyed by the government, for it still belonged to the Indians, from whom it would have to be obtained by treaty.

Having staked their claims, the founders of Seattle began to make preparations to move across the Bay—then known both as Elliott Bay and Duwamish Bay. It had been named Elliott Bay in 1841 by Captain Charles Wilkes in honor of the Rev. J. L. Elliott, chaplain of the Wilkes exploring and surveying expedition.

On the 23rd of March, before their preparations were completed, the *Exact* returned from her trip to the Queen Charlotte Islands. Incidentally on board were the disillusioned gold-seekers, the same who had sung "Three Blind Mice" so merrily. David Denny and Carson Boren took passage on the ship for Olympia; and then went on to the Willamette Valley for their stock which they had left to winter there after their trip across the plains.

On the very last day of March, three days before the pioneers left "New York" for the east side of the Bay, a stranger who was to play a very vital part in the history of Seattle came into the little settlement—Dr. David S. Maynard, whom Chief Seattle had brought from Olympia. Dr. Maynard had a wonderful scheme for salting and packing salmon for the San Francisco trade. The Indians were to help him that summer, and he was looking for a good place to carry on the work.

He had had a small store in Olympia, but, as the story goes, he was too good to his customers, selling at very low prices, or, if he was in an especially jovial or convivial mood, bestowing his goods upon them as gifts. This was fine for the customers but not so good for his competitors who finally asked him to betake himself and his belongings elsewhere.

Chief Seattle, a very good friend of Dr. Maynard's, was familiar with Elliott Bay and he advised the doctor to come farther north, to open another store, perhaps, when he saw the opportunity; or, at any rate, to carry on his immediate plan to pack fish. They stopped at "New York," but Dr. Maynard did not care for that location.

Bell and Arthur Denny—Boren and David Denny not having returned from Oregon—were glad to welcome a man with an industrial enterprise, and immediately invited him to join them in the new settlement on the east side of the Bay. They offered to move their stakes north in order to give him a claim. But the doctor was not eager to take up land; he was looking only for a temporary place to pack salmon. He chose "the Point" south of Yesler Way for this industry probably on the advice of Chief Seattle, who with his tribe had often used this point for a camping ground. However, after thinking the matter over, Dr. Maynard decided to accept Bell and Denny's offer. This was Seattle's first move to encourage outside industry.

On the 3rd of April, Bell, Boren's family, and Dr. Maynard packed their household goods into canoes and moved over from "New York-Alki" prepared to camp until their cabins were built. Alas for Arthur and Mary Denny! The ague from which they had been free all winter again attacked them, and they were too ill to move. Fortunately when summer came, the famous climate that they had come west to find had its healing effect. The ague left them never to return. The climate also benefited others of the little band, who, as we remember, were not very strong when they landed.

According to the Washington State Historical Society Boren's was the first cabin built in Seattle. It stood on what is now the northwest corner at Second and Cherry Streets Seattle's first home!* And that tiny cabin, in one man's lifetime, gave way to the tall Hoge Building that stands on the same site today. A plaque on the side of the building reads as follows:

> Carson D. Boren built here the first cabin home of white man in the city of Seattle in April, 1852. It was made of split cedar puncheons. This tablet was erected by the Washington State Historical Society Nov. 13, 1905.

Bell's cabin was built "away out" in what has been known ever since as Belltown. Maynard built his on "the Point" at Commercial — now First Avenue South — and Main Streets. His was larger than the other cabins, being 18 by 26 feet, with an attic in the front. The front part of his dwelling he made into a combination drug and general "store"—the first store in Seattle.

With true pioneer camaraderie, the settlers built a cabin for Arthur Denny—who was still sick at Alki—on the bluff near the gulch at the foot of Battery Street. But when he moved into it, the site was found impracticable, for there was not sufficient water in the forty-foot well which he dug in the gulch. Besides, the bluff was so high at this point that it was difficult to get down to the beach where their supplies were brought in. Several months later, Mr. Denny built another cabin on a lower bluff on the southwest corner of his claim. He chose the spot where he had seen a clearing

---

*It is but fair to say that historians differ as to whose cabin was built first. I am not prepared to say definitely as my research gives credit to both. Inez Denny and Bancroft say it was Bell's.

that day in February—the northeast corner of the intersection of First and Marion Streets.

It is characteristic that he chose to build on the water front and Carson Boren back a little in the woods. Boren was more interested in farm land and in hunting than in town lots. One of my childhood memories of Uncle Dobbins is of his love of the woods and of hunting.

When the claim adjustments were made to allow Maynard "the Point," Boren and Arthur Denny moved their boundaries north and east, Denny retaining his original extent of water front. "The Point" was the land south of Yesler Way that ended abruptly at Jackson Street and was separated from the land to the east when the tide backed up into what is now Occidental Avenue.

The pioneers had just moved into their new cabins when there came sailing into the harbor the brig *John Davis*, Captain George Plummer, looking for lumber for the San Francisco trade, and bringing the new settlement much-needed provisions—just as the *Leonesa* had come into Alki at the opportune time. The little group went right to work attacking the great forest that grew to the water's edge. Again their immediate economic problem was solved by the giant firs and cedars.

EARLY DAYS OF THE SEATTLE SETTLEMENT

During the summer of '52, a few immigrants—venturesome spirits from the crowds that were streaming into California and the Willamette Valley—arrived on sailing vessels or by canoe from Olympia. One family was that of a brilliant young lawyer, George N. McConaha, whose little daughter Eugenia, born soon after their arrival, was the first white child born in Seattle. Another newcomer, who paddled up from Olympia, was a physician, Dr. Henry A. Smith, a young man of twenty-two, who told afterwards of his difficulty in finding the little settlement from his canoe.

He finally discovered along the deep-forested water front one lone cabin, which turned out to be Dr. Maynard's "store."

For a while the settlement was known as Duwamps; then during the summer the name Seattle was chosen. There seems to have been very little discussion and no controversy over its choice. It was probably suggested by Dr. Maynard in honor of his friend. All readily agreed that "Seattle" after the Indian chief was appropriate, euphonious, and practical. The name, as we pronounce it, is a corruption of the original "Sealth" pronounced with a guttural sound that only an Indian can utter. "Seattle" was easier for the white man's tongue; so Seattle it became.

The old chief was not favorably impressed by the honor conferred upon him. He was very angry at first that such liberties should have been taken with his name, fearing, according to an Indian superstition, that harm might come to his spirit—that after death, every time his name was spoken on earth, he would turn over in his grave. Then after a time, he bore the affront in dignified silence. Later he became very proud of his namesake.

The pioneers accomplished an amazing amount of work that first summer. With their bare hands and the few tools they had among them—one or two augers, a few handsaws, axes, adz, and a broad axe—they had built their cabins and then set to work getting out piling and timbers for wharves and buildings that were needed in San Francisco.

Of that summer Arthur Denny writes:

Our first year on our claims (1852) was spent in building homes and getting out piles and timber as a means of support.

That year we were visited several times by the brig *Franklin Adams*, Capt. L. M. Felker, and about as regularly by the brig *John Davis*, owned and commanded first by Capt. Geo. Plummer and next by Capt. A. W. Pray. Each lumber vessel carried a stock of general merchandise and upon them we depended largely for our supplies. Our pork and butter came around the Horn and flour in barrels from Chili; sugar mostly from China in mats.

Fortunately for the little group of settlers, the heavy forest grew right to the edge of the bluff; so they were able to push much of the lumber over the bluff into the water where it could be rafted to the ships. Those who were skilled in the use of the broadaxe squared timbers while others got out piling and split cedar into shakes.

There was no record kept of the amount of lumber shipped that summer. We only know that on the *Franklin Adams* alone they shipped 12,000 feet of squared timber, besides 8,000 feet of piles, 10,000 shingles, and 30 cords of wood.

While the ships were in, the skippers and sailors assisted in logging. Four yoke of oxen were used in hauling along the water front. Captain Plummer owned two yoke which he subsequently sold to Arthur Denny, and Boren and Bell each had one yoke.

Meanwhile Dr. Manard was carrying out his original plan of curing salmon which he bought from the Indians. At times the harbor—especially down around "the Point"—swarmed with Indian canoes when they were bringing in the fish. The fish were salted and packed in barrels—barrels probably made of fir with hazel hoops, since this method of cooperage later became quite an industry here.

Nearly a thousand barrels of salmon were prepared that summer and sent to San Francisco. Unfortunately, when they reached that city they were spoiled and a complete loss. The doctor had sold part of the pack to Captain Felker and part to Captain Plummer; so probably the three of them shared the loss.

The intrepid doctor was undaunted, however, and cheerfully turned his attention to other enterprises. He called his store the "Seattle Exchange," and that fall he advertised in the *Columbian* that he was "now receiving direct from London and New York, via San Francisco, a general assortment of dry goods, groceries, hardware, crockery, etc..

suitable for the wants of immigrants just arriving. First come, first served."

There was little play for either men or women that summer. Nevertheless they were experiencing the beauty of their first summer on the shores of Elliott Bay. What a contrast to inland summers! How different from the preceding summer when they were crossing the plains! No scorching sun and alkali dust now. But instead, the smell of salt water; the fragrance of fir, of broken earth, of fallen timber; and the sight of the royal Olympics against the sunset sky. Green of the firs, blue of the water, and white of the snow-capped mountains! This was the Promised Land! New hope —new energy—new life.

No one was busier nor happier than David and Louisa. In all the hard, sweaty toil, David still found time for his courting. In the long twilights and moonlit evenings, he and Louisa sat at the water's edge and planned the future —Seattle's first lovers. David would be twenty-one in the spring. He was clearing land for their cabin on the claim he had staked north of Mr. Bell.

Perhaps these lovers felt the complete isolation of the little colony less than the others; yet all found it one of the hardest things they had to endure those first months. Even when mail from dear ones back home had reached Olympia after coming across the plains or by way of the Isthmus, it had to be brought to Seattle by canoe. A man named Bob Moxlie was engaged as postman to bring the months-old letters stroke by stroke from Olympia to the eager pioneers around Elliott Bay.

Days of the month meant little to them, but when "the Fourth" came, they did not forget. There were no firecrackers, but the day had to be observed in some way; so some of their precious powder was put into logs and set off, making a good patriotic noise. Striking an anvil ringing blows took the place of bells. Isolated and away out on the last frontier, they still remembered their American origin. What a joyous event it must have been when Mrs. John Denny and her little daughter, Loretta, came to visit them late that summer! How she arrived is best told in an account given by E. B. Maple, who had just crossed the plains to join his father on the Duwamish:

After I had been at Olympia several weeks, Dr. Maynard with four Indians and a large canoe came from Seattle to Olympia to buy goods for the Indian trade. Mrs. John Denny, mother of A. A. Denny, and Retta, her little daughter, and Mr. Latimer came from Oregon to Olympia and went on to Seattle with Dr. Maynard. On our trip down, head winds and strong tides compelled us to go ashore and camp until the wind ceased. Crossing from Vashon Island to Alki point, we came near swamping. It kept an Indian busy bailing the water to keep the canoe from sinking. We were all glad when we got ashore. We reached Seattle about two o'clock that night and let Mrs. Denny and Mr. Latimer out at A. A. Denny's near the beach. I went home with Dr. Maynard and stayed all night.

Another account of this same incident is furnished in an interview with W. G. Latimer by Samuel L. Crawford which appeared in the *Post-Intelligencer*, November 22. 1896:

While knocking around the beach at Olympia I met a dapper looking man who in company with a lot of Indians was loading a canoe with provisions such as flour, potatoes, beans, bacon and molasses. I entered into conversation with him, told him of my acquaintance with the Dennys and my desire to reach Seattle. He said his name was Dr. Maynard, that he lived in Seattle and that if I wished I might accompany him down the Sound, provided I had enough money or provisions. I told him I had no provision and but 50 cts. in cash. He said that was enough and advised me to buy hardtack, or sea biscuit, as that would go farther than anything else. I did as he suggested and my first journey on Puget Sound was made in an Indian canoe. We were two or three days making the journey and at night camped on the beach, Indian fashion.

In October, the whole character and outlook of the settlement was changed and determined by the arrival of Henry Yesler. All the men of the settlement—only a handful—were "down in the sag cutting spar timber"—the sag being where Pioneer Place is today. Landing in a canoe, the

newcomer walked along the beach in the direction of the
chopping. When the choppers looked up, they saw a robust.
ruddy-faced stranger, a man of about forty-five, standing
before them. They stopped work to greet him and he wasted
no time in telling them he was looking for a site for a sawmill.

Now, there were other sawmills on Puget Sound at this
time and the idea was not new; but to have the offer of a
sawmill come walking along the beach to meet them was a
matter for rejoicing. Whether or not they worked any more
that day I do not know; but I do know that Arthur Denny
invited the stranger home to dinner, and Mary and Louisa
welcomed him to the little cabin and did their best to cook
a good dinner with their meager fare. They talked and plied
their guest with questions of the doings of the outside world.
Mr. Yesler seems to have liked the dinner, the people, and
the place, for he decided to stay.

Since all the land along the immediate water front had
been taken, he went over toward West Seattle and staked a
claim and began making arrangements to clear a site for
the mill. The settlers did not want that mill to escape them;
they wanted it right in their midst and, although they had
no Chamber of Commerce, that little group knew exactly
how to treat a man who wanted to start an industry. They
went to him and said, "Come over here and pick out the
land you want and we will make room for you." So he
chose the same sag where he had first met them and for the
second time, they moved over to make room for industry.

Yesler's donation claim of three hundred and twenty
acres consisted of a long, narrow strip on either side of Yesler Way, Maynard contributing a strip one hundred and
twenty feet wide along his claim and Boren three hundred
feet including the street. This shaped Yesler's claim like a
shovel with a long handle, but it gave him his mill site on
the water. Maynard and Boren extended their claims far-

ther east to make up for what they had given him.

The settlers welcomed Yesler not only for his mill but for himself. They saw in him a real addition to the town. He was a man older than most of them, a man of means a millwright who knew his business and had come to Puget Sound for the express purpose of locating a mill.

They went right to work and helped him build the first unit—a log cookhouse, larger than the cabins. Soon after that Yesler set out for San Francisco to buy machinery for the mill.

At that time there were water-power mills at Whatcom and at Tumwater, but no steam mills on the Sound. Yesler's was the first steam sawmill on Puget Sound.

In the very same month of October, Seattle found her name in print for the first time. The *Columbian* announced the location of a new sawmill at "Seattle, north of the Duwamish," and added:

"Huzza for Seattle! It would be folly to suppose that the mill will not prove as good as a gold mine to Mr. Yesler besides tending greatly to improve the fine town site of Seattle and the fertile country around it by attracting thither the farmer, the laborer, and the capitalist. On with improvement. We hope to hear of scores of others ere long."

Snowden calls attention to the fact that the fifth issue of the *Columbian* was the first number to mention the settlement at Seattle, although the names of "New York" and Whidby Island had both appeared previously. Prosch says that the Seattle settlement was called "Duwamish River" in the first issue.

The same October that brought Henry Yesler to Seattle brought Thomas Mercer. Back in Illinois, Mercer had heard Dr. J. P. Richmond, a returned missionary tell about "Northern Oregon," the rich country north of the Columbia River. He became so much interested in it that when he started for the West, this country was his destination.

That summer of '52, he and Daniel Bagley and Dexter

Horton with their families crossed the plains in an overland train known as "the Bethel party." Since all three became prominent in the earliest history of the city, they may
well be called Seattle's second covered-wagon expedition.

Bagley and Horton stopped in Salem, but Mercer hurried right on to "Northern Oregon," to the settlement on
Puget Sound which he had doubtless heard about. He came
on despite the terrible loss he had suffered at the end of
the long journey across the plains when his wife died and
left him with four little daughters.

Leaving them in Salem, he came to Seattle and staked
his claim north of David Denny's. It extended to the western shore of Lake Union and was separated from David's
by a line now known as Mercer Street. Since he had no
wife to claim her share, he could take only one hundred and
sixty acres. He then went back to Salem and prepared to
return in the spring.

Soon after Henry Yesler's cookhouse was finished, another stranger—Bishop Demers of the Catholic faith—arrived in a canoe paddled by Indians. The bishop had heard
of this new settlement, and stopped to hold service on his
way to "assume at Fort Victoria, the Bishopric of New Cal-
edonia, with Russian America and Alaska included." He
stayed that night with Arthur Denny, and the family always remembered with pleasure the genial, kindly guest.
Bishop Demers and the Rev. F. N. Blanchet had introduced
the Catholic religion in the Oregon Territory in 1838.

The next day after the bishop arrived service was held
in the new cookhouse and everybody in the settlement attended the first religious service ever held in Seattle. The
cookhouse was swept clean, a table was brought from one
cabin, stools and boxes from others. The children's faces
were scrubbed shiny bright. Everybody tidied up for the
meeting. I like to look back upon that handful of pioneers.
seated on their stools and boxes, eagerly listening to the

white-robed priest. They did not understand the Latin phrases but drank in every word of the sermon.

The bishop's subject was "Charity." One of the little covered-wagon girls said afterwards, "I was a very little girl when I heard this sermon—the first I remember. But the speaker's earnestness impressed me deeply as he repeated his text in a deep, sonorous voice, often saying 'Charity, my friends, charity'." This listener was my Aunt Lenora. She was only five years old at the time but she never forgot those ringing words, "Charity, my friends charity," which became the keynote of her life.

Challenging words, those—spoken in the new-timbered cookhouse on the edge of the forest—to be incorporated in the upbuilding of the little settlement.

CIVIC BEGINNINGS

The locating of Seattle was not accidental nor the result of a streak of good luck. The town did not "just grow." Its site was searched for, chosen, and then worked for. Those pioneers on Elliott Bay did not sit and wait for people to come or for things to drift in.

From the beginning they shaped their course. The first summer, Seattle was platted and laid out in city blocks by a young surveyor, not yet thirty years old, whom many think of only as an old man and whom I think of as my grandfather. This young surveyor realized that they were laying the foundations for a great seaport. This foundation made all the difference in the world with the superstructure we have today.

As we remember, Mr. Denny had been surveyor and county supervisor of Knox County, Illinois. His instruments were his most ready tools. He surveyed for Terry at Alki and an old travel-letter of an early pioneer reads, "As I approached Alki point, I saw a white man standing on the beach with a surveyor's staff who turned out to be Arthur Denny."

If we would appreciate what it meant to survey and plan a city on Puget Sound in 1852, let us visualize the young surveyor standing on the beach with his staff in hand, facing the unbroken forest. Up from the beach rose the hillside with a sky line of giant cedars and firs. As he visioned the city, it was the logical thing to project the streets at right angles to the beach, as we see them now outlined at night by electric lights. He used his cabin at First and Marion Streets as a starting point.

Dr. Smith's arrival must have inspired the pioneers in their dream of city building, for he came enthusiastic over the rumors of Congressional appropriations for the exploration of railroad routes across the continent. If one route terminated at Puget Sound, as it seemed reasonable that it would, Dr. Smith felt, after considering all of the little settlements, that Seattle was the logical terminus for such a road. That was his reason for coming from Olympia to Seattle. He even went so far as to choose what is now Smith's Cove as the point where the railroad would touch the Sound, and took up his claim accordingly away out from the other settlers.

Though he never lived to see them, the long piers of the Great Northern Railroad which jut into the Sound at Smith's Cove, alongside which Oriental liners come to rest. attest the soundness of his judgment.

No doubt he and his good friend, David Denny, discussed many times just where the railroad, which they felt certain was coming to Seattle, would terminate. In David's plat which he filed later, we find the name "Depot Street" for the present Denny Way.

At that time, practically all of what is now the State of Washington was unsurveyed. Much of the western part of this territory was known as Thurston County, named after Samuel R. Thurston, Oregon's first delegate in Congress.

In the summer of '52, there was no voting precinct north of Steilacoom; consequently, when an Oregon territorial election was held in June, the settlers around the Duwamish could not vote. However, Arthur Denny was appointed one of the county commissioners for Thurston County by the legislature.

In July the legislature lumped the three vigorous groups —"New York," Seattle, and the Duwamish settlement at the mouth of the river—into one precinct, and for want of a better name called the precinct "Duwamps." Perhaps Seattle has nothing to be more grateful for today than the fact that the name "Duwamps" did not endure. This same legislature appointed David Maynard justice of the peace for Duwamps, with authority to write "J. P." after his initials on any legal papers.

The new justice of the peace held the first trial in Seattle in the old cookhouse. A charge was brought against the mate of the brig *Franklin Adams* for misappropriating money and goods belonging to the vessel. The man was found guilty, but Dr. Maynard let him off with the admonition never to do the like again and to keep his books in better order.

Shortly after the June election, Arthur Denny met with the other Thurston County commissioners, and the result of this meeting was the first effort at building a road in what is now King County—a road from "Steilacoom City to Seattle." William Bell, Luther Collins, and John Chapman were appointed viewers of the road. The term "viewers" is much used in the early accounts of road building.

On the Fourth of July, 1852, Arthur Denny went to Olympia to an important meeting in the interest of "Northern Oregon." A movement was on foot at this time among the settlers of this section to become a separate territory with the Columbia River as a natural boundary. A meeting for the same purpose had been held at Olympia on the previous

Fourth, but nothing had come of it. The pioneers were
more determined now to accomplish their purpose.

Mr. Denny writes that the meeting was held "on the hill
where the old schoolhouse stood, but it was then new and
unfinished." All was "new and unfinished"—the village
the political organization. The men gathered there were
young and ambitious. The tang of spicy new-cut lumber
was in the air as they gathered about an improvised platform to listen to the orator of the day—Daniel R. Bigelow
a lawyer, who had sailed for Olympia on the *Exact* with
the Seattle party.

An excerpt from the speech is given to show, as Professor
Meany says, *"the spirit applauded by those pioneers."

> We are now assembled on the verge of United States soil—no
> monumental shafts erected on revolutionary battle-fields meet our
> eyes to stimulate our patriotism and awaken our sympathies. We are
> far removed from all such scenes, farther than the most enthusiastic
> actors in those scenes ever expected the results of their labors to
> extend. But the scene exhibited here today shows that the great na-
> tional heart sends its pulsations actively, healthfully, patriotically even
> to this distant extremity. We see the flag of the Union waving over
> us, and we feel that beneath its ample folds we are at home.

The big thing accomplished at this Fourth of July meeting was the establishment of the first newspaper north of
the Columbia, the *Columbian.* The pioneers had realized
that in order to spread the idea of the new territory it was
necessary to have a newspaper. The effort made the previous Fourth had apparently died out for want of a paper
to spread the idea. Mr. Bigelow's speech in full was printed
in the first issue.

Arthur Denny returned to Seattle fired with new ambi-
tion for the commonwealth envisaged by the pioneers.
Speaking later of the disadvantages under which "Northern
Oregon" labored, he said whimsically:

---

*From *History of the State of Washington* by Edmond S. Meany. By permission
of Macmillan Company, publishers.

We were like two sisters; Oregon was the big sister, and of course must be served first, and I will do her the justice to admit that she was always willing that we should have what was left after she was served and would try to help us get it. But we were thus, as it were, clad in cast-off clothes.

Doubtless as a result of the call sent out by the *Columbian* a convention was held, October 25, 1852, in Monticello — at that time one of the little aspiring towns of "Northern Oregon," now part of the present city of Longview—to draw up a petition to Congress for the formation of a separate territorial government. It is significant that eight of the forty-four delegates were from Duwamps: Low and Terry from "New York"; Collins and R. J. White from the Duwamish settlement; Bell, A. A. Denny, Maynard, and McConaha from Seattle. Not much of a journey now, but a long two weeks' trip for those men from Duwamps, going by canoe to Olympia and then overland by way of the old trail of the Hudson's Bay Company to Monticello.

Of their sleeping accommodations after their arrival, Edward J. Allen of Olympia wrote afterward:

Monticello did not offer much in the way of hotel accommodations and the delegates quartered themselves the best way they could. As everyone brought his own blanket, going to bed meant simply finding a dry place big enough to spread it on. Some fifteen or more of us found happy lodgment in an attic where we camped down miscellaneously on the floor.

George McConaha made the principal address of the convention—an address distinguished for its oratory and brilliance. In the memorial to Congress, the petitioners called the new territory "Columbia," as they had planned. They also described "Northern Oregon" as having "a large population constantly and rapidly increasing." Commenting in after years on this presumption, Mr. Denny admitted that they "drew it rather strong," but thought that they might be pardoned "for we had so much room and were starting in to build an empire."

After signing this historic memorial, all of the delegates
returned home except Dr. Maynard who went on to Oregon
City where the territorial legislature was in session. Here
he obtained a legislative divorce from his wife who was in
the East. Legislative divorces were not uncommon in the
territorial government. A month later Dr. Maynard married "the widow Broshears," whom he had met on the journey across the plains and whom he had assisted very greatly
after her husband died of the cholera. She became the Catherine Maynard of Seattle history.

At this same session of the legislature that granted Maynard's divorce, Thurston County was divided into four other
counties: Pierce, King, Jefferson, and Island. The first two
were named by this Democratic legislature in honor of
President Pierce and Vice-President King, who had just
been elected; the third for their favorite, Thomas Jefferson.
Three commissioners for King County were appointed by
the legislature—J. N. Low, Luther Collins, and Arthur
Denny.

Dr. Maynard, strongly Democratic, had influence in the
legislature, and when the new counties were formed a clause
of the law read that "the county seat of King County be
and the same is hereby located at Seattle on the land claim
of David S. Maynard." The doctor was appointed a notary
public for King County.

The need of organizing a separate territory was emphasized in a graphic manner soon after the delegates returned
from Monticello. "Northern Oregon," at this time, had
two representatives in the Oregon legislature—Colonel
Isaac Ebey and Columbia Lancaster. Mr. Lancaster did not
favor the contemplated removal of the capital from Oregon
City to Salem and resigned. A special election was called
for December 6th to elect a representative to fill immediately his unexpired term, which expired with this session.
Two candidates were nominated: Seth Catlin, a Democrat

known as "the sage of Monticello"; and Arthur Denny. Mr. Denny received sixty of the ninety votes cast: all of the seventeen votes cast in what is now King County; all of the thirteen cast in Steilacoom; and thirty of those cast in Olympia.

But the successful candidate never took his seat. So inadequate were the means of communication, that by the time he had received the official notice of his election, that session of the legislature had convened and adjourned. It was high time that "Northern Oregon" became the separate territory of "Columbia."

The *Columbian*, a new newspaper in a new field, mentioned the candidates impartially and tactfully with a few kind words for each in the courtly phrasing of the Fifties. Of Mr. Denny it wrote:

Mr. Denny is a farmer, plain and unostentatious, highly esteemed as a citizen and neighbor, straightforward in business transactions and eminently qualified to discharge with credit any civil duties he may be called upon by the people to perform. He is a young man of good, general intelligence and a steadfast friend of northern Oregon.

By the first of December, 1852, the Seattle pioneers were entering upon their second year in the Promised Land. The first year had been, to put it very conservatively, a busy year. Frederick Grant says:

Although the acts of but a handful of pioneers, they nevertheless made up a very considerable aggregate, moving along with something of the rapidity which has characterized Seattle during her entire career.

In one year they had survived their first winter among the Indians, established a lumber trade, explored Elliott Bay, founded a city, surveyed and platted a portion of it into city blocks. They had increased their lumber output, made an attempt at packing salmon, and procured a sawmill. They had made plans for a wagon road, taken a most active part in forming a new and separate territory, and had acquired a very definite ambition to become the western terminus of a Pacific railroad. When, in later years, Arthur Denny was asked how they ever did it, he answered, "By muscle and timber."

Throughout that eventful first year on the east side of Elliott Bay, the pioneers intended to explore the country to the northwest of their settlement, for the Indians had told them that there was grassland in that direction. They were in need of range for the stock which David Denny and Carson Boren had brought back from the Willamette Valley in the spring. They had accomplished so much that year that we can very well understand why Arthur Denny says in *Pioneer Days on Puget Sound*:

> We were too busy to explore until December, 1852, when Bell, my brother, and myself determined to look for the prairies.
> It was slow and laborious travelling through the unbroken forest, and before we had gone far, Bell gave out and returned home, leaving us to proceed alone. In the afternoon we unexpectedly came to a body of water and at first thought we had inclined too far eastward and struck the lake [Union], but on examination found it to be tidewater.
> From our point of observation we could not see the outlet to the Sound. Our anxiety to learn more about it caused us to spend so much time that when we turned homeward it soon become so dark that we were compelled to camp for the night without dinner, supper or blankets. We came near being without fire also, as it had rained on us nearly all day and wet our matches, so that we could only get fire by the flash of a rifle, which was exceedingly difficult to do under the circumstances.

Inez Denny tells us how the fire was started.

> Arthur Denny pulled some of the cotton wadding out of his coat, and then dug into a dead fir tree that was dry inside and put it in with what other dry stuff they could find, which was very little, and David fired his gun into it, with the muzzle so close as to set fire to it.

Mr. Denny continues:

> Our camp was midway between the mouth of the Bay [Salmon] and the cove [Smith's], and in the morning we made our way to the cove and took the beach for home.
> Of course, our failing to return at night caused great anxiety at

home. Soon after we got on the beach, we met Bell coming on a hunt for us and the thing of most interest to us just then was that he had his pockets full of hard bread.

Their failure to return home did cause the greatest consternation. That night was one of the longest nights that Mary Denny and her sister Louisa ever spent. My mother remembered how they kept the candles burning; how Grandmother would go to the cabin door and listen. All night long she waited and prayed. At that time they were living in their first cabin on the bluff at the foot of Battery Street.

At daybreak, Grandmother sent my mother and her sister to Uncle Dobbins' cabin at Second and Cherry for gunpowder with which to fire bombs. She also wanted him to go to look for the wanderers. He hurried back with the little girls; set off some gunpowder bombs; and then started out firing his gun and calling. Before he had gone far he met the lost ones returning with Mr. Bell, who had also started out at the first glimmer of dawn to search for them, since they had not passed his cabin on their return, as he was sure they would have done. A warm welcome and a hot breakfast awaited the explorers, and a morning of joy and thanksgiving followed the night of anxiety.

Mr. Denny wrote later of this experience:

The narrative of our travels and discovery in this case doubtless sounds strange to some now. but it was not uncommon for inexperienced persons then to get lost between the bay [Elliott] and the lake [Union], and in some cases it was necessary to look after them to prevent suffering. . . . .

This was the last exploring expedition for that winter. which was as unusually cold as the preceding one had been mild. After that, the pioneers struggled for existence, for winds and storms on the high seas prevented the sailing vessels from coming in with supplies. The settlers were entirely cut off from any source of provisions outside Puget Sound.

That winter Arthur Denny described later as "a time of great scarcity amounting almost to distress."

A twelve-inch snow fell and lay on the ground for two or three weeks. Ice formed in the Bay, seriously interfering with boats and canoes going back and forth to "New York." Mr. Denny says, "I had the misfortune to break my thermometer before it got coldest and I could not replace it and cannot, therefore, give the temperature."

In the fall Arthur Denny had bought two barrels of salt pork for ninety dollars—they too had their high cost of living—and while they were using one barrel, the other was left on the beach in front of his cabin, as he supposed, above high tide. But one night there was a heavy wind and an unusually high tide and in the morning the pork was gone.

According to Mr. Denny:

It was the last barrel of pork in what is now King County and the loss of it was felt by the whole community to be a very serious matter. There were different theories about it. Some said it would float and had gone out to sea. Others thought it had rolled down by the action of the waves into deep water. We all turned out at low tide in the night with torches and searched the beach from the head of the bay to Smith's Cove, but the pork has never yet been heard from.

Snowden suggests that it may still be somewhere at the bottom of the sea preserved by the brine, and like old wine growing better with age.

The loss of salt pork would not mean much to us, but to them it meant that all the shortening, seasoning, butter substitute, and all the pork for frying salmon were gone.

We do not know whether they had any milk at this time. for there is no mention of it. My impression gained from Mother's accounts of the hardships of that winter is that they went without, substituting clam broth as they had at "New York" the previous winter. We know that they had the cattle that David Denny and Carson Boren had gone back to the Willamette Valley to get in March, but the problem of finding pasturage in the deeply-forested surroundings was a grave one. Scanty pasturage and no supply of hay and grain would easily explain the lack of milk.

As winter wore on, the supply of flour grew less and less. The fall before Arthur Denny had paid twenty dollars for a barrel and that winter the price rose to forty dollars. At last there was none to be had anywhere on Puget Sound. Even the supply of hard-tack gave out, and for six weeks they were without bread of any kind.

Fortunately they had a good supply of sugar, syrup, tea, and coffee; nor did they lack for fish, venison and fowl. David Denny and Carson Boren, the trusty huntsmen, found good hunting in the forest and often brought in grouse, pheasants, ducks, and wild pigeons. All of this supply did very well, even without bread, as long as they had potatoes. But finally they too were gone. With neither bread nor potatoes, it did indeed amount "almost to distress."

Something had to be done, so John Low from "New York" and Arthur Denny started out in search of potatoes. They set out in a big canoe manned by four Indians and went up the Duwamish hoping to get "wapatoes" from the Indians on the Black River, who had been trained by the "King George" men (Englishmen) at Fort Nisqually to do some farming.

Their mission was successful and they returned in three days with fifty bushels of "little round red potatoes." Nothing in pioneer days was remembered more vividly than that return. One remembered that the potatoes piled on hides spread on the bottom of the canoe were wet, for the Bay was rough. The children, starved for fresh food, grabbed the "little round red potatoes" and ate them as if they were apples. The men piled the potatoes on the ground, washed the salt off, and then divided them among the several families.

Some time later, one morning at two o'clock, the blessed sound of chains and anchor woke the pioneers. They wasted no time in rowing out to the ship for supplies. And then, in the night, the women got up and baked bread—probably "quick biscuit"—and roused the children with the joyful news that at last they had bread, the first they had had for months.

In commenting on this experience, Mr. Denny says:

This was the hardest experience our people ever had but it demonstrated the fact that some substantial life-supporting food can always be obtained on Puget Sound, although it is hard for a civilized man to live without bread

CHAPTER IV

THE SWEETBRIAR BRIDE AND OTHER PIONEER WOMEN

THROUGH ALL the stress of that hard winter, the romance of David and Louisa, the John Alden and Phiscilla of the Seattle Pilgrims, had been ripening to a happy climax. Storms on the high seas which had cut off their supplies had not interfered with their courtship, begun back in Illinois and continued across the plains. David would soon be twenty-one and now they were to be married.

Louisa had had many suitors. Among them was one of the skippers of the little ship *Exact*, who wrote to her and sent her a ring, but she sent it back saying it did not fit. When he found that she and David were engaged he said. "You're a mighty lucky boy, Dave."

David built a little log cabin on his claim at the foot of Denny Way. It had no windows and the door was cut in half. As soon as it was finished, he and Louisa were married on the 23rd day of January, 1853, in Arthur Denny's cabin.

The bride was as fair a one as Seattle's sun has ever shone upon, with her wealth of black hair and wonderful coloring. She was dressed in soft white mull, which her own deft fingers had fashioned before she left the States.

The cabin was decorated with evergreens. She and David, like two children, had gathered the greens and made the little cabin a bower. Louisa helped cook the wedding dinner of wild duck. In her own words, as she told it long afterwards:

After everything was ready, I went upstairs; or rather I climbed up a ladder to the loft where the roof was so low I couldn't stand up without bumping my head, and put on my white dress. The belt was so tight I couldn't fasten it, so I came downstairs for Mary to help me, but she was busy; so David had to fasten it for me.

The ceremony was performed by Dr. Maynard, justice of the peace, with Henry Yesler as clerk and recorder. Besides Mr. and Mrs. Arthur Denny and their children, Mr. and Mrs. McConaha were present, also a few Indians who crowded around the door to see how the white man got his "klootchman."

After the ceremony and wedding dinner, the bride and bridegroom went down the bluff to their canoe carrying their few wedding gifts, among which were an old hen and a rooster given them by Dr. Maynard. Chickens were scarce in those days and were considered very valuable wedding presents. Their few household goods with the hen and rooster flapping on top were packed into the canoe and they were off. The waves were heavy and the canoe lurched badly; so their wedding journey from Marion Street to Denny Way, was not without thrills, but they reached their cabin in safety.

There they put skins and Indian mats on the floor; curtained off a pantry with blue calico; tacked on the walls some steel engravings and some pictures cut out of an old Godey's *Lady's Book*, that Louisa had brought across the plains; and hung the precious mirror that she had packed against her elders' wishes. On the bedstead, which was made of cedar poles with slats, they put their feather bed and gay quilts and then covered it with a hand-woven counterpane. that had once graced a four-poster in the old home. On a table nearby was a brass candlestick which the bride had carried to singing school back in Illinois. The furniture was all homemade excepting a stove and a chair, which David had bought from a sailing vessel. The stove was a regulation ship's cookstove with a railing around it.

When the room was arranged, the bride prepared the supper of salt meat and potatoes, and when the table was spread, she and David sat down to their first meal in their own home. And in that little one-roomed cabin with the earth for a floor, a bunk for a bed, a stool and a chair, and two pegs behind the door—one for the cap and one for the sunbonnet—in that little room they bowed their heads and gave thanks for their many blessings.

THE SWEETBRIAR BRIDE

The old hen that Dr. Maynard gave the "newly-weds" made a nest under the doorstep, and went to sitting as soon as the nest was full of eggs. Both she and the rooster seemed to realize that there was no time to waste in this new country, for when the eggs were hatched the rooster took full charge of the chicks while the hen filled the nest again and soon came forth with a second brood.

David was young and strong and that splendid energy that later made him a leader in city building went into providing for the new home. He supplied his table with meat from the forest—deer, elk, and bear. To support his family he cut and hewed square timber and hauled it to the beach to be sent to San Francisco.

It is fitting that the first flower garden in Seattle should have been planted by the first bride. One day in spring she planted around the cabin door a few of the precious sweetbriar seeds that she had picked when she bade Pamelia Dunlap good-bye in the garden in Cherry Grove. The sweetbriar grew and scattered over the town, and the old settlers called Louisa Denny "the sweetbriar bride."

This sweetbriar continued to grow at the foot of Denny Way until a short time ago—seventy-seven years after the seeds were planted—when the last trace of it was uprooted by the jaws of the steam shovel.

I always think of "the sweetbriar bride" when I read of a beautiful wedding. The wedding may be more elaborate. the gifts more costly; but, I am sure, none is happier than was Seattle's first bride. Then in the springtime, when thoughts of gardening are in the air, I try to picture that first little garden about the cabin door.

PIONEER WOMEN

"The foundation of Seattle was laid in a mother's tears." Tears of discouragement and disappointment; yet those tears of Mary Denny and of the other women who landed at Alki

in the rain, washed away the pent-up fears and doubts, re-
cruiting their strength, and enabled them to carry on.
Seattle's history reads heroic because of the pioneer women's
bravery.*

The cabins of the Seattle settlement were scattered from
what is now Pioneer Place to Mercer Street. Not far apart.
it seems to us when we locate them by the populated streets
of today, or dash from place to place in motor cars, but then
the thick forest closed in upon each and made it lonely and
remote. Sometimes two settlers were able to live near each
other when they held adjoining claims; but, for the most
part, they were obliged to live several miles apart in unprotected places in order to perfect the titles to their claims.

That is why "the sweetbriar bride" was forced to live so
far from her sister Mary, why the Bell cabin was set in the
wilds of what is now Belltown, and why Thomas Mercer
had to take his motherless daughters so far into the forest
to live.

On those days when her husband was out felling timber
for the San Francisco trade, the pioneer woman was alone
many times from early morning until late at night ever in
the shadow of danger, always anxiously awaiting the safe
return of her husband. At bedtime, when her little ones knelt
at her knee and trustingly lisped the words, "If I should
die before I wake," she did not know but that an Indian's
arrow or bullet might pierce them before morning.

This fear of unseen foes was probably the hardest thing
in her life, for what is more terrifying? The forest about
her might at any time send forth a crouching beast or a
stealthy Indian. The children were never allowed to wander
far from the cabins and were taught to blow out the candle
at any unusual sound after dark so that they might not be
too easy targets for arrows. Paradoxically, the silence of the

*From *History of the State of Washington* by Edmond S. Meany. By permission
of Macmillan Company, publishers.

forest and the stillness of the night were filled with a thousand sounds many times magnified; the falling of a leaf, the fluttering of a bird, or a soft tread of a furry foot might be a creeping Indian. Little wonder that the pioneer woman's nerves were often tense and her ears strained as she worked with her gun by her side.

When she lay down at night, instead of trains and street cars, and the whistling of steamboats, she frequently heard the chanting of the Indians as they "momoked tamanuse"— drove away evil spirits—or perhaps she was startled by their midnight wailing for the dead. Cries of wild animals and the hooting of owls came out of the depth of the forest, now First, Second, and Third Avenues. Even these sounds were sometimes alarming, for the Indians signaled each other by imitating the cries of birds and beasts. Sometimes, the Duwampsh war cry was heard—a loud, harsh bawl, warranted to strike terror to the most courageous heart.

A story of Louisa Denny and Mrs. Bell illustrates how entirely the women were at the mercy of the Indians in their lonely cabins while their husbands were away hunting or cutting timber.

David and Louisa's cabin at the foot of Denny Way was a mile from their nearest neighbors, the Bells. One morning, Mr. Bell found some pheasant eggs which Mrs. Bell decided to take to Louisa as a great delicacy, since she was not well. After walking along the beach she came to the Denny cabin and found Louisa in bed. She did what she could for her and then sat down to visit. While the two friends talked, two Indians came skulking around and looked in over the half-door. Friendly Indians told David afterwards that these Indians had intended to murder Louisa and rob her cabin. but on seeing another woman there, feared that the men might be near, and so abandoned the idea and went away.

Then I remember the story Mother used to tell of an old Indian who entered the house in a threatening manner one day when she sat sewing. She never stopped sewing but stood up and talked to him in Chinook, all of the time edging her way toward the back door. When she reached the door, she darted out and ran to the nearest neighbor.

Probably the loneliest of the women was Lydia Low who, for a whole year after the others had moved to Seattle, was the only white woman at "New York." She lived in the first-built cabin. Where yachts and power boats, steamers and plains pass today, then Indian canoes nosed their way upon the beach. Now and then a great whale came in close to shore. One night Mrs. Low was startled by a commotion in the water and found that it was caused by a school of black-fish passing the point. Furthermore, while her husband was away cutting timber, she was alone with her children among the Indians for weeks at a time; in fact, she was the only white adult on the beach except for a kind old Scotsman whose name we wish we knew.

At this time the accessible timber at Alki had been cut; so the men went to Port Orchard to cut a second cargo of piles for the *Leonesa*. Low stayed at the logging camp, occasionally going home to visit his family.

In an old account of Mrs. Low's experiences we read:

On the second or third trip of the *Leonesa* that vessel brought from San Francisco a stock of general merchandise for Low & Terry which was kept in the shed room of Mrs. Low's cabin. Terry had also received a keg of whiskey which was kept in the same shed room. Mrs. Low was afraid the Indians would break in, obtain this whiskey, get drunk and kill them all while the men were across the Sound. So she had Terry train her in the use of a Colt revolver until she could hit a tree a good distance away; but she never had occasion to use it.

Many times she would become frightened at the number of Indians encamped there from all parts of the country. Her fear would be greatest when the Northern Indians came. At one time thirty canoes full of these Northern Indians came in there. All the Indian women and children, as soon as they saw them, ran to the woods crying, "Stickine! Stickine!" while the Indian men took their Hudson's Bay muskets and ran to the beach. It was a long time before they would allow any of the visiting Indians to come ashore and then only part of them landed. They claimed to be peaceable and professed to be on their way up the Sound to trade and sell their furs at Fort Nisqually. After getting fresh water they passed.

That summer of '52 would have been lonely indeed for Mrs. Low if Captain Howard of the *Leonesa* had not presented her with several of Dickens' novels, bought in San Francisco. When she had a little spare time she would take her treasured book, steal out to her favorite spot overlooking the Sound, and read while the children played around her. I love to think of that pioneer woman being lifted from her life of toil and loneliness and apprehension into another world. I wish I knew just which characters were her companions during those golden moments of forgetfulness—David Copperfield, Oliver Twist, or perhaps little Dorrit. Precious books—precious moments—linking her with the old days back home.

In October of this year of isolation, in the original cabin that David Denny and Lee Tracy had begun, Mrs. Low gave birth to her fifth child—the first white child born in King County outside of Seattle. A doctor was called from Fort Steilacoom, but who paddled down to get him and then took him back, no one is left to tell. We do know that Mary Denny went over from Seattle to care for her friend and that she stayed for a week. What a week of companionship it must have been for the two friends! When she left, Mrs. Low was again the only white woman at "New York."

Charles Terry was allowed to name the new baby. He chose "Amelia Antoinette" and Amelia Antoinette she became, although she was called "Nettie." She became Mrs. George Foster and is still living today.

When we think of Mrs. Low's lonely months at "New York" before her child came, and of the fact that Mary Denny's baby was born twelve days after her arrival in Portland, after a four-months' journey across the prairies and that she had no food except clam broth for her babe for several months after reaching Alki; when we learn that Louisa Denny's second child was born in the blockhouse during the thick of the Indian War, and that Catherine Blaine, the wife of the first resident minister, was carried on board the *Decatur* in a rocking chair with her new babe to escape the Indian's arrow, we women of today sense slightly —only slightly—something of the hardships attendant upon bearing and rearing children in pioneer days.

Perhaps it was fortunate that the pioneer women had little time to sit down and think of the dangers surrounding them. Their lives were filled with the usual household cares and with the arduous task of making something out of next to nothing. This was their greatest achievement.

They made the children's shoes out of buckskin, with the tops of men's boots for soles. Flour sacks were used for the children's clothing. The men's jumpers and coats were sometimes made of buckskin which shrunk whenever they were caught in the rain.

The only oil for the little tin lamps was obtained from the dogfish. If lamps were lacking, rags were braided for wicks and stuck into cups of oil. The light was dim and the oil smelly. Those pesky fish-oil lamps, which were always leaking or being upset, tried the very souls of the women. One little girl remembered long afterwards of spilling the oil from one down the front of her "pink rosebud delaine dress." Poor little girl! It was her best dress. Tears would not wash the oil away. Whenever she came near the other children they held their noses.

Today, "hello, hello!" and an order over the telephone bring the supplies of the "butcher, the baker, and the candlestick maker" to the modern housewife; but not so then. The housewife then depended upon the incoming ships for staple supplies; fresh food was supplied by some one of her own family who went to the woods and waters for it, or by an Indian who brought it to her door to sell.

The abundance of edible game, and some that was not

edible, is pictured vividly for us in a letter which the Rev. David Blaine sent to friends in the East shortly after his arrival in '53:

> There is an abundance of game in the woods, consisting of deer, wild cattle (these belong to the Hudson's Bay people and have run wild) bears, wolves, panthers, squirrels, skunks and rats. Pheasant, grouse, gulls and ducks and crows are as tame here as the hens at home. They are very numerous. There are also a great many eagles, ravens and cranes. Our Sound or inland sea beside its many other excellent qualities, abounds in fish of almost every variety. Salmon are very abundant, cod fish, herring, sardines, oysters and clams. Whales come spouting along now and then. Halibut are caught at certain seasons of the year. The Indians do most of the fishing. The oysters here are of an inferior quality and small size.

These inland women learned readily how to prepare sea food to the delight of all. Clams were especially enjoyed; in chowder or fritters, fried or "straight." Roast wild goose and wild duck, and baked salmon were also favorite dishes. Wild berries were abundant and added much to their diet. In this same letter, Mr. Blaine exults over the wonderful substitute they have for the fruit to which they had been accustomed in the East:

> As for fruit, we can very well live without it as the superabundance of berries here will do as a substitute. These abound during nine or ten months in the twelve. We have strawberries, raspberries, dewberries, salal berries, salmon berries, cranberries, whortleberries, and wild grapes of a superior kind. These ripen successfully and are picked by the Indians and brought in by the barrel. Cranberries and whortleberries are still hanging on the bushes in abundance. (This was in December.) They are larger and more solid than our berries at home in the states.

Ingenious were the makeshifts when the supply of flour ran low or was entirely exhausted: potatoes were combined with flour to make it go further; biscuits were made of potatoes alone, and pudding of hard-tack and berries. Sometimes, when flour did arrive after having traveled up the coast from Chile, it was caked several inches inside the barrel where the water had seeped in.

Even in those days of privation, the feminine love of the beautiful and personal adornment could not be entirely quenched. One among them, Mrs. Bell, always managed the dainty touch that is so dear to the feminine heart. What she accomplished with her little was almost the impossible. One day, she appeared in a lace cap trimmed with new blue ribbon. Where did she get the blue ribbon? They all knew only too well the limited stock of her finery. She did not bring it with her and there were no shops to buy from. Where did she get it? After enjoying their amazement and admiration for a while, she told them she had taken some of the paper that lined the sugar barrel, cut it into strips, and put it under the lace.

Mrs. Bell was one of the appealing figures that moved through those early pages. Delicate and dainty, she was like a fragile windflower growing among the stumps. Frederick Grant writes of her, "Mrs. Bell like most of the mothers of Seattle was a woman of good education and refinement. She was the daughter of a clergyman."

Then there was little Louisa Catherine Denny, my mother, who longed for a black silk apron. She hunted the scrapbag over but there was no black silk. At last she found just what she wanted—one of her father's handkerchiefs, which had a hole in it, however. Nevertheless, she made the apron and when asked what she was going to do about the hole, replied, "I will keep my hand over it." So the child wore the apron, primly holding her dear little hand over the hole, and was happy.

Polished shoes were as much desired then as now, but there was no real shoe polish. The black off pots and kettles, mixed with grease made an excellent substitute.

Odd bits of calico, especially pink, were used to cover the boxes in which the emigrants had brought their plunder across the plains. The boxes became china closets and dressers. When the interior of the cabins became too monotonous the women resorted to the timeless feminine remedy; they changed the furniture about.

When a ship brought bolts of cloth there was little joy for the pioneer woman in having a dress of the new material, for every "klootchman" in town would have one from the same bolt. The old dress, turned, patched, and pieced, was preferable. Hats, which are either a woman's joy or her despair, were blocked and re-blocked by their own home methods; the straw sewed and re-sewed, trimmed and re-trimmed until there was nothing more to turn or trim. Then they turned to the lowly but ever-trusty sunbonnet, which shed the sun in summer and the rain in winter.

Even after there were stores in the village, only the sternest necessities were carried at first. The luxuries had to wait. When they could send to San Francisco in a few years for clothing and furniture, it was like sending to Paris today. Articles from Victoria were also thrilling. We still have my mother's brooch, earrings, and shawl that came from that place.

And what a joy it was to the women in later years when Henry Van Asselt began making curly maple furniture! He was kept busy, for, as soon as possible, the homemade furniture was cast aside and replaced with the new maple. A few four-posters and chests are still in the possession of the descendants of those first settlers.

The Bell family had the first bathtub in Seattle. Mr. Bell and Arthur Denny made it from a cedar log split into boards which were planed smooth and made into an oblong box. The seams were filled with swamp grass. Washtubs were easily made by sawing barrels in half. The fireplaces which they used until the vessels brought them stoves were made of sticks and stones daubed with blue clay, with stones for andirons and a flat rock for a hearth. On a chain and hook a kettle was hung. Some of the women had Dutch ovens for baking bread and a "gold pan" from California made a very good mixing bowl.

As time went on, the women trained the squaws to do the housework. At first, they seemed hopeless and were exceedingly trying, but after much training, they learned to scrub and wash fairly well. But the greatest trouble with their laundry work was that they were either likely to rub holes in the clothes or, if they did get them clean, soil them again by laying them on the floor or ground. If they were set to scrubbing the floor, only the center would be scrubbed—the corners meant nothing to them. The white woman might remonstrate and scold, but the squaw remained unmoved and scrubbed the center and nothing more.

Few household treasures were carried across the plains. but tiny flower seeds took so little room that many varieties were brought for future flower gardens. Louisa Boren Denny started a number of flower favorites other than the sweetbriar. Her daughter, Inez Denny, tells us in *Blazing the Trail*, that everywhere her mother made her home, even for a few years, she planted a garden of old-fashioned flowers. Roses and hollyhocks, pansies and tiger lilies, honeysuckles and sweet William, and mignonette ran riot about her door.

Pink mission roses which her brother Carson had brought from Steilacoom, where the Mission Fathers had introduced them in the early days, were later added to her collection of flowers. Her flower garden was outlined with white pebbles from the beach and filled with black dirt brought from the forest by a "klootchman."

Louisa was an ardent nature lover. The story is told that in those first hours after landing at Alki on the cold, desolate beach, the eager young curiosity of this inland-born girl led her to examine the shells and pebbles, the ferns and firs. It had been her delight to look for new plant life along the westward trail. She said afterward that she had left Illinois when violets were in bloom and had reached her journey's end when only rose hips and snowberries were left.

Catherine Blaine, the bride of the pioneer minister, grew the first apples in Seattle. Whether she carefully packed the seeds before leaving her New York home or whether, as an afterthought, she saved the seeds of the apples they may have eaten on the way, I cannot say; but we do know that on their lot at Second and Cherry Streets she planted the seeds that grew into the first fruit trees in Seattle. According to an old settler she had "the finest apples on Puget Sound."

Red clover was also planted by a woman's hand, the first clover seeds having been scattered by Mrs. John Denny.

Even the irrepressible, gadabout dandelion, which we vainly try to eject from the lawn, was not a native of Puget Sound but was actually planted here. The great, gloomy forest was no place for the sun-loving little flower but, after a clearing had been made, Mrs. Maynard planted it for medicinal purposes. I reluctantly write this for fear that every time you see that unconquerable weed fairly daring you to dig it up, you may harbor an unkind feeling for the one who planted it. Let the many greater things she did stay that thought. Nevertheless, the dandelion blooms on, a constant reminder of the indomitable spirit of that pioneer woman.

As it was with "the sweetbrier bride," and with Mrs. Low, so it was with all of the pioneer women; they dwelt in their lonely cabins and worked from early dawn till late at night. Many times one pair of hands had all to do, sometimes a man's work as well as a woman's. Those hands sewed, baked, washed, and scrubbed; soothed and caressed. Wonderful hands! If all the work those hands did could be piled into one great mound, oh, what a mountain it would be! I rejoice that some in the evening of life rested, sweet and tranquil like the hands of Whistler's mother. I grieve that others toiled on to the end; but perhaps their reward in the Beyond is greater and brighter for the waiting.

CHAPTER V

SINCE THE ADVENT of the white man, no springtime in Seattle has ever come as joyously and with such a sense of resurrection and hope as the spring of 1853, because none has ever followed such a lean and hungry winter. In January the pussywillows began to bud with larger catkins than our pioneers had ever seen before; in February the warm glow of wild currant bushes in bloom appeared.

No sooner had the rough seas subsided than vessels began to appear on the Sound. One ship from San Francisco bore its weight in gold, for it came laden with the machinery for Yesler's sawmill.

Mr. Yesler wasted no time in setting it up, not even waiting for a roof over its head, and on March 28, 1853, began sawing the first lumber to be used for building the structure around the machinery. Probably no sound has ever been more exciting to Seattle ears than the first buzz of that circular saw. Every man in the community was needed to operate it. Arthur Denny, I happen to know, tended the screw that gauged the sawing of the boards and David Denny drew in the logs. Even the Indians were trained to help. Then as spring advanced, other immigrants arrived as if they had been sent for to fill a need.

A slim, young man of eighteen, George Frye, my father, arrived with Mr. and Mrs. Hillory Butler. He and Mr. Butler had crossed the plains together, endured the ravages of cholera together, worked together in the Willamette Valley during the winter, and then had come on to Puget Sound. They were put right to work getting out timber to supply the saw.

William Gilliam, another newcomer, and Mr. Butler subcontracted the work of getting out the timber from Dr. Maynard, who had contracted to supply the mill. The versatile doctor was killing two birds with one stone, for he wanted to clear a piece of land on "the Point," which was covered by a grove of firs. He wished to get them out of the way so that his lots south of there in "Maynardtown" could be seen.

Affairs of state were also getting on, for the settlers received word on April 25th that their petition for the organization of a separate territory in "Northern Oregon" had been granted by Congress. The news was received in the newly created territory with fitting ceremony. Guns were fired and speeches made.

But the new territory was not named "Columbia" as the pioneers had planned. Some Congressman, thinking that name would be confused with the District of Columbia. named it after George Washington, apparently not realizing that a city and state of the same name would be equally confusing.

President Franklin Pierce immediately appointed a governor, secretary, marshal, chief justice, and other officials for the new territory. Isaac I. Stevens was appointed governor and superintendent of Indian affairs.

In May, Arthur Denny received a letter from the newly made governor explaining what was planned for the new territory. Certainly no letter ever received in Seattle was weightier with plans for big development.

Washington, D. C.
To A. A. Denny Esq.,   April 18, 1853
Dear Sir:

Herewith you will find a printed copy of my instructions from the secretary of war, by which you will see an exploration and survey of a railroad from the head waters of the Mississippi to Puget Sound is intrusted to me. To avoid the delay such expedition might occasion in the organization of the territory, Colonel Anderson, the marshal, will take a census preliminary to an election for members of the legislature. He will be found to be a very worthy genteman, will consult with his fellow citizens on all subjects of interest to the territory, and for him and his brother officers I bespeak your good offices. A military road is to be built from Fort Walla Walla to Puget Sound. Captain McClellan, distinguished for his gallantry in Mexico, has command of the party who will make the exploration of the Cascade range and the construction of the military road. His undertaking of the task is a sure guaranty of its accomplishment. I expect to pierce the Rocky Mountains and this road is to be done in time for the fall emigration so that an open line of communication between the states and the Sound will be made this year.

Desiring to know your views on these and kindred topics, inviting your consideration of a proper location of the territorial capital, I am,

Yours truly,

ISAAC I. STEVENS

The news that the government was to make a railroad survey to Puget Sound was indeed inspiring; but the news that a wagon road was to be built through the Cascade Mountains and that Captain McClellan, later of Civil War fame, was coming out that very summer to begin operations was almost too good to be true. More than anything else. Seattle needed roads that would lead immigrants to Puget Sound; consequently, the news of the building of this military road was highly encouraging.

The Congressional appropriation of $20,000, which was made at this time for this road through the mountains, was secured through the efforts of the pioneers of Olympia and Steilacoom, who had felt the urgent need for such a road. before Seattle was founded.

A year had passed after the founding of Seattle and the plats of the little settlement had not been filed. The United States Land Office in Oregon City was so far away that the filing had been deferred. Now, in '53, it could be done at home, for local government had been established in the new territory.

In *Pioneer Days on Puget Sound*, Mr. Denny writes:

The policy of laying off a town and the name had been discussed and agreed upon by us before Yesler came which accounts for the fact that he does not appear as one of the proprietors in the first plat which was filed for record.

Of that day on which the plats were filed, he says:

All had gone smoothly until the time when we (Boren, Maynard and myself) were to record a joint plat of the town of Seattle, when it was found that the Doctor, who occasionally stimulated a little, had that day taken enough to make him feel that he was not only monarch of all he surveyed but what Boren and I had surveyed as well. Consequently, Boren and I on the 23rd day of May, 1853, filed the first plat of the City of Seattle. When, in the evening of the same day, his fever had subsided sufficiently, the Doctor filed his also.

The plats were filed before Henry Yesler, the newly appointed clerk of probate, and the records were kept in a cheap account book.

Dr. Maynard's plat of the tract south of "The Sag," or Yesler Way, shows Commercial Street as the first street along the water front and parallel to that: Second, Third and Fourth to Tenth. Streets running east and west were named: Washington; Main; Jackson and King for prominent Democrats—Andrew Jackson and Vice-President King; Weller for the governor of California; and Lane for Joseph Lane of pioneer fame in Oregon. Dr. Maynard's tract consisting of fifty-eight blocks, extended to Judkins street.

Boren and Denny's plat of the section north of "the Sag" began with Front Street, that ran along the bluff in a northerly direction—the present First Avenue—which was paralleled by Second and Third Avenues. At Yesler's mill Front Street merged into Commercial Street with a jog of half a block west. At right angles to First Avenue the streets were platted north to Spring, which was fittingly named for the spring that had trickled down to the beach below and given refreshment to the explorers on the day they made their momentous decision in locating their claim sites.

Why Mr. Denny named the streets in alliterative pairs. no one knows. It was doubtless just a fancy. James and Marion Streets were named in loving remembrance of his brother, James Marion, who had died in Oregon not long after crossing the plains. Madison, named undoubtedly after President Madison, paired with Marion; Jefferson with James, Jefferson probably named by Yesler who was a Jeffersonian Democrat. Columbia was a name that was much in their minds. The origin of Cherry is not known. It may have been chosen to harmonize with Columbia; or as one old settler suggests, the street may have got its name from the wild cherry that grew thereabouts abundantly; it may have been inspired by two settlers named Cherry, who lived on the Sound, but probably it was named for Cherry Grove, Illinois.

Later in '69 when Mr. Denny filed his second plat of an additional tract, this same pairing of names was continued. Seneca to go with Spring, probably chosen out of courtesy to the Rev. and Mrs. David Blaine, who came from Seneca Falls, New York; University and Union, the former as the street on which the territorial university was built. and the later named at the close of the Civil War; Pike for John Pike, a prominent pioneer, and Pine to go with Pike. the naming of streets for trees being the custom of the day.

This filing of the plats must not be mistaken for the legal transaction of securing title to the land. The legal patents were not obtained until a number of years later when the Indian title was relinquished. This filing was for the purpose of granting deeds of the lots to those who were expected soon to buy.

For the time being, the seller of a lot gave bond assuring the purchaser that he would receive the deed to his property when the title became clear by virtue of the Indians relinquishing their rights.

It is worth emphasizing that these original plats were the plans of a city which had been surveyed and laid out that first year. The streets and alleys for the most part are identical with those of today, even their original width of sixty-six feet remaining the same except where the avenues have been widened.

On May 28th, five days after the filing of the first plat of Seattle, the plat of "New York Point" was filed, but the record was subsequently destroyed. According to Arthur Denny's survey "New York" was divided into six blocks of eight lots each.

On March 5th, the King County commissioners, appointed the preceding winter by the Oregon legislature, held their first meeting. Mr. Low did not qualify since he was preparing to leave "New York"; but Collins and Denny met with Boren, sheriff, and Yesler, county clerk. All during that year these four men met and slowly, painstakingly. conscientiously laid the foundations of King County.

At the first meeting, they affected only an organization but in April they planned seriously for some road building. The county was divided into two road districts; all of the county "north of the Duwampsh" being district No. 1 with William Bell supervisor, all "south of the Duwampsh" being district No. 2 with George Holt supervisor.

This division of the county sounds illogical until we use our imagination to see King County as they did, as one big. unknown forest with the mouth of "the Duwampsh" as a tangible point to mark a dividing line between the north and south.

At this April meeting, Luther Collins, having given "requisite notice," was granted a license to operate a ferry across the Duwamish. He paid two dollars for his license and was to charge "footmen" 12½ cents, a man and horse 50 cents, wagon and team $1.50, oxen 12½ cents, and sheep and hogs 5 cents.

Another important thing the commissioners did was to arrange for the first King County taxes. Until a regular election could be held, they appointed a temporary assessor and a treasurer. We read this significant item in their records: "ordered that a tax of four mills on the dollar be levied for county revenues." Taxes had begun.

In April, true to his plans, Thomas Mercer returned from Salem to attend to his claim and to make arrangements

to bring his children later. This time he was accompanied by
Dexter Horton, a young man of twenty-eight, who, as we
know, had crossed the plains with Mercer and Daniel Bagley.

Mercer went back to Salem very soon, but Horton remained for a while to earn some much needed money before going back to Oregon for his wife and daughter. This
young man, who later became the dean of Seattle bankers
at that time penniless and depleted by a siege of the ague
was glad to go to work for Bell, shaving shingles, getting
out piles, and even grubbing the stumps that were very
thick in Mr. Bell's front yard. All of this he was glad to
do for $2.50 a day.

John C. Holgate and Edward Hanford, who were to
leave their names permanently on the map of Seattle, also
arrived that spring. Mr. Holgate had been in this locality
before. As early as 1850, accompanied by Indians, he had
ascended the Duwamish and chosen a claim site on the river
near the present Georgetown. This made him, in a measure, the original pioneer of King County. He then left
the Puget Sound country, intending to come back later and
settle.

The story of John Holgate is one of the romantic chapters in Seattle history. As a frail, imaginative boy, he had
been so fired by stories from Lewis and Clark's *Journals*
which his sister, Abbie Jane Holgate, had found in their attic and read to him, that he came west at the age of nineteen. And then, the spirit of adventure leading him on, he
explored the Puget Sound region and selected the Duwamish Valley as the best place in which to locate.

Mr. Holgate brought with him from the East a load
of carefully selected nursery trees among which was a much
admired little fir. It is said that at one time while crossing
the plains he refused five dollars for it. Very tenderly did
he care for the tiny evergreen, thinking it would be a rare

and valuable tree in Oregon—only to find that he had come to a land of towering firs.

Young Holgate was so eloquent in his letters back home describing the new country that his sister and her husband. Edward Hanford, sold their farm in Iowa and came to Puget Sound.

On his return to the Duwamish Valley in 1853, Holgate found his original tentative selection of land taken by Collins; consequently he staked another claim, the next one south of Dr. Maynard's. Edward Hanford took the one south of Holgate. These two claims extended over the steep slopes of Beacon Hill with only a narrow bench of beach along what is now Ninth Avenue South—all the vast industrial section of today west of Beacon Hill being tide flats at that time.

With the arrival of spring came changes at "New York." John Low sold his interest to Terry and moved with his family to Chamber's Prairie near Olympia, where he bought a farm on which he lived for many years. Later he moved to Snohomish County. Although he drops out of the Seattle picture, he remained on Puget Sound. It is not surprising that the Lows moved away, for Lydia Low had passed long, fearful months at "New York-Alki" alone with her little family among the Indians.

Charles Terry was now the dominating figure at "New York." As we know, his brother Lee had left for his native state the preceding spring. But Charlie Terry was fully able to carry on alone. Due to his salesmanship, as we would call it today, "New York-Alki" began to hum that spring, many immigrants stopping there in preference to coming to Seattle. With unlimited energy this young man of twenty-three was shaping the wilderness into what he believed was to be a great city.

Before they settled on White River, Samuel Russell and his family lived at "New York." For a time they were the only family there, the rest of the population being bachelors and men without their families.

The big thing that happened at "New York" that spring was the coming of Captain William Renton looking for a site for a steam sawmill. Alki Point looked like a good place; so there he built his mill.

The spirit of "New York" in that spring of '53 is reflected in the name of a store which advertised in the April *Columbian* as the "New York Wholesale and Retail Store and Ship Chandlery." In the same paper is a notice of a new cooper shop and another grocery, which advertised "a full supply of groceries, flour, and liquor."

It must have been shortly after this that Terry decided to change the name of the settlement from "New York" to "Alki," for the *Columbian*, commenting on it, says:

Our enterprising friend, C. C. Terry, has made an excellent change of name for his flourishing town at the mouth of the Duwamish Bay, hitherto called "New York." It is henceforth to be known by the name of "Alki." We never fancied the name of New York on account of its inappropriateness but Alki we subscribe to instanter. The interpretation of the word Alki being "by-and-by," "in a little while," or "hereafter" we must approve its application to a growing and hopeful place. Well done, friend Terry, success to thee and thy Alki. We are informed that a steam sawmill and several business houses are being erected at Alki. An extensive square timber and pile business is being done there and good assortments of merchandise are kept by the merchants.

Although "success to thee and thy Alki" was not to be realized soon, it looked very near that spring.

Nor was romance lacking in the "growing and hopeful place." Samuel Russell had a pretty daughter, Mary Jane. and Charles Terry was young and handsome. We have only time and place for facts, but fancy fills in between the lines. Again on the beach at Alki do lovers plight their troth.

At Alki and at Seattle the shores are flooded with tender spring sunshine. Between the settlements the wake of canoes threads its way across the water.

THE SUMMER OF '53

Spring quickened into a prosperous summer. Nearly every brig and schooner that came into the Sound brought a few immigrants, some for Seattle, others who were planning to found settlements elsewhere. Some came looking for good locations for sawmills, for the news of the San Francisco building boom was now bringing to the West, Argonauts, not seeking gold, but lumber. Many came from as far east as Maine, and joined in the upbuilding of the great lumbering industry of the Northwest.

Among the newcomers were: Timothy Hinckley and Franklin Matthias from Olympia, who became identified with many of the useful undertakings in the village; Henry Adams, a carpenter, who helped build many of the early homes; Charles Plummer, who at once entered into the life of the village as one of its most active pioneers; and David Phillips with his motherless girls, the oldest of whom, Dorcas, kept house for him. J. H. Nagle took up a donation claim east of what is now Broadway and John J. Moss took up a claim between Hanford and Collins. Some of the men who had come the year before sent for their families; Dr. Smith, for one, whose mother and sister Ellender arrived on one of the brigs.

As new settlers arrived many of them took up claims along the rivers in preference to penetrating the forest. The rivers were their only roads and the Duwamish was the main arterial. "White River," "Black River," "Green River" were spoken of as today we speak of important towns.

On the Duwamish, south of the Collins, Van Asselt, and Maple settlements, donation claims were taken along the river banks down as far as Mox La Push, the junction where the Black and White Rivers joined and formed the Duwamish at the present Renton Junction. Another group of settlers took claims on the site of the present city of Renton.

The Black River, so important in pioneer history, is today nothing more than a dry river bed and all that is left to mark Mox La Push is a filling station bearing the sign "Black River Junction." Black River at that time flowed from Lake Washington into the White River but was drained in 1916 when the level of Lake Washington was lowered by the opening of the canal into Lake Union. Mox La Push was an important point for trade and transfer as well as for settlement. Black River was so called in comparison to the white, glacier-fed waters of White River.

The Seattle settlement that a few months before had been isolated and hungry now hummed to the tune of the sawmill. The new arrivals added their vitality and energy to the village group. All worked from sunup to sundown to supply trade, and, though they worked for revenue, they were at the same time clearing the town site of its heavy forest—accomplishing two tasks with one axe.

Trees were coming down and buildings were going up now that sawed lumber was available. Yesler built a wharf where all the men gathered when a ship came in. He also built his house near the mill. Hillory Butler bought land and built on Second Avenue at James Street, where the Butler Hotel stands today. Young David built a second home; this time a small board one near Arthur and Mary Denny's. These two little homes stood near the "big laurel," as they called the great madrona that overhung the bluff near First and Marion. Bell continued to live in Belltown. South of town Edward Hanford and John Holgate were building cabins on the beach preparing for the coming of their families who were still in Oregon.

This was undoubtedly one of the busiest summers in all Seattle history. The insatiable sailing vessels kept coming for more lumber faster than it could be cut. There were about twenty ships that plied between the Sound and San Francisco that summer.

The hardest work was getting the timber for the mill to saw into lumber. Even the farmers up the Duwamish went to logging. Young Maple wrote of the summer:

My father and I took a contract for getting 7,000 telegraph poles and 5,000 boat poles; these we packed out of the woods to the water on our shoulders. We rafted them by hand alongside of the ship as there were no steamers to do our towing.

This was the method used by all at that time.

Henry Yesler wrote of it, "A great deal of the earliest logging on the Sound was done exclusively by hand, the logs being thrown into the water by handspikes, and towed to the mill on the tide by skiffs."

When we stop to realize that the forest was in its first-growth condition and that these men, without the donkey engine or modern equipment of any kind, were logging giant firs and cedars, our admiration and amazement increase.

Clarence Bagley describes their accomplishment very aptly in his *History of Seattle*, when he says:

By sheer strength of their bodies the men laid low the stately trees that made the site of the future city a forest, rolled them to tidewater and towed them with small boats to the mill. There was no other way to do the work and full advantage had to be taken of the accommodations that the gods had provided, as the steep hills back of the waterfront, presented grades that eased somewhat the work of handling logs without the equipment that makes them the playthings of the machinery of today.

Splitting cedar shingles and shakes did not require so much labor. After the tall, straight-grained cedar trees, that grew so plentifully here at that time, were sawed into short lengths, they could be split by hand. Bagley says of this industry:

The ease and rapidity with which these shingles could be split from fine clear cedar was a surprise to the newcomer to the country. Good prices were obtained and the business was one yielding fair returns, especially as very little capital was required.

An eventful incident in the industrial development of Seattle was the discovery of coal. Dr. R. M. Bigelow, while clearing land on his claim at Black River, came upon signs of coal which led to further discovery. From that time on, coal played a part in Seattle's plans for future growth.

Although they had little capital, Dr. Bigelow and three of his friends—H. H. Tobin, O. M. Eaton, and Joseph Fanjoy—formed the Duwamish Coal Co., recorded in old King County records on October 20, 1853. Unfortunately, due to lack of capital, they were not able to develop the project.

It is one of the ironies of pioneering that Dr. Bigelow, who discovered and opened up the first coal mines that brought such wealth to the new country, should have spent his last days in poverty.

I should like to omit one event of this summer of constructive activity, for it mars the splendid record. A murder, which had a far-reaching effect on pioneer history, was committed by "Masachie Jim" (bad Jim), an Indian. He killed his "klootchman," and a few white men in Seattle took the law into their own hands and lynched him the same evening.

Not only was the hanging a lawless thing to do, but an unwise one, for it loosed a stream of hatred that, as all historians of that period agree, contributed to the flood of resentment that caused the Indian War.

Another murder occurred shortly after this tragedy, but the white people, going busily about their work, knew nothing about it until a year later. The Indians knew, but they kept the secret; and the beautiful forest around Lake Union did not betray the grave of a white man buried on its shores. This was the famous "McCormick murder" always included in the history of '53, but not discovered, as we shall see, until the following year.

The sight of a white sail coming around the Point was *the*

great event of those years. Aside from the revenue derived from the cargo which it carried away, it brought the things which today we get by train, telegraph, radio, and newspaper. It brought groceries, hardware, news, and immigrants and took away cargoes of piles, squared timbers, ships' knees, cordwood, shingles, and hoop poles. San Francisco's gold boom was Puget Sound's lumber boom.

The ships brought a regular supply of articles for barter with the Indians, articles such as calico, red flannel, beads. blankets, shawls, knives, and tinware, especially tin pails. The Indians loved shiny, new tin pails. They gladly exchanged "wapatoes," clams, salmon, berries, crabs, and mats and baskets of their own weaving for these things or for foolish trinkets.

Furthermore, the white sails brought good friends, for their masters became influential men in the settlements. Try as one may, it is hard now to recapture the romance and importance of those early sailing vessels.

After the shipmasters had disposed of what goods they could, they left the remainder with Arthur Denny, who sold it on commission. He kept these supplies in the only place he had—his little two-room cabin on Marion Street. When a householder's provisions gave out, he went down to the cabin, and from the sugar barrel, the pork barrel, or the keg of molasses, Mr. Denny would measure him a portion.

In those days whiskey was one of the big items of merchandising. Grant tells a story of Arthur Denny, who was strongly opposed to the traffic in intoxicants and found himself in somewhat of a dilemma when the master of a sailing vessel sent a young man ashore with merchandise to be stored, among which was some whiskey. Grant says:

Mr. Denny finally consented to store the goods until the owner came and it was accordingly brought ashore and placed in safe corners about his cabin. Speaking of the incident Mr. Denny naively says, "It was a hard kind of goods to hold on to in those days but there was never a drop of it escaped until the owner came and removed it to Steilacoom." A large profit could have been realized from its sale at this time and Mr. Denny was a small capitalist in those days, but then, as throughout his entire career, he never engaged in any business which a high sense of duty to his fellow men or his conscience did not approve.

Early in the summer both Alki and Seattle had a visit from two young men by the name of Meeker, who were looking for a good farm site on Puget Sound. These two came, not in a canoe, but in a flat-bottomed boat. Although "Brother Oliver pointed to the fact that Indians navigated the whole Sound in these canoes," Ezra, as he tells the story in his *Pioneer Reminiscences of Puget Sound* "would not trust his carcass to a craft that would tip so easily."

Ezra Meeker, who had crossed the plains the summer before in '52, writes of this visit:

Just then we spied a cluster of cabins and houses on the point to the east, and made a landing at what proved to be Alki Point, the place then bearing the pretentious name New York.

Here we met the irrepressible C. C. Terry, proprietor of the new townsite, who was keenly alive to the importance of adding to the population of his new town. But we were not hunting town sites and of course lent a deaf ear to the arguments set forth in favor of the place.

We soon pushed on over to the east where the steam from a sawmill acted as a guiding star, and landed at a point that cannot have been far removed from the western limit of the present Pioneer Place of Seattle near where the totem pole now stands.

Here we found the never-to-be-forgotten Yesler, not whittling his pine stick as in later years, but as a wideawake business man, on the alert to drive a trade when an opportunity offered, or spin a yarn, if perchance time would permit. I cannot recall meeting Mr. Denny, although I made his acquaintance soon after at my own cabin on McNeil's island.

In fact we did not stay very long at Seattle, not being favorably impressed with the place. There was not much of a town, probably twenty cabins in all, with a few newer frame houses. The standing timber could scarcely have been further removed than to have been out of reach of the mill, and of course, scarcely the semblance of a street. The lagoon presented an uninviting appearance and scent, where the process of filling with slabs and sawdust had already begun. The mill though, infused activity in its immediate vicinity and was really the life of the place.

So did he who was to become the patriarch of covered-wagon pioneers, pass Seattle by and row off in his flat-bottomed boat. The "lagoon" with the "uninviting appearance and scent" was the same which made "Maynardtown" an island at high tide, and at low tide revealed the rubbish and garbage that was dumped there. It was gradually filled with sawdust from the mill.

In August, the *Columbian* gave this new settlement a few kind words of encouragement, although even then it is plain to be seen that Alki was the more important of the two towns. It said:

Seattle is thriving. All the accounts that we receive from thence tell us of new buildings and other improvements. Yesler's steam sawmill is working finely. Alki is full of vigor and goaheaditiveness; her commerce is increasing and her men of business are doing well. Renton's steam sawmill will be in operation in a few days. The enterprising inhabitants of these two places, near together as they are, seemed determined that their full, high and important destiny shall be achieved as soon as possible. Success attend them, say we.

This was Alki's peak summer. On the Fourth of July the settlers had a celebration with dinner in "the grove," with speech making and a dance in the evening. Alki was much the livelier and gayer of the two places at that time.

Of this period Bagley says:

The two villages retained their separate activities and were jealous rivals for more than five years. They had their own stores and trading posts and sawmills. Each of them had seagoing boats plying to and fro between the bay and San Francisco, carrying lumber, piles and other products of the forest, as well as fish.

But for all of Alki's "goaheaditiveness," it lacked the essential of a protected deep-water harbor. No sooner was Renton's mill finished than he discovered that the strong, northerly winds and high tides that sweep around Alki Point made the site impossible. Today that point is protected by a lighthouse.

It is hard to understand how Captain Renton could have

made such a mistake. In commenting on it and the fact that others of those early sawmill men, as well, passed up the better locations at first, Arthur Denny says, "I suppose it was on the theory that Puget Sound is all a harbor and it was not necessary to be particular."

The failure of the mill was a hard blow for Alki. The mill was moved to Port Orchard the next spring and, although Terry remained in his dream-city another year, there were no more flowery comments in the newspaper. It had been nip and tuck between Seattle and Alki for a while and if Terry's dream had come true, the sky line of the city would be at Alki and over the hills of West Seattle today.

The ships brought news of other settlements on Puget Sound, for gradually brave little groups were venturing up the rivers and along the shores. There were new ones up the Puyallup River, on Whidby Island, at Utsalady, Dungeness, Port Townsend, and Whatcom (Bellingham).

Steilacoom and Port Madison were entering on a period of prosperity that threatened to make them rivals for place as the most important town on Puget Sound.

It is amazing how these groups came to know each other and about each other despite the distance and lack of communication. Arthur Denny says, "At this time all white men were supposed to know each other and their location and occupation, between the mouth of the Cowlitz River and Cape Flattery."

It was not idle curiosity that made them seek news of the other settlements, but a bond of pioneering. These gallant founders of the State of Washington were so few and the Indians were so many, the forest so deep and the waters so wide, no wonder each was solicitous of the other. In their histories of those days both Inez and Arthur Denny speak of the people at Port Townsend and Olympia and Whidby as if they were near neighbors.

A matter of intense interest to the entire territory during

the summer of '53 was that J. Patton Anderson, the newly appointed United States marshal, a tall, striking-looking Southerner, was in their midst, taking the census in preparation for the election of members to the first territorial legislature.

The result of that first census was as follows:

Counties	Population	Voters
Island	195	80
Jefferson	189	68
King	170	111
Pierce	513	276
Thurston	996	381
Pacific	152	61
Lewis	616	239
Clarke	1,134	466
	3,965	1,682

Less than four thousand people in all of Washington Territory at the close of that busy and prosperous summer. In King County only 170 white people, of whom 111 were men and voters. In every community the Indians outnumbered the whites by large numbers.

The city's founding and growth did not depend upon the numbers as much as upon the calibre and substantiality of the men who had the hardihood and vision to struggle as far north as Puget Sound. By the time they got here, it was a survival of the fittest. They were men who sought not gold, but land; men who came to settle—empire-builders.

CHAPTER VI

A PARSON AND A SCHOOLMA'AM

OTHER NEWCOMERS in the autumn of '53, who were to add color and texture to the pattern of Seattle, were the Rev. David Blaine and his wife, Catherine. During the previous summer, the Rev. Benjamin Close, a Methodist and the first Protestant minister in Washington Territory, had made several visits to Seattle and had held the first Protestant service in the settlement; but now it was to have its own resident minister. Mr. and Mrs. Blaine were young bride and bridegroom when they left Seneca Falls, New York. and set out by way of the Isthmus of Panama for the far frontier.

From the letters which these two wrote home, which have been preserved, we get one of our most authentic and colorful accounts of those years. On their arrival on Puget Sound. they first spent a few days at Olympia where they were entertained by "Brother Close," and then stopped at Steilacoom a day or two. From there, as Mr. Blaine wrote:

We came on some 25 miles down Sound to Seattle—our Home. We reached Alki, a little place six miles distant across the bay, on Saturday, November 26, and as it was late in the day and the wind was high, we concluded to remain there until Monday. We were very kindly received and hospitably entertained at a Mr. Russell's, the only white family in the place, which contains 8 or 9 houses and a sawmill. The houses are used as stores and homes for bachelors. I preached in the afternoon and evening. In the evening after the sermon, a young man took his hat, of his own accord, and passed it around among the auditors, of whom I should think there were 30. He turned out the contents on the table and I scraped them off and put them in my pocket. When we counted the money it amounted to $12.50.

The impulsive and generous young man was Charlie Terry. One account says that he exclaimed as he passed the hat, "I don't know much about Methodism, but I do know about this."

From Alki, the new minister and his wife were paddled

over to Seattle in Bob Moxie's canoe. Mr. Blaine wrote in his first letter back east, "It rained hard most of the way from Alki to this place. We came to Mr. Denny's and were kindly received. Here we are yet. This house contains two rooms."

In after years, Mr. Blaine wrote of their arrival:

One needed some hopeful ardor not to be a little depressed by the, to us, unusual and not altogether attractive surroundings of gloomy and unbroken forests. But the cordiality with which we were received by Mr. A. A. Denny and family were very cheering and no chronicler of the beginning of church work on Puget Sound can neglect to mention the unvarying kindness and helpfulness of his family.

For three weeks the newcomers were entertained in that cabin of two rooms. Arthur and Mary Denny now had four children. Four adults and four children in two rooms for three weeks in winter!

Mr. Blaine began at once to organize his work. The very first Sabbath, he "preached two sermons and organized a church [Methodist Episcopal] of four members of whom Catherine was one." Mary and Arthur Denny, and John Nagle were the others.

The Blaines were entirely without Western or pioneer experience, their trip by water not having prepared them for roughing it as the trek across the plains had prepared the settlers. They were in every sense of the word, tenderfoot missionaries.

Mrs. Blaine, who had a keen sense of humor, used to love to tell this story on her husband in after years. He spent much of his time on that tedious ocean voyage from New York writing sermons of a missionary cast, so that he would be ready to convert the heathen when he arrived at his new field. With his first sermon all written, he was prepared for his first service. Not realizing that these rough- and-ready looking pioneers had but recently come from the East. where they had had advantages of church and school, he

started to read, telling the people who he was and that he
had come to tell them of a Savior who had died to save
them. This was too much for his audience; there was a
smile; and a wink passed around, which Mrs. Blaine was
quick to see. She finally caught her husband's eye and
frowned at him, disconcerting him somewhat, but having
the desired effect of causing him to skip several pages and
proceed in a different vein.

As the community had welcomed industry, so it welcomed the first minister. Carson Boren donated land for a
church and a parsonage at the southeast corner at Second
and Columbia Streets. The enterprising young minister
solicited funds for his church everywhere possible, even on
board every vessel that came into port. Captain Howard of
the brig *Leonesa* is said to have contributed the first money.
Some of the settlers gave money. Those who had no money
gave saw logs which Hillory Butler hauled to the mills.

Writing back home of the generosity of the people Mr.
Blaine said:

I am offered a lot anywhere in town to build our house upon
without charge. I have not selected it yet. One man here has donated
thirty acres of land for a seminary just outside the village survey.
Another has given me a lot for a church and parsonage. Brother
Denny offers a lot for a first, best garden where it will not require
much labor to clear it. We shall not need to secure a claim.

I am not sure whether Mr. Blaine refers to Dr. Maynard
or to Carson Boren as the donor of a tract for a seminary,
for we find in old records that both made such a donation.
The seminary was never built, however.

Though he made a mistake in his first sermon, the young
minister was not long a tenderfoot, for both he and his wife
soon won the hearts of old and young by bravely accepting
the frontier life and becoming a part of it. Ere long he was
in the midst of everything; clearing land, digging stumps,
planting a garden, building his house and church, and taking part in all of the pioneer activities.

In one of her letters to her sister, Mrs. Blaine tells of her husband's soiling and wearing out his clothes in doing hard, rough work. Finally she made a hickory shirt for him to wear while he did the roughest work. She goes on to say that she helped him clear and burn the stumps and bushes in their yard, and plant the garden. She adds that his hands were rougher and coarser than any farmer's and his clothes to match; but she does not speak of her own hands and clothes.

Until the church was built, services were held in a building near First and Cherry, which had been built by W. G. Latimer for a men's boarding house, later known as "Bachelor's Hall."

While their own home was being built, the Blaines lived part of the time in a small rented house—"a mere frame enclosed"—which they found very uncomfortable when an unexpected cold spell came; and the rest of the time, in the unfinished wing of their house—a room 13 by 14 feet. Mrs. Blaine's description of their living conditions in this room is typical of the way in which many of the pioneers were obliged to live:

In this room we have our bed; stove; two tables; three trunks; and four boxes, each larger than our trunks; a half barrel of sugar; a half barrel of flour; a firkin of butter; a box of soap; another of candles; a stool for our wash-pail; another for our wash-dish; and half a dozen chairs, besides a rough cupboard in one corner for our dishes etc. Then we have no place for our clothing but hang it up around the room, as there is no space large enough to make a rough cupboard for it . . . . . we have plenty of room and have entertained two strangers one night.

Such crowded conditions in one-room houses did not quell the hospitality of the pioneers. Travelers carried their own blankets. Mrs. Blaine tells of their guests rolling up in their blankets and sleeping on the floor at the foot of the bed. She also says, "It seemed funny at first to undress and go to bed in a room where are men and women, but I have got used to it."

When their house was finished in May, 1854, Mrs. Blaine wrote, "Our house is now painted outside and is the admiration of the whole town. The people say it is by far the handsomest house in town, that it looks like a house in the states."

Soon after the Blaine's arrival, the settlers started subscriptions for money to employ Mrs. Blaine as a schoolteacher at sixty-five dollars a month. In one of his letters. Mr. Blaine comments on the "generous-hearted men here."

The first term of the first school began early in January, 1854, and closed in the middle of March. It too was held in the Latimer Building. McGuffy's reader, Mitchell's geography, and Davis' arithmetic were the textbooks.

The second term of school began in February, 1855, in the minister's new house on Second Street between Cherry and Columbia, and lasted until the first of April. Shortly before it began, Mr. Blaine wrote home:

> Catherine is intending to go into her school next Tuesday. Were not the necessity imposed upon us, she would not incline to take another school, but her health is good and her school will be at home. Besides it is the urgent wish of those who have children that she should teach.

It was not accidental that school was to open on Tuesday. Monday was wash-day, and Mrs. Blaine did not wish her weekly schedule upset; so all through that term, the children had their Saturday holiday on Monday.

I have heard my mother tell how Mrs. Blaine taught school and did her cooking and housework in the same room; how the children, in their keen way, noticed that their teacher did her work differently from the way their mothers did. Many times, when they should have been busy with their sums or spelling books, their bright eyes were upon her.

Those attending this first school were: the Mercer girls, Susie and Eliza, and part of the time, Mary Jane, the fifteen-year-old homemaker, who really preferred to keep house and care for her little sister Alice; the Bell girls. Laura, Virginia, and Olive, who with the Mercer girls came trudging in by the woods trail with their dinner pails, or sometimes got a ride with "old Tib," Mr. Mercer's horse; two McConaha children, Ursula and George; Hulda Phillips, known as "Huldie," the daughter of David Phillips; William Smith, whose father was the first town treasurer; Rebecca or "Becky Horton, the daughter of Dexter Horton; Robie Willard, who was staying with Dr. and Mrs. Maynard and who was a younger sister of Dr. Rufus Willard of Olympia; and the two daughters of Arthur Denny. my mother, Catherine Louisa, known as "Kate," and Lenora, whom everyone called "Nora."

From a letter written by Seattle's first schoolteacher, we read:

> I am now in my school room and obliged to have a care over my scholars at the same time I am in mind present with you. My success in school has been very satisfactory to me. My scholars have improved in mind and manners. . . . . . I shall not regret having engaged it. . . . . . I think I have accomplished more in this way than I could have done in any other way.

Mr. Blaine had not been in Seattle long when he was called upon to perform a marriage ceremony. William H. Brannan and Elizabeth Livingston were married on December 29, 1853, in the parsonage, if the Blaine's first little rented "frame enclosed" could be called that. Early in '54 the minister and his wife went over to Alki and there in the home of her father, Samuel Russell, Nancy Russell was married to John Thomas. Not long after, Timothy Grow and Elizabeth Johns were married. After that there were no marriages for many months, marriageable girls being very scarce.

The Blaine letters—written, of course, with no idea of publication—record little incidents that reveal the customs of those first years in the new territory. For example, when

Mrs. Blaine hesitates to write more in a letter because it will make it "too heavy for a single postage," it is because at that time even "single postage" was an expensive luxury. Postage was determined by both weight and distance. A letter might cost anywhere from twenty-five to fifty cents besides the twenty-five cents a letter that was paid to Bob Moxlie for taking it to Olympia for posting. Nearly all of the settlers subscribed to support Mr. Moxlie's weekly canoe express in addition to paying for each letter.

Mrs. Blaine writes: "Stamps are most acceptable to us as we cannot obtain them here. Neither can we obtain three-cent pieces, pennies nor six pences. Our smallest coins are ten-cent pieces and shillings."

We learn from Mrs. Blaine's letters that the "home paper" not only carried news across the continent to the eagerly expectant pioneer minister and his wife, but carried in its folds at one time a few caraway seeds, at another some seeds of summer savory. A pair of mits arrived, in a letter or in a copy of the magazine, the *Lady's Repository*, which elicited this response from Mrs. Blaine, "Only the Sunday before as I was putting on a pair I had brought from home, I thought, where shall I get another pair when these are gone."

The climate, the wealth of wild berries, the new kinds of flowers impressed these newcomers just as they had Louisa Denny and the others. Of the weather Mr. Blaine writes. "The weather is so genial, the changes so gradual and moderate, I cannot help being pleased with it." And then in this same spring of '54 he discovered the wild syringa and spirea and his wife writes:

He said the woods are full of these syringas and the bushes grow to a wonderful height, about like trees from 15 to 20 feet. Then there is another white flower I should call the feather flower. It is a good deal handsomer than the fringe tree.

From the wild raspberries and dewberries, Mrs. Blaine

made jam and jelly. She learned from the Indians how to make "hiyou" (dried berries), which process she mentions in a letter in this way, "We went out yesterday and got 10 or 12 quarts of raspberries which I am drying in sugar." She describes herself and the minister scrambling over logs much as modern berry pickers do.

Descriptions of their food are typical of pioneer fare:

We had clam soup, turnips, and potatoes, lettuce, and gooseberry pie for dinner. I have learned to cook clams so that they are very good and I can get a plenty for us a meal in exchange for a slice of bread, from the Indians.

We usually get up about 6 o'clock, have breakfast about 7, dinner about 12, supper about 6, go to bed from 9 to 11. Our living is plain and simple, our breakfast more often consisting of warmed over potatoes, Indian pancakes and cold water; for dinner we have a good variety of vegetables with always pie or pudding for dessert; for supper, bread and butter, plain cakes, stewed apples or berries and cold water. I sometimes cook for breakfast and dinner some fresh, wild meat or some of the excellent salmon.

Of the styles that were then in vogue we get some hints. Mrs. Blaine writes back anxiously, "Mary writes that spencers are worn. Do they have lining in the waist, how long and full is the frill to be? What kind of sleeves, if any?"

The clothes of the period are again mentioned when she writes about a trip she and her husband took up the White River:

And we were quite a sight I can assure you. I had on my black delaine and for two fingers up my pantaletts were so thickly covered with mud you could not have guessed what color they were.

On this same trip she lost a pair of "morocco boots," which loss left her only "buskins" to wear. In another letter "Congress gaiters" are mentioned.

On one occasion when Mr. Blaine went up the Duwamish to preach, Mrs. Blaine went with him. They arrived at their host's home after dark on Saturday night. The loft of the milk house was the guest room—individual, at least, if not aesthetic, judging from Mrs. Blaine's letter:

We got up to it by a ladder and through a hole in the floor so small I bumped my head. The roof is made by putting boards on logs which serve the place of rafters and then logs on the outside to hold them down. There were three beds in the room. . . . . And oh, such beds. You should have seen them, the sheets of thick, unbleached drilling which looked as though they had been used for years without washing, the pillows cases of dark calico knotted on the ends and so thick with dirt we could almost rub it off with our hands, and the bed covers, blankets that might have been used for we know not what, and how they smelt.

We knew not what to do but after a consultation we decided to cover our skin as carefully as possible and get in. . . . .

Besides keeping on our drawers and stockings, we took my petticoat (fortunately I had worn that green delaine and so had a long skirt) and put it on to both of us completely covering our necks, hands, etc. Mr. Blaine tied a pocket handkerchief on his head and arrangements were complete. We managed to pass the night and I think escaped pollution. I think I shall not go up there again soon to spend the night.

In all fairness to the pioneers, it must be explained that this was the unusual condition in the early homes. A few settlers succumbed to the privations of the frontier, but most of them kept up their standards of home-making. Mr. Blaine continued to hold church services in the Latimer house for a year and a half, the church building not being finished until the spring of '55. The seats in the Latimer building were twelve-inch boards supported by blocks of wood. There was no pulpit, until Dr. Maynard had one built and put in place as a surprise. Those active in church work. according to Prosch, were: John Nagle, Edmund Carr. Jacob Maple, Henry Van Asselt, David Phillips, Dexter Horton, Mr. and Mrs. Edward Hanford, Thomas Mercer. and Arthur and Mary Denny.

The teachers in the Sunday School, which Mrs. Blaine describes as "small but interesting," were Edmund Carr and Olivia Holgate—whose love for each other developed as they worked there together—and Dorcas Phillips, or "Miss Dorcas" as she was called.

The faithful supporters of the church were a small part of the village. Judged by the standards of the East of that period, it was not a religious community. The Blaines, not yet adapted to the frontier, often bemoaned the lack of interest. Mr. Blaine writes, "We mourn the absence of a revival. We are low in the scale of spirituality . . . . . even those who moved in refined society at home . . . . . now show no respect for religion, no regard for the Sabbath."

Mrs. Blaine writes, "would you think you could sustain in a prayer meeting with four? That is as many as we usually have including Mr. B. and myself and if by any means we have six we think it a pretty large meeting."

But the influence of that first young preacher and that first school-teacher was greater than they realized at the time. They have ever occupied a place deep in the affection of Seattle.

Some there were, although absent from prayer meeting, who helped support the church. Such gifts as the tract of land in "Maynardtown" which Dr. Maynard offered for the site of a Methodist Seminary and the land which Carson Boren gave for the church and parsonage showed that the donors were interested.

On the 12th of May, 1855, the dedication of the new church was held. No one can hope to describe it as Mrs. Blaine did when writing of it a few days later:

We had our dedication last Sunday. All went off pleasantly notwithstanding the day was very rainy and unfavorable. Neither Br. Devore nor Br. Morse were here. . . . . Br. Roberts was here and preached. His subject was the origin and advance of Methodism. After the sermon Mr. Blaine offered the dedicatory prayer and then proceeded to raise money to pay off the debt on the house (the church house). He has succeeded in getting enough money and what he considered reliable pledges to pay expenses already incurred but designs to go on and try to raise enough to paint it and finish the inside. He will probably finish the inside by ceiling with planed boards as plaster is liable to crack and fall off on account of the lath swelling and shrinking by reason of the damp weather. There is some doubt about his being able to do all this summer as money is very scarce.

I wish the people could be made to feel some pride in it. I mean enough to make them care to keep it looking nicely. The windows did not get washed. You know I told you how hard I worked to clean the floor. The people came in with all the mud on their shoes and stuck them up on the seats before them. Mothers let the children stand on the seats, the nasty tobacco chewers squirted their juice around and the umbrellas were set all running with water right in the seats, so that by night it looked worse than before I cleaned it. We have no sexton and cannot afford to hire one, but nobody made any move toward cleaning it again and so I went at it today and made it quite tolerable. I do not know but I am foolish but I could not bear to see it so dirty. I am hoping they will take the hint after a while and if they will not clean it, at least will not make unnecessary dirt for others to clean.

Besides the regular attendants—who I know were not tobacco chewers, knowing the pioneers as I did—the dedication, which was a unique event for the settlement and the surrounding country, had apparently called out an audience more accustomed to lumber-camp ways than to church decorum.

Mrs. Blaine's letter continues in a more cheerful vein:

I tell you it seemed real good to go to meeting in a comfortable house after we have been without so long. Br. Roberts was very much pleased with the church, says he has seldom seen so small a house that combined so many excellencies and so few defects. It is 24 ft. by 36 ft. with 14 ft. posts. It has no basement except the hall which is 10 ft. wide and each end has winding stairs. The hall floor is on a level with the ground outside. In the audience room between the stairs are three seats, each raised one step above the other. These are for the singers. At the other end of the room is the pulpit which is small and neat. On each side of the pulpit are three seats. There is but one aisle, a center one three feet wide. The house would comfortably seat 150 persons and more could find seats. On the top, in front is a low, square steeple designed for a bell as soon as the people can afford one. When the house is finished it will be quite an ornament to the town.

When the church was finished by Jacob Maple and painted white by Henry Adams, it was indeed "an ornament to the town." For ten years, through all their vicissitudes, this first little M. E. Church was the only one in King County. All through pioneer history "the White Church," as it was known, played a historic part.

CHAPTER VII

GREAT THINGS FROM SMALL BEGINNINGS

ON FIRST AVENUE at Marion Street on the side of the Stevens Hotel is an inconspicuous bronze tablet on which is inscribed:

Arthur A. Denny in his log cabin home on this spot opened the first post office of Seattle, August 27, 1853.

The crowds hurry by; but the few who linger to read may let their imagination translate the high buildings into tall firs and cedars, and vision a tiny log cabin among the trees. In front of it is a trail that leads down to the beach where naked Indian children play and roll in the sand.

Inside the cabin, which is only 18 by 24 feet, a man of thirty-one sits before a little mahogany desk, which he had bought from the master of a sailing vessel. "This desk will be handy now for a post office," he says, as he opens a packet of letters which have just come in from Olympia—old-fashioned letters sealed with wax.

This new postmaster sorts the twenty-three letters and fourteen newspapers, while about him are gathered his fellow townsmen eagerly waiting for mail. Mary Denny and the two little covered-wagon girls are interested spectators. It is fitting that Mary and Arthur Denny who had decided on the quest of the four wagons should now be a part of such an important scene as the opening of the first United States mail in Seattle. Heretofore all mail sent to Seattle or Alki had been addressed "Olympia," and the people of these settlements depended upon Bob Moxlie's canoe-express for their weekly mail delivery.

For many years this little desk, which for a time held all the mail for Seattle and the surrounding country, stood in a corner of my mother's room. When I pass our present postoffice with its many clerks within and with a stream of people passing in and out, I think of that modest desk in its quiet corner.

Arthur Denny was the first postmaster in Seattle, but he was not in office long. Even as he sorted the first mail an effort was being made to relieve him of the position Strange that out here on the farthest frontier there should have been partisanship. Although President Pierce was a Democrat and must have known that Mr. Denny was a Whig, he nevertheless appointed him. But Dr. Maynard and other Democrats wrote secretly to the Department that Denny was not only a Whig but an "offensive partisan." In October, word came back from Washington that another postmaster had been appointed. Other Democrats headed by the young attorney, McConaha, made such a protest that in the following May Mr. Denny was reappointed, but he declined the position.

All of this is significant of conditions at that time. While the feeling about slavery was not so partisan as in the East. the lines between Whigs and Democrats were drawn just as sharply. Lines were also drawn on fundamental questions other than politics. Some of the settlers were puritanically religious men, strongly temperate, stern in their sense of right and wrong, others were more liberal religiously. not teetotalers, less exacting in behavior. The latter were unquestionably "better mixers." Both elements contributed much to the development of Seattle. Each fitted into the pattern. Later when the need arose, they stood together as one man.

Early that same fall of '53, Thomas Mercer and Dexter Horton returned from Oregon whither they had gone for their families. The arrival of newcomers was always an event and Mr. Mercer's arrival with his four little daughters, Mary Jane, Eliza, Susannah, and Alice, was certainly no exception. The children were tenderly welcomed by the pioneer women, whose hearts ached for the motherless girls

Regardless of how well known some of the pioneers became subsequently, this newcomer had the honor of attracting the most attention at the time of his arrival because he brought Seattle's first team of horses, Tib and Charley which came in for more attention than their owner. All the men and boys gathered round, examined the team's good points, looked at their teeth, guessed their ages, measured how many hands high they were, examined their feet, and remarked how well they had stood the trip across the plains

A favorable quip of Thomas Mercer's was that Tib and Charley were "a splendid match." Tib was glossy black; her mate Charley, snowy white. Tib was a nervous beast; Charley, good natured. Tib was no ordinary horse. On the journey across the plains the Indians had recognized this and had tried several times to buy her. Once a party of them tried to steal her. Tib truly belongs to pioneer Seattle history. She lived a long, useful life of over thirty years and at her death was buried on the Mercer place, and her grave was marked. Charley seems to have been less deserving, or perhaps shorter-lived, for his name has not endured so conspicuously in the chronicles of the past.

The Indians first called Mr. Mercer's wagon the "Boston kaynim" (canoe), and when they heard the creak of the wagon they called it a "chik chik."

While the others were admiring the horses, Dexter Horton wandered along the beach wondering what to do next. He hadn't a cent in his pocket and was indebted to "Uncle Tommy"—as he called Mr. Mercer, who was at the ripe old age of forty—for again bringing him to Seattle. Let any man who enters this city penniless and in debt remember that Dexter Horton preceded him in the experience.

On the beach, Mr. Horton met some men from Port Gamble who offered him and his wife one hundred and thirty dollars a month to manage the cookhouse for a camp of men who were working there in the sawmill. This offer he gladly accepted. He and Mrs. Horton remained in Port Gamble nine months, when they returned to Seattle with

$1160 in gold which they had saved. Mr. Horton then went to work in Yesler's mill and Mrs. Horton took charge of his cookhouse.

Thomas Mercer started at once to build his house on his claim near Lake Union where the fourteen-year-old Mary Jane was to keep house for her father and little sisters. Kind pioneer women had offered to take the children and care for them, but Mary Jane said that they must all stay together. While their house was being built, they lived in Bell's first little cabin.

The whole town turned out to build a road through the forest for "the team." This was Seattle's first road, grubbed through the stumps and tough salal from Yesler Way to what is now the corner of Roy and Taylor Streets.

Mr. Mercer became at once the town teamster, and for a long time had a monopoly of all the town transfer business. In later years he became the first milkman.

A description of this first transfer business was given by Dexter Horton in an interview years afterward:

That summer Uncle Tommy spent most of his time on his place near Lake Union, clearing the land, and I did the teaming. There was only one wagon and team in town then. After I ate my dinner I went around to the shed where he kept "old Tib" and "Charley" and hitched them up and did whatever teaming there was to do. This usually took a couple of hours; then I went to bed. I hauled the lumber for Plummer's store and several other buildings that season. If any one had some lumber, wood, or goods to haul he knew he could find me at the Mill so he came there and told me what to do.

It is said that before Mr. Mercer left Illinois he was so charmed with the stories of Puget Sound and had become so familiar with the subject that people often invited him to talk about this section of the country as if he had actually been here. In his dreams of a home in the West, he always visioned a place with a lake in front of his property, much like the spot on Lake Union which he later chose in the new country.

Lake Union was "a mirror-like lake surrounded by the

deep, dark evergreens of the primitive forest" when Mercer first saw it. But this beautiful lake had no name. Mr. Mercer, who lived close to it, first realized that it should be properly named; consequently, he called the attention of his townsfolk to the matter at a Fourth of July picnic in 1855.

The picnic was held on the Mercer place at the south end of Lake Union, an occasion on which Old Tib doubtless did good service in transportation. When it came time for speeches, Mercer recommended that "Hyas Chuck" (big waters), or Lake Duwamish, should be named "Washington" for the Father of his Country, and that "Tenas Chuck" (little waters) should be called "Lake Union," for, as Mr. Mercer predicted, "This smaller body of water may sometime provide a connecting link uniting the larger lake with Puget Sound."

As Thomas Mercer's transfer business developed naturally out of a need, so did another important enterprise. As the town grew, Arthur Denny found that his commission business that had originated as an accommodation, was developing into a thriving business. More and more frequently the skippers brought in goods to sell on commission and the people came to buy, until the enterprise outgrew his cabin and he decided to build a store.

The homes were north of the mill; the business section south. When Mr. Denny decided to keep store in earnest. he put up a 20 by 30 foot frame building on the waterfront side of Commercial Street, a stone's throw from the mill—on the present northwest corner at Washington and First Avenue South.

Mr. Denny's store is important, not only because it was the beginning of the first permanent store, but because it developed into the first bank, which grew into the great First Seattle Dexter Horton National Bank, now the First National Bank of Seattle.

For a time after moving into the new building, Mr. Denny continued to sell on commission, but discontinued this method of business in the fall of '54 when he took into partnership Dexter Horton and David Phillips. This general store of "Denny-Horton-Phillips" handled groceries, hardware, dry goods, notions—everything from a thimble to a plow.

Another general store, which figured prominently all through the early years, was opened in '53 on the east side of Commercial Street between Main and Washington by Dr. Joseph Williamson, "a widower who was a very successful merchant" according to Grant.

And yet another general store, for which Dexter Horton speaks of hauling the lumber, was Charles Plummer's, or Plummer & Chase's as it soon became, which stood at the northeast corner of Main and Commercial on the opposite corner from Dr. Maynard's. Plummer was postmaster for a number of years and during this time his store was also the post office.

Seattle's first store, which Dr. Maynard had conducted in the front part of his cabin, had been short-lived; but with unfailing resourcefulness the doctor used this part of the log building as an office in which he dispensed both drugs and real estate. His knowledge of medicine was of great service to the community, especially to the Indians, who had great faith in him, but there was not sufficient practice in a community both small and healthy to keep a doctor occupied; hence he was obliged to turn his attention to other pursuits. This was also true of the other pioneer doctors. Dr. Williamson practised very little; Dr. Bigelow, who was a skillful surgeon, worked on his farm at Black River; and Dr. Smith, a man of letters as well as a physician, had to spend his first years on Puget Sound in clearing land.

Dr. Maynard was Seattle's first realtor. He devoted much

of his energy to developing "Maynardtown," sometimes selling his lots for very little — anything to encourage growth. For the first twenty-five years the business of the village was done on "Maynard's Point" or "Maynardtown."

The following story is characteristic of the doctor's methods of doing business. There was need at this time for a blacksmith shop. The doctor knew nothing of blacksmithing, but, with his usual enterprise, he bought and installed a forge and tools. One day in September, 1853, while he was engaged in some repair work, a newcomer, a tall, young fellow, sauntered in and made critical remarks on the work being done.

"Well, perhaps you think you can do better yourself!" snapped the peppery doctor.

"Yes, I can, for that's my trade," answered the stranger.

When Maynard discovered that the stranger, Lewis Wyckoff, was a blacksmith, he threw down his tools, and offered to sell the shop, tools, and business "cheap" and "on terms to suit." Wyckoff had but a few dollars but he asked the price. The doctor replied,

"If you will keep the shop open and do the people's work, I'll give you the entire outfit and sell you the lot for ten dollars."

"There's the money, give me the deed," shouted the astonished young man.

This lot that was sold for ten dollars is the southeast corner at First and Washington Streets. The record of the sale can be found in the court house.

Bagley says of this blacksmith shop:

With the building of Yesler's sawmill Seattle obtained her first iron-working establishment. True it was but a blacksmith shop in which were made the things necessary for the building of the mill and the operation of the logging camps of that day but upon this primitive shop all of Seattle's iron and steel and brass working plants may well be said to have had their foundations.

Another enterprise in the little pioneer village grew out of a definite need—the need of an adequate place in which to entertain strangers. Save for limited accommodations in the cookhouse and at the first restaurant, conducted by David Maurer, a German, the homes were the hostelries. No stranger was turned away, but, if he remained, he usually had to sleep on the floor. Frederick Grant makes special mention of the hospitality of Mr. and Mrs. Hillory Butler —Virginians, whose home on the site of the present Butler Hotel was always open to the stranger.

David Maurer first served his meals early in '53, in Dr. Maynard's building and later across the street, where he also provided lodgings.

But the time had come when the need of accommodations for newly arrived immigrants, for transients, and bachelors had grown beyond the scope of Maurer's accommodations and private hospitality. Consequently the Felker House, Seattle's first hotel, was built on "the Point" on what is now Jackson Street at Western Avenue. It was two stories high, lathed and plastered, the first hard-finished structure in town. From all accounts it was as grand to the pioneers' eyes as the latest metropolitan hotel is to us. It was built by Captain Leonard M. Felker, master of the brig *Franklin Adams,* whom Grant describes as a fine type of man, who later made his mark in California.

This hotel was also known as "The Conklin House" because it was managed by Mrs. Mary Ann Conklin. Mrs. Conklin—also called Mary Ann Boyer—is generally spoken of in pioneer history by the name by which seafaring men all up and down the coast knew her—Mother Damnable. On an old map her place is labeled respectfully, "Madame Damnable."

Mother Damnable always furnished a topic of conversation for the town. She was noted for her good cooking, nasty temper, and her rough tongue. Swear, oh, how she could swear! Her husband was an old sea captain, and true to the traditions of the sea, and by nature, no mild man was he; but, poor old salt, years with his shrew of a wife must have discouraged him, for she could outswear him any day. At last he gave up, left the honors to her, and became a mild, inoffensive husband.

Years later Mother Damnable's tongue was stilled and they laid her away in the little burying ground on the hill. Stormy and impervious in life, in death too she resisted time, the elements, and the way of all flesh, for in after years when it became necessary to move the pioneer cemetery, the workmen could not lift the coffin. On opening it, they found that her body had turned to stone.

Now, 377 hotels shelter Seattle's guests. In the memory of men still living, Mother Damnable was the only hotel proprietor in the place.

Some means of administering justice was found necessary in the settlement when the first burglary was committed. The pioneers had to make their own law and mete out their own punishment; so they went about it in a most conscientious manner. In Charles Terry's old account book are found the following resolutions signed by thirty men including most of the responsible citizens of Seattle and Alki at that time:

> We the undersigned are in favor of whipping the two Indians, cropping their heads and making them leave the place, forthwith, the said Indians having acknowledged breaking into and stealing money and goods from Dr. Williamson's store.

This is followed by the signatures and two laconic statements:

> One Indian received twenty-five lashes by Hillory Butler.
> One Indian received twenty-five lashes by C. D. Boren.

Another case of flogging was provoked by the first "boot-

legger" and "rumrunner." The story is best told as Arthur
Denny told it with a hearty laugh at the memory:

There was a worthless fellow here on the Sound who owned a
sloop with blue drilling sails. He made it a business to sell whiskey
to the Indians and every time we saw those blue drilling sails come
into port we knew there was going to be trouble. We got along with
the Indians all right when they were sober but when drunk they
were very dangerous. Some of us talked the matter over and concluded that we would lay in wait for that blue drilling skipper the
next time he came into port, and give him a sample of our "primitive
justice."

We did not have long to wait, for the next day I saw the sloop
with the blue sails round West Point and notified the neighbors to
get ready for business. The sloop sailed into the Bay, came to anchor
near the beach and the skipper with his wares started on shore in a
small boat. On his arrival we received him with open arms and after
giving him a good sound flogging took him down to the beach and
bid him farewell. We notified him that he had received only a fore-
taste of what he might expect when he returned, but we never afterwards saw the man or the sloop with the blue drilling sails.

CHAPTER VIII

SAWMILLS, SHIPS AND WAGON ROADS

THE GROWTH of Seattle in '53, '54, and '55 was steady and strong, and the atmosphere of those years was happy. New people arrived. The mill hummed. Gardens of the pioneers' own planting were beginning to produce. White fences enclosed flower gardens, and kept the children in and the cows out. The Indians were friendly, some working in the mill, others peddling clams, salmon, and berries. To be sure, there were rumors of discontent among some of the tribes, but these were not alarming, for Governor Stevens, superintendent of Indian affairs, would settle all of them.

Seattle was by this time a well established sawmill village. The life of the community centered about the mill, for no one wanted to live far from it. The noisy clang from beating an old circular saw that hung on the side of the cookhouse startled the pioneers from their sleep in the early morning, and sent the men to their day's work. Later a bossy little whistle regulated their very lives; they got up by the mill whistle, they ate by the mill whistle, and they set their clocks by the mill whistle. It broke the silence and loneliness, and gave a cheerfulness to the little town.

San Francisco building continued and so did the prosperity of the lumber business on the Sound. From the time the settlers had loaded the brig *Leonesa* at Alki, they had never lacked a market or good prices for their lumber. Furthermore, every newcomer was certain of finding work either in the manufacture of the lumber or in providing logs. George Frye, a newcomer of '53, became Yesler's sawyer and continued to be for years. It was said that he was "the best saw filer on Puget Sound." Dexter Horton, who had also found ready employment in the mill on his return from Port Gamble, said years later of his position, "The mill was running two twelve-hour shifts and I went on duty at 12 midnight and worked till noon next day. We had no eight-hour regulations those days." Of the nature of his work, he said:

> My work was to turn one of the screws and help carry away the slabs. After a slab had been cut off, we set the screws and while the saw was making another cut we took the slab and put it on the great fires that were always burning in Yesler Way.

Those fires never went out. By day the blue smoke curled aloft; by night the shadows danced about the glow. Then, too, each householder had his own little fire in his own yard, burning a stump or log that interfered with his garden patch. Such innumerable cords of wood as the pioneers burned! Always the odor of smoke and fresh burning wood mingled with that of fresh-cut timber and up-turned earth.

To the north of the village, Thomas Mercer and David Denny were doing their bit in burning and clearing while they cut logs from their claims for the mill. Again David built a cabin in the forest and moved Louisa and Baby Inez out there to live.

To the south of town, Edward Hanford and John Holgate, who had returned from Portland early in the summer of '54 with their families, were logging off the steep sides of Beacon Hill. Each had two brothers—George and Ebenezer Seymour Hanford, and Lemuel and Milton Holgate; consequently, they had a substantial logging crew. Timothy Hinckley drove the oxen, which were invaluable help in hauling the logs along the beach to the mill. Edward Hanford had driven these work cattle to Seattle from Portland after bringing them across the plains from his large herds in Iowa.

Sometimes the logs were rafted to the mill—a method which apparently had its disadvantages. On one occasion, Yesler found John Holgate's diary which he had dropped. The last item read, "Started for Yesler's mill. Fell off into the water." Yesler, always a wag, added "and drowned," and returned the diary without comment to Holgate.

There was considerable danger to the cabin homes from falling trees, as one of many stories told of the fortitude of Mrs. Holgate (John Holgate's mother) illustrates. Her sons were hewing down a monster tree which fell in the wrong direction and crashed into their cabin. Horrified, the sons ran to the cabin, fearing their mother had been killed. Venturing in, they saw her calmly preparing dinner over the stove in the unharmed end of the cabin. Answering the anxious inquiries, she calmly said, "No, I was not hurt and as soon as the crash was over I was thankful and my fright was over."

Even though Henry Yesler's sawmill had been a money-maker from the first, somehow or other, the genial mill owner was always hard up—perhaps because he was too easy going. Later he became rich, not from the mill but from the sale of his property as it increased in value. During those sawmill years he lived in his little white house close by, and, as town employer, presided over the mill, the cookhouse, and the wharf in a friendly, hearty fashion, that made him the popular leader of the industrial life of the town. He was always whittling. Nearly all accounts picture him with his trusty jackknife, whittling — usually a piece of white pine.

The cookhouse was not only the mess hall for the mill hands, but for years was also lodging house, town hall, military headquarters, and a place for social gatherings for the settlers along the Sound. Everybody was welcome whether he had money or not; no man was ever turned away hungry. It was the general lounging place for the men where they met to exchange the news of the day or while away the evenings at cards and stories. Within its weathered and smoke-blackened walls men "ate, drank, laughed, sang, prayed, wept, and slept."

Later on, Judge Lander had his desk in one corner of the dining room, and the auditor's office was in another. The first lawsuit was tried in the old cookhouse and the first sermon was preached there. Long after all other log buildings in the town had been replaced by houses of sawed lumber. it was left standing, the last log house in the business section of Seattle.

A second sawmill, also equipped with two circular saws. was built "up Black River"—or "down at Renton" as we should say—and operated by Tobin, Fanjoy, and Eaton. The six-foot dam above it was fed by the water from Cedar River which at that time flowed into the Black. The great difficulty was getting the lumber down to the vessels on the Sound, but even so, this mill did considerable work until it was burned during the Indian War.

A third sawmill was built and operated by the young settlers, Edmund Carr, William Strickler, Francis McNatt. and John Ross, who lived near Salmon Bay. The summer before they built their own mill, these young men lost a season's work when their raft broke and got away from them while towing their logs from their claims to Yesler's mill.

Their mill was built near the present Fremont bridge. where the owners had built a dam across the outlet of Lake Union. A road for hauling timber to the mill was just begun when the Indian War came and the mill was destroyed.

The sawmills augmented the romance of the ships in pioneer history, for the two are inseparably linked in the beginning of Seattle industry. The history of the different ships and their masters is vital and romantic. "Yesler's wharf," which ran out from the mill, became Seattle's point of contact with the great world outside. It was the most animated spot in town.

I have spoken of the *Exact*, which brought the Seattle Pilgrims; of the *Leonesa*, which started industry; and of the *John Davis* and *Franklin Adams*; but there were many other ships interwoven with the life of the early days. These

I have mentioned were all sailing vessels. The first steamer on the Sound was the famous *Beaver*. Mr. Denny writes, "We occasionally saw the Hudson's Bay steamers, *Beaver* and *Otter*, passing to and from the stations at Nisqually but as yet no American steamboats had ever navigated these waters."

But it was not long before a steamer flying the Stars and Stripes arrived. She was a small side-wheeler named *Fairy*, brought to Olympia on the deck of the barque *Sarah Warren* by her master, Captain D. J. Gove, in October, 1853. She was rightly named *Fairy*. Her cabin was just the size of a feather bed. My grandmother, Mary Denny, told of making a trip to Olympia to join Grandfather, who was then in the legislature, when she put her feather bed on the floor of the cabin, and the whole family piled in.

Speaking of travel on the Sound before the arrival of the *Fairy*, Prosch says:

People had travelled up and down the Sound in canoes, skiffs, scows and small sail craft, the most popular boat for several years being the sloop, *Sarah Stone*, Captain Slater. L. M. Collins had a scow in which he made trips carrying freight and passengers, boarding the latter when they would furnish their own provisions and do the cooking.

However, steamboat travel was not to be depended upon for several years, for the *Fairy* was too small for real service. The need for such service was keenly felt, especially dependable mail service. In March, 1854, Catherine Blaine wrote to her family in New York:

I have just heard that there is a possibility of my having an opportunity of sending a letter to Steilacoom and that it can be mailed to you.

On May 19th of the same year, she wrote:

The mail that left N. Y. April 6th has been due a week. . . . . It will probably come in during the night or to-morrow and as we do not think it best to go to the office on Sunday, I shall think of little else to-morrow.

However, on Sunday she wrote that a "good brother"— who apparently had no scruples about going to the post office

on the Sabbath—"brought our mail to us." She was not the
only one eager for mail, for she said in one letter:

> You ought to see how the men act when the mail comes. Every-
> thing is dropped and off they run to the office as if their lives de-
> pended on it. Some come away looking quite happy and others quite
> dejected.

In July of '54, Mrs. Blaine is hopeful of a change:

> The government has not formally allowed enough for mail to pay
> expenses of it and the people raised enough more to hire a carrier. His
> time is now out and we expect hereafter that Government will carry
> mails for us. . . . . It has formerly been sent to Oregon, from there to
> Olympia (up the Cowlitz River) and brought from there by canoe.
> This subjects us to much delay and embarrassment and it has been
> the earnest wish of the people of the whole territory to have it sent
> from San Francisco. Judge Lancaster has written to some one here
> that he thinks this will be done and that the steamer will be here
> next month.

One day in August of the same year, the people of the
village thought that the expected steamer had arrived, but
it turned out to be the government survey steamer *Active*.
Commander James Alden. Mrs. Blaine describes this occasion when the chug of a steamboat was enough to set Seattle agog:

> We were quite elated one morning this week at hearing the puffing
> of a steamboat coming up the Sound and into our bay. We thought
> surely the mail steamer had come and we, that is the women, imme-
> diately planned rides for ourselves. But, alas, our hopes were like
> those of the milkmaid in the spelling book. As soon as she anchored a
> large company of men went out to see her and learned that she was a
> vessel belonging to the government and is out surveying the Pacific
> coast and harbors.

In September, however, the steamer for which they had
so fervently hoped, arrived. This was the *Major Tompkins*, which was to do service between Olympia and Victoria.
She was received with rejoicing all up and down the Sound.
and greatly praised as "commodious and seaworthy" and a
"propellor of seagoing qualities."

But the *Major Tompkins* was disappointing as a mail carrier. She would chug her way from Olympia to Seattle; on

to Victoria; and then back to Seattle and Olympia. Mrs. Blaine wrote, "Before this letter can speed to the Isthmus and thence via New York to Seneca Falls, the steamer must take her tedious trip to Vancouver Island and back."

Mail carrying was a side issue with the *Major Tompkins* when she could get odd jobs to do. She did considerable work towing vessels, being the first steamer on the Sound to do this work. One of her first exploits was "chasing Indians," as Grant describes it, when she made a vain pursuit of Indian murderers to Hood Canal.

Professor Meany says that the Indians were afraid of this "fireship" and were delighted when in February '55, she was wrecked while entering Victoria harbor, and sank.

"A MANIA FOR ROADS"

Sawmills and ships alone could not make a great city. From the first the Seattle founders realized that unless they had roads as a means of intercourse with the surrounding country, not even a good harbor would make them a great seaport.

Immigrants into Portland and the Willamette Valley had made their roads as they entered and had brought with them the teams to make other roads, for they could go all the way in their wagons by way of Barlow's Pass. Immigrants into Puget Sound settlements were obliged to leave their prairie schooners behind in Oregon and come to the Sound in seagoing schooners. What Puget Sound settlements needed was a road through the Cascade Mountains. Until there was such a road, the majority of immigrants would continue to go to the Willamette Valley.

We recall how the three Thurston County commissioners —Ford, Shelton and Arthur Denny—appointed in the summer of '52 before King County was established, were immediately interested in the building of a road from "Steilacoom city to Seattle." The viewers of the proposed road handed in this quaint report in the spring of '53:

From Seattle to Collins on the Duwampsh river; thence on the dividing ridge most of the way, striking the Puyallup river one mile above Adam Benson's claim; thence to crossing of Steilacoom creek, thence to Steilacoom, the terminus.

Following "the dividing ridge most of the way" whenever possible was typical of pioneer roads, for the deep mud of the lowlands was thus avoided. Mr. Denny says of this report:

At the time this report was made Thurston County had no longer jurisdiction of the case, having been divided. . . . . We, however, did not abandon the effort to get the road, but proceeded to open it by volunteer work, and also a road from Alki to intersect it near Collins'. These roads were traveled but little, and after the first year were allowed to go out of use for want of work to keep them open.

"A mania for roads" was what Ezra Meeker once called this obsession of the county commissioners after talking with Arthur Denny. And this "mania for roads" obtained in all of the Puget Sound settlements, for all were handicapped by the same need.

The pioneers of Olympia and Steilacoom were anxiously anticipating the road from Fort Walla Walla to Steilacoom that Governor Stevens said in his inspiriting letter to Arthur Denny would be built by Captain McClellan in the summer of '53.

But McClellan was disappointing both in the construction of this road and in the railroad survey which he was to make. He reported that from twenty to twenty-five feet of snow lay on the pass in the winter time; that the whole Cascade range was impassable; and that it would be necessary to follow the course of the Columbia River in building a railroad to the coast. Professor Meany says:

*Captain George B. McClellan had been sent ahead with a party of men to survey a road through the Yakima Valley and the Naches Pass to Puget Sound, and he was directed to let contracts to construct a wagon road from Fort Walla Walla to Fort Steilacoom. He failed

---

*From *History of the State of Washington* by Edmond S. Meany. By permission of Macmillan Company, publishers.

in both, though he reached the summit of the Cascade Range before turning back toward Walla Walla. His excuse was that the mountains were impassable. . . . McClellan was again sent from the west to push through Snoqualmie Pass and complete the line of his surveys. He turned back with more excuses.

Opinion is divided on the efficiency of McClellan but the consensus of opinion is that he was sorely lacking in ability, and manifested many of those traits of indecision and delay that later characterized his work in the Civil War.

The pioneers of Olympia and Steilacoom were keenly disappointed in McClellan's failure, for they had been very anxious to receive some part of that year's immigration. With their own funds and voluntary labor, under the supervision of Edward J. Allen, they started out on the formidable task of building the road themselves through the Naches Pass. They hewed a rough road and built primitive bridges as far as the summit. Here they met Indians who told them that no parties were coming through the mountains that fall; so they turned back and did no more, since it was late in the season.

But a company known as "the Biles party," made up of twenty-nine wagons and one hundred and forty-eight people, had heard that the "Northern Oregon" settlers were building a road through to Puget Sound and came on through the mountains that way. The hardships and suffering of that first immigrant train through Naches Pass is an epic of pioneer history. Some of the oxen were killed in order to obtain rawhide for ropes for lowering the wagons over the precipices. To quote one of the party, it was "so fraught with hardships and peril and misery as to make all that had been suffered before scarcely worth mentioning."

Most of the party went through to Nisqually; but A. L. Porter, who later became famous in the Indian War, stopped at the prairie that is to this day called Porter's Prairie, on the present highway to Enumclaw. These prairies were open, grassy meadows in the midst of the dense forest and, since they needed no clearing, were much desired for claims by the pioneers. Muckleshoot Prairie near by was also taken up at this time.

The Naches Pass was miles from Seattle, but its opening vitally concerned her progress. Arthur Denny writes that in order to divert some of the stream of immigration which they expected toward Seattle, "Our people at once turned their attention to opening a road from Seattle to intersect this military road and practically accomplished it."

Early in '54, according to old records, Thomas Mercer Henry Van Asselt, and Richard Tobin were appointed viewers of this road, described as "a territorial road from Seattle to intersect the emigrant road from Steilacoom to Fort Walla Walla." A copy of their report and the petition for the road is to be found in the office of the county engineer in the first King County road book in which "the petitioners pray and will ever pray" for such a road.

This road was not only viewed but it was surveyed by William Strickler, for which service the county paid him ninety dollars. According to the plan of the road in the road book, it ran in a general direction between the White and Green Rivers to the Pass.

In the summer of '54 Naches Pass was used to some extent, but, according to Arthur Denny, "it was found that the military road was not a success as a wagon road across the mountains." Ezra Meeker went back that summer by this route to meet his father's family. On the way he met the weary families of Harvey K. Jones and George E. King and directed them to the rich valley of the White River little realizing the hideous fate that awaited them in that fair valley.

In the same old King County road book following the record of the viewing of the territorial road to intersect the emigrant road through Naches Pass, there is another petition which also prays "as in duty bound to ever pray," this time for a road from the land claim of Henry Van Asselt along the Duwamish and White rivers to meet the territorial road "at crossing of White river on claim of John Thomas." Later the viewing of this same road is accepted by the county commissioners who describe it as running from "the claim of John M. Thomas to Joseph Foster thence down Duwampsh river on south side to crossing said river at claim of C. C. Lewis terminating at or near claim of Henry Van Asselt."

Work on these roads was done by volunteer labor; those who did not volunteer were fined. Luther Collins was put in charge of the collection and according to another road book did a thorough job. Apparently no remote settler or transient bachelor or mill worker escaped, for the list includes many names that do not appear in the permanent lists of settlers. Each was fined nine dollars besides costs amounting to five dollars.

Unfortunately these early efforts at road building were frustrated. The covered wagons the pioneers had expected did not come lumbering in to keep the trails open; consequently they were soon overgrown by the lush, quick growth of the Northwest. And then came the Indian War which obliterated them. However, the routes were well chosen, for today, broad, paved highways cover them. Not emigrant-wagon pioneers but tourists now come through the pass.

The pioneer effort to build roads, to reach out and make way for population helped determine the future greatness of Seattle. If the pioneers had been merely squatters, they would have been content to live on their claims, fishing and hunting, and depending on the sailing vessels for their supplies. If they had not looked beyond the sawmill for their livelihood, they would have had just a sawmill town, prosperous only as long as the timber lasted. But from the first they were conscious that they were builders of a great seaport and to this end they worked and planned.

CHAPTER IX

THE COMING OF THE GOVERNOR

THE NEW Washington Territory awaited the arrival of its first governor, Isaac Ingalls Stevens. The governor was coming with three distinct and highly important missions: to start the machinery of the territorial government, to act as Indian agent with authority to adjust differences between the races, and to make a report of his survey as to the best route for a new northern railroad to the Sound. Besides, he came as a link with the parent government, making these Northwestern pioneers feel that they were a unit in that government. Not only were they three thousand miles away from Washington City, but they were isolated by the barrier of the Cascade Mountains. The new governor would determine where that barrier should be pierced. Anxiously they awaited his coming.

No radio and not even a telegram announced the exact time of his arrival, but the little village of Olympia made preparations just the same. And then when he came—on November 25, 1853, they didn't recognize him! Professor Meany tells the incident delightfully in his *History of the State of Washington:**

He had pushed ahead of his party and when he arrived alone he was tired, dirty, and hungry. He sought the only place that looked like a dining hall, but was refused admission.

"We are going to have doin's here," said the chef, "and we can't feed strangers until after they're over."

"Well, see here. I am hungry. Can't you give me some of the scraps at the kitchen table?"

"Oh, yes. I guess we can do that."

After satisfying his hunger the governor walked out into the street. There a man accosted him and complained about the slow arrival of the governor.

"Then I suppose I am the man you are looking for."

"You!"

"Yes."

When satisfied that the small travel-stained man was really the

*From *History of the State of Washington* by Edmond S. Meany. By permission of Macmillan Company, publishers.

new governor, the man began beating a discarded circular saw hung on a post. This was a signal. Men swarmed from cabins and forest. They filed into the dining hall, placed the governor at the head of the table, but there he sat unable to eat a mouthful. He was chock-full of scraps.

This travel-stained arrival of the governor was not in keeping with the importance and magnitude of the survey he had made. The government had equipped him with a small army of soldiers and civilians for what was the first investigation of the routes to the Northwest. Crossing the continent with Governor Stevens, who had come by way of Portland, were eleven army officers, seventy-six enlisted men, thirty-three members of the scientific corps, besides teamsters, packers, guides, herders, and voyageurs; in all. two hundred and forty men. The reports of this survey fill volumes, which include data on the faunal, floral, and mineral characteristics of the Northwest.

The new governor immediately set about his task. He first made provisions for a territorial election in January. and for the convening of the legislature, and then began acquainting himself with the Indian situation. Early in January, 1854, he started on a trip around the Sound. His object was to visit the Indians and take census of them, to examine the harbors, and to visit the representatives of the Hudson's Bay Company and negotiate with them about relinquishing their holdings in Washington Territory. Although he made the trip in winter in an open sailboat, the *Sarah Stone*. known as a "plunger," he visited Steilacoom, Seattle, Skagit Head, Rosario, and Victoria, returning by way of Port Townsend, all in the month of January.

Concerning this trip, the governor wrote in his diary, "I became greatly impressed with the important advantages of Seattle and also the importance of the disputed islands." The "disputed islands" were those of the San Juan group that had been claimed by both England and the United

States ever since the settlement of the "fifty-four forty or fight" dispute.

The governor's visit to Seattle is recorded in letters which David and Catherine Blaine wrote at the time. Mrs. Blaine said in one, "The governor is as rough in his appearance as any backwoodsman. He wears a red flannel shirt, no white one, coarse clothes and unshaven beard." No picture of the governor could illustrate more clearly the kind of task he had to perform and with what energy he went to work.

In *The Life of Isaac Ingalls Stevens,* his son, Hazard Stevens, wrote that upon his father's arrival, he found "a great wooded country without roads, the unrivalled waterways without laws, and the Hudson's Bay Company's possessions without settlement." The author speaks of the country as "fraught with difficulties and dangers where everything was to be done and nothing yet begun."

Mrs. Blaine also wrote of the new governor, "He unhesitatingly declares the advantages of the northern route and thinks, as we all know, that if such a road is ever built, its western terminus will be somewhere on the Sound."

Something of the young governor's indefatigable energy is reflected in this paragraph from Mr. Blaine:

I have just seen the governor. He came to Seattle last night; is expecting to go up our river tomorrow to visit our coal mines and make arrangements for the exploration of our country back to the pass in the Cascade range, with a view to ascertaining the most feasible situation for the terminus of the Pacific Railroad. Many in this territory are very sanguine in the opinion that this terminus will be at some point on Puget Sound.

If the governor was ambitious, the townsfolk were equally so. They gathered about him and told him eagerly about the coal which Dr. Bigelow had discovered on his land, and then took him up the Duwamish to see for himself. They also gave him information which they had obtained from the Indians about passes through the Cascades. It was January; the great barrier of mountains was snow-covered and formidable; the little group of men appeared puny in comparison, but already their eager minds were conquering this great obstacle.

Their zest increased when the governor told them that he had been dissatisfied with Captain McClellan's report that the Cascades were impassable, and that he had given orders to one of his surveying party, A. W. Tinkham, a civil engineer, to get Indian guides and cross the Cascade Mountains. No wonder, as Catherine Blaine wrote, that he "gave the people new life and vigor."

A short time after the governor's visit, it happened! With five Yakima braves Tinkham crossed the mountains in early February through seven feet of snow. How the news quickened the pioneers' ambition! Down around the cookhouse, where they gathered and talked, their dreams soared until they saw the forest cleared, a city built, and a train roaring into the station. From that moment, the little town began to build in the direction of that dream. Mr. Tinkham's success in crossing the mountains was unquestionably a determining event in Seattle history.

While the governor was touring Puget Sound, the Territory was preparing for the election on January 30th of members of the first territorial legislature and for a delegate to Congress. Apportionment was based on the census that J. Patton Anderson had taken the previous summer. King and Pierce Counties jointly were entitled to two members in the upper house or Council; King, one representative, and Pierce, three in the lower house.

The Democrats in King County took their politics so seriously that they held a "convention" to prepare for the election. Theirs was the first ever held in the county. Dr. Maynard, Plummer, and Collins were among those who met in Maurer's eating place and nominated William Heebner for representative and George McConaha for the Council.

The two candidates for delegate to Congress were William H. Wallace, Whig, a prominent pioneer attorney; and Columbia Lancaster, Democrat, an early pioneer who had worked hard for the welfare of "Northern Oregon." Prosch writes that the two of them "stumped the country" in their campaign.

Dr. Maynard, Henry Yesler, and Arthur Denny were election judges. Columbia Lancaster was elected to Congress; George McConaha to the Territorial Council to represent King and Pierce Counties jointly with Captain Lafayette Balch of Steilacoom; and Arthur Denny—not because he was a Whig but in spite of it—was elected representative from King County, receiving eighty-seven of the county votes; Heebner, nineteen.

The legislature convened in Olympia, February 27, 1854, at ten o'clock. George McConaha was elected president of the Council. On the following day, the governor delivered his message, which is characterized by Professor Meany in this way:

*From the very beginning Washington Territory felt itself to be an important part in the American republic. The spirit of bold, self-conscious aspirations was summarized in the first gubernatorial message to the territorial legislature.

Governor Stevens said in that message:

The outpost of the great Northwest, having the elements of a great and varied development, commerce, manufacture, agriculture and the arts, has received the name of the Father of his Country and has had the impulse of its life at a great era of American progress and civilization. . . . . In this great era, we can play no secondary part, if we would. We must of necessity play a great part if we act at all.

He emphasized the immediate need of dealing with the Indians in order to prevent serious trouble which threatened. Most of the Puget Sound Indians were friendly with the whites; still there was a growing feeling of discontent

---

*From *History of the State of Washington* by Edmond S. Meany. By permission of Macmillan Company, publishers.

among the tribes of the whole Northwest as a result of the steady immigration of the white man into their territory. They did not resent the trappers; but immigrants with wagons, plows, and families made the natives realize that the white man had come to stay. The governor reminded the legislature that the Indians owned the land until their title to it was nullified by treaty and recommended that the members memorialize Congress to provide money with which to buy the lands. He advocated the removal of the Indians to reservations with definite laws in regard to their rights to hunt and fish. In the same address, he spoke of "the unrivalled harbors of Puget Sound, due to control the trade of China and Japan."

Gathered in the upper story of a plain, two-story frame building, reached by a stairway on the outside, these twenty-seven men listening to this message were filled with "bold, self-conscious aspirations" that made them able founders of the proud state of Washington.

The eighteen members in the lower house and nine in the Council, whose average age, according to the *Columbian,* was twenty-eight years, went to work drafting a constitution and making laws. Meany says that *"The very first law shows the wisdom that actuated them. It embodied a request for the three judges of the district court to act as an advisory code commission to help them enact the first fundamental body of laws." These judges said afterwards, "No legislative body ever met who evinced more decidedly a determination to be governed in all their acts by a desire to promote the public good."

Before they adjourned the first of May, these aggressive young legislators memorialized Congress on several matters: they advised that the Sandwich Islands (Hawaiian) be annexed to the United States; they asked for certain fish-

---

*From *History of the State of Washington* by Edmond S. Meany. By permission of Macmillan Company, publishers.

ing privileges along the coasts of Russian America (Alaska); and they demanded that the dispute over the San Juan Islands be settled. They also voted on a bill which Arthur Denny had introduced that all women over the age of eighteen be allowed to vote. The measure was lost by one vote. that of a man who had an Indian wife.

With all the boldness of youth these law-makers handled matters both great and small. They voted large sums of money for any worthy project that came to their attention; nor was it beneath their dignity to regulate such a matter as the keeping of swine and to pass a law against their promiscuous running at large.

Until there was a regular election in the counties in the Territory, the legislature appointed county officers. This procedure gives rise to some confusion as to who were the first county officers, for the county commissioners also made appointments. The King County commissioners chose William P. Smith for their first treasurer, and he was also appointed by the legislature. C. D. Boren, sheriff, and Henry Yesler, auditor, who had been appointed by the Oregon legislature, were reappointed. Thomas Mercer, Luther Collins, and George W. Loomis were appointed county commissioners. A school law was passed providing for the establishment and maintenance of schools. Regardless of the fact that there were only one hundred and seventy people in King County and no money for either schools or teachers, Dr. Smith was made the county school superintendent.

Before the legislature had been in session thirty days, Governor Stevens asked for, and the legislature passed a resolution declaring that "no disadvantage would result to the territory should the governor visit Washington, if, in his judgment, the interests of the Northern Pacific Railway survey would thereby be promoted."

So in March the governor left for the East, going back by way of San Francisco and the Isthmus. His main object

in returning so soon was to report on his survey and to further the plans for a northern route for the proposed Pacific
railroad, which he had learned was being opposed by Southern interests. These interests did not want the railroad to
pass through anti-slavery territory.

When Governor Stevens made his glowing report to Jefferson Davis, Secretary of War, Mr. Davis was not at all
pleased. Snowden says of this interview:

> But Secretary Davis was in no kindly humor with this evidence
> of efficiency, or with the demonstration that this route was not only
> practicable but desirable. . . . . He would give but scant attention to
> what ' e had to say, and finally, in laying his report before Congress,
> raised the estimate of cost of construction . . . . . magnified the phys-
> ical difficulties; depreciated the agricultural resources of the country;
> described that part of it west of the Rocky Mountains as one of gen-
> eral sterility. . . .. He ignored Tinkham's report of a reconnaissance
> he had made in Snoqualmie Pass, but quoted McClellan's with ap-
> proval.

The same author says further:

> By the unfavorable comments, not to mention the misrepresenta-
> tions, with which he submitted Governor Stevens' report of his rail-
> road work to Congress, Secretary Davis also deprived the country of
> that immediate benefit that might and probably would have resulted
> from it.

Although the governor found his efforts in behalf of the
railroad balked and discredited, he was still able to accomplish much. He assisted Delegate Lancaster in getting
through certain measures for the new Territory; two townships of land for a university were appropriated by Congress; an appropriation of $10,000 was made for extinguish-
ing the Indian title to the land in the Territory; and Governor Stevens was given the commission of dealing with the
war-like Blackfeet Indians and other tribes in what is now
Montana.

The governor also called attention to the need of settling
the San Juan Islands dispute and of settling with the Hudson's Bay Company for their holdings in the Territory. One

of the most important things that he accomplished was bringing the new Pacific Northwest with its advantages and rich possibilities to the attention of Congress and the East.

On his return to the Territory he brought Mrs. Stevens and their children with him. They left New York on September 20, 1854, on an overcrowded steamer bound for Panama. Here they crossed the isthmus by railroad, by mules and in chairs carried by Indians. Then after fourteen tedious days, with many on board sick and dying of fever, they reached San Francisco, where they were detained by sickness. When able to travel they went on to Portland by water, and then up the Cowlitz River and on over the primitive road with wagon wheels deep in mud, until early in December from the "top of a little hill" they looked down upon the twenty wooden houses of Olympia. Again the governor had arrived.

CHAPTER X

HAVING BEEN far afield with the legislature at Olympia and with the governor at Washington, D. C., it is good to get back to Seattle; back to the cookhouse where the community life of the village centered.

Here in the cookhouse the settlers gathered after a hard day's work in the mill, and swapped yarns. They had to make their own fun. They had no vaudeville, no movies. no radio, no daily newspaper, and no magazines for entertainment. If the cookhouse walls could have borne record in later years, what choice stories on the pioneers and on town characters would have been disclosed. As it is, many have come down to us, each having been colored a bit in the retelling, no doubt.

Stories of Mother Damnable—of her violent temper and profane tongue. Stories of Dutch Ned, a funny old character who was a bit queer because of some injury to his head, whose work it was to cart the sadwust away from the mill and spread it over Mill and Commercial Streets, making a so-called "sawdust town." Much of the town's merry-making and loitering and town talk took place "down on the sawdust."

Of all the cookhouse stories, probably the best known was a story on Dr. Smith, which was told and retold many times as a great joke on the doctor. He had cleared the land for his home near what is now Smith's Cove. One day in the summer of '54, he started out to blaze a trail to the village of Seattle, having gone back and forth by canoe heretofore. After working his way through the forest, he found himself in a clearing and thought he must have worked as far east as John Nagle's claim. He sat down to rest and as he looked about, noticed how similar this clearing was to his own. The buildings looked familiar. Even the rooster was like his rooster. There he sat for some time pondering on the strangeness of it all when a woman wearing a blue dress came out to feed the chickens. She, too, looked famil iar. Where had he seen her before? Then it flashed upon him that he had been working in a circle and was back at his own home. The woman was his own mother.

But they were not all jokes that were told in the cook-house. Public matters were threshed out there and this discussion of their common problems developed a community spirit that stood the pioneers in good stead in the dark years that were to follow.

The year of 1854 gave them plenty to talk about. No modern moving picture could be more crowded with exciting incidents. On the very first day of January, as if to start the sensational year appropriately, came the weird news that a crazy man had been found wandering on the beach. Seemingly out of nowhere, this nameless derelict was suddenly in their midst—their responsibility. He was in a pitiable condition, his frozen toes indicating that he had been exposed to the weather for many weeks. For food he had been eating raw mussels gathered from rocks on the beach. He was not dangerous, but an extremely unpleasant addition to their small community.

There was no public fund for the care of paupers; consequently, the stranger within their gates had to be supported by voluntary subscription at a time when money was scarce. His board and care and doctor's fee were paid until spring when the town sent him to board with a doctor in Steilacoom—by a coincidence, to the town that has since become the seat of a large state hospital for the insane. The understanding was that the legislature was about to appropriate money for the care of such paupers and the doctor in Steilacoom expected to get his pay from that source. This, the town thought, was the last it was to see of the demented stranger; but the legislature failed to appropriate funds for his care. After the Indian War, in the settlement's darkest hour, he was returned.

On February 13th of '54, the first term of court convened in the cookhouse. With the coming of the new governor, the machinery of federal law had been set up. Edward M. Lander, who had been appointed Chief Justice of the new Territory by President Pierce, presided over this first district court.

Mr. Lander was a native of Massachusetts, a graduate of Harvard University, and a man of handsome and distinguished bearing. "United to extensive legal and literary acquirements, he possessed dignified and polished manners," according to Grant.

This session of court brought into the frontier village other brilliant lawyers of the territory—J. S. Clendenin, the prosecuting attorney, Elwood Evans, Frank Clark, and William H. Wallace.

In the cookhouse where the good citizens had arranged a table and chairs at one end of the room, these distinguished visitors gathered. A wood fire in the stove made the place hot and stuffy. The room was crowded, for pioneers from all up and down the river settlements had come in, many with their clothes muddy and wet and steaming in the heat. Indians hung around the outside staring curiously. Up in front, with his steel-rimmed glasses now on, now pushed up on his forehead, sat David Maynard, clerk of the court.

A grand jury was impaneled composed of Charles Terry, foreman; William Bell; David Denny; Lewis Wyckoff, the town blacksmith; E. A. Clark, later the town photographer; S. B. Simmons, who kept a rooming house; Franklin Matthias, a carpenter; Charles Walker, who lived at the mouth of the Duwamish; John Buckley, Timothy Grow, and George Holt from farther up the river; and H. H. Tobin and Dr. Bigelow from the Black River.

The first accomplishment of the court was the granting of citizenship to Henry Van Asselt, a Hollander, one of the first settlers of King County.

The first case was the trial of four shipmasters who were found guilty of dumping ballast in the harbor. They were reprimanded and warned not to do it again, and the case dismissed.

At the end of three days, court was adjourned until October. Not much had been accomplished, but the law of the federal government had been set in motion, as some of the townspeople found out before the next session of court.

Shortly after court was adjourned, George McConaha and Arthur Denny set out in a canoe—always in a canoe—to attend the first session of the legislature. Both Democrats and Whigs watched the slim canoe, manned by Indians, disappear around Duwamish Head bearing Seattle's first representatives to Olympia.

In March the pioneers had their first unhappy experience with the Indians. William Young, the engineer in the new Terry-Renton sawmill at Alki, went to Whidby Island accompanied by Indians and failed to return. Fearing that he had met with foul play, Thomas Russell, deputy sheriff at Alki, set out with a posse to arrest the Indians who were suspected. He encountered them at Holmes Harbor on Whidby Island. Several Indians were killed in the altercation and all of the white men wounded, one of whom, Dr. W. G. Cherry, died on reaching Seattle. Mr. Blaine conducted his funeral, and he was buried on Dr. Maynard's "Point." The town was in a furor of excitement. After the services a company of volunteers was formed to go and attack the Indians; but on sober second thought, the citizens met and drew up resolutions requesting the governor to take immediate action.

Their great concern is shown in one of Mrs. Blaine's letters.

They sent it [the message to the governor] off in a sloop, but unless the wind should be fair we cannot hope for aid from him before Saturday. Meantime we feel considerably alarmed for ourselves.

The Indians are well armed with guns, knives, and more ammunition than the whites.

The sloop sailed its slow way to Olympia. Without delay the governor ordered a squad of soldiers sent to Whidby from Fort Steilacoom; but on the way, the boat, small and frail, capsized and all but two were drowned.

Before the pioneers had recovered from the shock of the Whidby Island disaster they learned, in April, of the so-called McCormick murder that had been committed the preceding summer, which the Indians had concealed all these months. It came with the shock of a fresh tragedy to the settlement. All of the Indians in the vicinity knew of the murder and were much troubled, for they felt that an evil spirit hovered about and would cast a spell upon them. They were relieved perhaps when David Denny stumbled upon their secret. One day on hearing much "wah-wah" (loud talking) in an Indian hut near his house on Seneca Street. he went to investigate. He heard one Indian accuse another of killing a white man. He walked into their midst and demanded an explanation.

The Indians were surprised and at first unwilling to talk; but since David was their friend, they finally consented to let "Salmon Bay Curley" tell him what had happened.

David informed the other settlers at once. Several went out to the spot, which the Indians pointed out—near the present intersection of Eastlake Avenue and Valley Street —and disinterred the body. According to the Indians it was the body of a man from a lumber schooner. Since an advertisement from people in Pennsylvan ı inquiring for a man named James M. McCormick had appeared in an Olympia paper about the time of the murder, it was thought that the stranger might have been he. The tragedy became known as "the McCormick murder."

Three Indians were arrested. A justice court was held and two of the Indians found guilty, the third held under suspicion. There was now much "wah-wah" in the cookhouse. Feeling against the Indians was bitter. Luther Collins, down from the Duwamish, expressed in forceful language his opinion as to the only method of dealing with the "Siwash." Some agreed with him; others urged that no violent action be taken. Nevertheless, a few of the hot-headed ones, with the aid of sailors from a sailing vessel, who furnished the block and tackle and were only too glad to take part in a "necktie party," broke into the cabin where the two convicted Indians were held, took them to a conveniently shaped tree south of the mill and hanged them.

The crowd then turned their attention toward the young Indian who was under suspicion; but Sheriff Boren, anticipating their intentions, had locked the badly scared young buck in his own house and stood guard over him. When one of the crowd called Boren away for a few minutes on a pretext of urgent business, the mob broke into the cabin and seized the prisoner. Just as they were about to hang him, Boren, having discovered the plot, came running up and cut the rope. The Indian was taken immediately to the jail in Steilacoom, where he was kept until his trial, in which he was found innocent. He lived many years in Seattle and was always grateful to Boren for having saved his life.

There was a law stronger than frontier methods in the land now. Besides the lynching of these two Indians, there was the hanging of "Masachie Jim" to be accounted for. As usual, much talk and conjecture went on in the cookhouse as to what would be done about it, if anything. It was April; court would not convene until October.

But the death of one of their own group—their own brilliant McConaha, of whom they were extremely proud—turned their minds from the lynching. Truly this was a year of tragedies.

The legislature adjourned its first session on May 1st. Professor Meany gives the story of that day as it was told

by Arthur Denny, and it is repeated here because it not only
tells of the drowning of McConaha but because it gives a
picture of those days. The legislators had proved themselves
a most conscientious body of men and had even considered
very seriously the passage of a prohibition law; yet on their
last day they held this "celebration." Mr. Denny says:

*I had made arrangements for a large canoe and crew of Indians
to take me home on the morning after adjournment, and was hurrying to the boat, when a "committee from headquarters" gave chase.
Headquarters was the place where the "boys" were having a high old
time. I was captured and taken back to headquarters. I was offered
a glass of whiskey, and upon declining, the crowd yelled:
"Make him drink! Make him drink!"
They grabbed me by the collar, and I settled back for what I supposed was going to be a nasty fight, when Elwood Evans spoke as
follows:—
"No, boys, don't make him drink. I propose that we drink to the
health of the only member of the Legislature who consistently lives
up to the principles of the Maine liquor law."
This seemed to satisfy the crowd. They drank most heartily to my
health, and I made my escape to the waiting canoe. As I hastened
along I noticed my good friend, George N. McConaha, president of
the first council, running like a deer with another "headquarters committee at his heels. They caught him, and the last time I saw my
friend the committee was marching him back to headquarters. Now
Mr. McConaha was a man of superior parts, and one I always held
in the highest esteem. He had been previously addicted to the liquor
habit, and I never saw a man make more heroic efforts than he did
to overcome that habit. So you can imagine with what feelings of sorrow I pushed off the Olympia beach with my canoe. On his return
Mr. McConaha's canoe was overturned in a storm off the southern
shore of Vashon Island, and he was drowned. The delay and the
liquor at the "headquarters" may have had nothing to do with his
death, but there are many people who will always believe that he
would have continued in a long life of usefulness if he had not been
overtaken by that unfortunate committee.

"The news of this calamity," says one writer, "cast a
deeper gloom over our little colony than a like disaster
would today; it was the occasion of Seattle's first sorrow."

McConaha's death was a public loss not only for his per-

---

*From *History of the State of Washington* by Edmond S. Meany. By permission
of Macmillan Company, publishers.

sonal magnetism, but because the town depended much on his gifted leadership. That was the day of oratory. It was said that McConaha's speeches were "models of elegant diction, power and grace."

In the summer of '54 occurred the suicide of Betsy, which involved one of the serious pioneer problems, that of the squaw man. The population at that time was made up largely of young men, many of whom had come West from good homes to take up land, but for whom there were no wives to help in making homes.

Thoughtful men in the community realized the gravity of the problem. Thomas Mercer especially considered it very seriously, well knowing that no stable community could be built without having home life for its foundation. The Blaines speak often in their letters of its seriousness.

In the midst of this population of lonely men the presence of many Indians was highly demoralizing. The contact of the two races was bad. Unscrupulous white people sold liquor to the Indians and taught them nothing good; on the other hand, many of the white men, who were away from the restraining influence of home life, were debauched in associating with the natives. The need of segregating the Indians on reservations was felt strongly.

The tragedy of Betsy is a significant squaw man story of the West. Betsy was the granddaughter of Chief Seattle; the daughter of Princess Angeline. Catherine Blaine tells the story in her letters in that year of '54.

I believe I have written about the men living with squaws. There was a man bought one from her folks about three years ago and has been living with her ever since just as if she was his wife. A part of the time he has been unkind to her but since their child was born which is now eight or ten months old and a fine little boy, he has, it is said, treated her very well. He has been living out on a claim all summer but moved into town a few weeks ago and they have been housekeeping. Yesterday for some trifling circumstances she became angry and when he had gone to work in the afternoon she hung her-self and when found was dead.

She never loved him nor wanted to live with him, and had run away several times but he had followed and brought her back. This time she was beyond his reach. He was in rather a peculiar position. The Indians claim the body to bury among their own people with their own ceremony and he is unwilling to let it go but uncertain whether the whites will allow her to be buried in their ground. There was some opposition to it but they consented. . . . . The Indians carried the coffin covered with a blue Indian blanket. The man who owned her accompanied by one or two squaw men (as we call those who live with squaws) and a number of Indians followed to the grave and this afternoon as Mr. B was passing his house the Indians were in it howling and wailing as they are accustomed to do. Now, what a situation he is in with his little half-breed child and despised by the whites and hated by the Indians who would kill him if they could get a chance in revenge for her death. He is, I believe, the son of a minister and well brought up.

As the story came down to us who were children of the pioneers, sympathy was always with Betsy, and her drunken husband was condemned; but Mrs. Blaine shows that it was a double tragedy. For those who want to know "what happened next," the little boy turned against his father and went with his mother's people. He grew up a "bad Indian" by the name of Joe Foster and was a constant sorrow to his grandmother, Princess Angeline.

This year of '54 was not all calamity, but it did bring home to the people the need of settling with the Indians. Much was expected of the governor after his return from Washington City. The pioneers sent him word of the Indian murders and he asked for a special stand of arms to be deposited at Fort Steilacoom with which to equip the militia in case of trouble, but Jefferson Davis, Secretary of War, refused his request. However, the governor had returned with authority to settle the Indian difficulties by treaty. The settlers' fear of an Indian uprising was thus somewhat allayed.

MORE OF EVENTFUL '54

The same wind and tide that had proved fatal to George McConaha forced Arthur Denny to land on McNeil's Island where he found shelter in the cabin of a stranger named Ezra Meeker. The bearded patriarch, as Ezra Meeker is remembered in history, was then a young man of twenty-three. The two talked far into the night. Meeker wrote of his guest, "Mr. Denny remarked in the morning that he thought there was a good foundation under my cabin floor as he did not find any spring under the bed."

After the storm had subsided, Mr. Denny went on his way. It was a busy, building settlement to which he returned. The tragedies of March and April and the drowning of McConaha, though they cast a shadow, did not interfere with the sober work of organizing the town and county into working units of the territory.

The first general election in the Territory was to take place on September 4, 1854, and the county commissioners were busy preparing for it by creating new polling places and appointing election officers.

Outlying precincts were established at Mox La Push, the election to be held in the home of Joseph Foster, a prominent Duwamish pioneer; at Stuck, the most southerly precinct near the present Sumner, the election to be held in the home of A. W. McCarty; and at Meig's Mill at Port Madison.

William Strickler, S. L. Grow, and David Denny were appointed election judges for Seattle. The names of all of the county election judges appear in a neat row in the county commissioners' records with $3.00 listed as the amount paid to each for his day's work at the polls.

Constables and justices of the peace were appointed and items like these appear in the records: "C. C. Lewis be and hereby is appointed justice of the peace for Mox La Push"; "Abram Bryant be and hereby is appointed constable for Mox La Push."

At the election, Charles Terry and William Strickler were elected members of the Territorial Council; John Carson, a prominent farmer on the Stuck River, and Arthur Denny, representatives—the latter for the second time; Henry Yesler, auditor; Dr. Smith, school superintendent; Thomas Russell, sheriff—the first *elected* sheriff in King County, Boren having been appointed.

Since it was the sheriff's duty to collect the taxes, and the tax list had just been completed, Mr. Russell went to work immediately after election. His Spencerian signature adorns many pages in the early treasurer's books, for he was in the office for twelve years, when he was succeeded by Lewis Wyckoff.

On October 23rd, the district court again convened in Seattle, this time for nearly two weeks. It was held in the Felker House, which was more commodious than the cookhouse. Again, distinguished guests arrived, and King County pioneers from the farms along the riverways gathered in the village.

As they passed across the porch of the Felker House on the point overlooking the Bay during those golden October days, they were a sturdy set of pioneers, although not so colorful as a group might have assembled on a similar occasion in the San Francisco of that period.

The twenty men who served on the grand jury, impaneled the first day, were: Charles Terry, foreman; Joseph Foster; William Gilliam and Abram Bryant, who had paddled down from Mox La Push; Bennet Johns and his neighbor, C. C. Lewis, from their farms on the Duwamish; Henry Van Asselt, who through his newly acquired citizenship was now eligible for jury duty; H. H. Tobin and O. M. Eaton from Black River; William Brannan, who had come all the way down the winding White River from what is now Auburn; Henry and Burleigh Pearce, Edmund Carr, and Francis McNatt from Salmon Bay; William Smith, the town treasurer; William Bell; Franklin Matthias; S. M. Holderness; William Heebner; and J. L. Foster. Dexter Horton and

Arthur and David Denny were among those on the trial juries.

The crowd milled in and out of the Felker House, but the actual excitement was down around the cookhouse, the general lounging place. After the grand jury had been charged, it became known that the men who had lynched "Masachie Jim" for the murder of his squaw, and those who had hanged the two Indians after the discovery of the McCormick murder were to be brought to trial. Frontier lynchings were not to go unchallenged. Federal law had arrived.

It was awkward for the grand jury to be called upon to indict their fellow townsmen, for the town was small and the population intimate. An especially embarrassing situation was the fact that one of their own members, William Heebner, was accused of having been an accomplice in the hanging of the Indians. This difficulty was met by excusing Mr. Heebner long enough to indict him. Two other prominent men—David Maurer and Luther Collins, county commissioner, known all over the countryside, were also indicted.

A subscription to raise money was started immediately in order that these men, all good Democrats, might have the services of the "smartest lawyers in the territory." Maurer's subscription list was headed by Dr. Maynard, who gave one hundred and fifty dollars.

Before the murder trial other matters were taken up—cases of whites selling liquor to the Indians, and again cases against sea captains for dumping ballast in the harbor.

At that time the skippers whose ships were heavily laden with lumber on the trip to San Francisco had no heavy cargo on their return. They were in the habit of using rock and dirt dug from the sides of Telegraph Hill in San Francisco harbor. The hill, to this day, shows the ravages made by those erring men. After arriving at Seattle those shiploads of Telegraph Hill were dumped in the harbor, until, after repeated arrests and fines, the masters were made to dump their ballast to the south of the harbor, near the foot of Main Street, where it accumulated and became known as "Ballast Island." For years this island was a gathering place for Indians. Now the place is entirely filled and the island is no more.

In the murder trial Elwood Evans was attorney for the United States government and Frank Clark of Steilacoom prosecuting attorney for the Territory. The attorneys for the defense were Joseph Cushman of Olympia and W. C. Pease, Captain of the U. S. Revenue Cutter *Jefferson Davis.* David Maynard was again clerk of the court, lacking only an official seal, and obliged to make one of his own by writing "D. K. C." and enclosing it in a zigzag scroll. The tall Virginian, Hillory Butler, was one of the bailiffs, and Thomas Russell, court crier. "Hear ye; hear ye; hear ye; the district court of the Territory of Washington is now in session."

Maurer, whom Prosch describes as a "simple-minded Dutchman," was tried first, and in his nervousness answered. "I suppose I ish guilty, Shudge." At this moment, as the old-timers told the story, Terry leaned over and whispered. "Not guilty, you fool, say not guilty." Maurer quickly changed his plea, and the judge disregarded the confession of guilt. A declaration of innocence was entered in the record.

While this may have been merely a cookhouse yarn, it illustrates very well the spirit that actuated the trial. They did show, as Cornelius Hanford says, "a disposition to enforce law without favor and without prejudice," but when it came to actually punishing members of their own race for hanging Indians, they faltered in their task. Both Maurer and Heebner were acquitted, and the case of Collins was discharged.

From the pen of Catherine Blaine we get the most illuminating account of the trial as it really took place:

Our court closed its session last week after a sitting of ten days. The two murder cases, or rather the trial of two men for the same murder caused a great deal of excitement. The first one tried was acquitted after a very short absence of the jury but the other case, the jury were out for nearly thirty hours and then acquitted the man only on the ground that the state had not proven the name mentioned in the indictment was the name of the murdered Indian. They had not labored to prove it because it had not entered the minds of any to dispute the name. But the jury wanted to acquit him and knew the people wanted they should, and the evidence of his having assisted to hang the Indian was so plain they could not acquit him on any other ground. There was another man indicted for hanging two other Indians but after the result of this trial the states attorney refused to prosecute him and so the matter was left.

Mother Damnable reaped a very good profit from this session of court. She charged $25 for the use of her best room as a court room; $10 for rooms for the jurors; and $4 for the use of the furniture. The jurors' meals came to $66 at fifty cents a meal.

The bill seemed rather steep to the prosecuting attorney, Mr. Clark. When he went to settle with her, he demanded a receipt. Mother Damnable could neither read nor write; besides, she did not care much for Clark, who, being a young lawyer trying to make a reputation, had worked hard for the conviction of the accused prisoners.

She told the young man that she would give him a receipt and stepped back into the kitchen. Returning with her arms filled with stove wood, she advanced upon Clark.

"You want a receipt, do you? Well, here's your receipt. I'll larn you for asking me for a receipt!" she said, and began pelting him with chunks of wood.

He ran and she after him, throwing wood at him until he was out of sight. No one ever asked Mother Damnable for a receipt after that.

A highly important and constructive event of the year of '54 was the development of the coal mine at Black River by outside capital. Bigelow, Fanjoy, Tobin, and Eaton, who had formed the Duwamish Coal Company in '53, had not had the financial means to do much; however, they had managed to get out some coal, for it was a scow-load of their coal that Captain William Webster saw in the harbor of Seattle that aroused his interest in supplying coal for the San Francisco market.

Mrs. Blaine writes in July that there is a rumor that the mine up the river has been sold for $24,000, and that "it is going to be a great benefit to our town as the company have means to work it largely and the coal is wanted by vessels." A few days later she wrote, "The report concerning the coal mine is true. The company have purchased it and will immediately build a wharf, get a steam tug to bring down the coal and do various things."

Exact information about the company purchasing the mine is not to be had—the little industry having been obliterated during the Indian War—except that Captain Webster, to whom it was bonded, according to Bagley, was responsible for its development. We do know, however, that during the summer of '54 the *Harriet Thompson* took three hundred tons of coal to San Francisco where it sold for thirty dollars a ton.

In December Mrs. Blaine wrote, "Last week a small steamer came to Seattle, lately brought from San Francisco to run on our river between this place and the coal mine to tug vessels that carry coal." This was the *Water Lily*, a tiny side-wheeler only forty-nine feet long, brought here by Captain Webster. A month later Mr. Blaine wrote of a brig in the harbor loading with coal for San Francisco.

Captain Webster became much interested in Puget Sound. and published a circular which he distributed in San Francisco, setting forth the possibilities and great advantages of settling in this section of the country. This pamphlet, issued by a sea captain, was the first piece of publicity about Puget Sound. The dissemination of such information was a fitting culmination of an eventful year.

CHAPTER XI

THE RETURN of Governor Stevens from Washington City in December of '54 with authority to make treaties with the Indians outshadowed all other events. To prepare the way for the treaty making, Dr. Maynard arranged with his friend, Chief Seattle, for a gathering of the Duwamish Indians at "the Point," at which meeting the Governor would be present and explain matters to them.

Dr. Smith has left this description of the event:

When Governor Stevens first appeared in Seattle and told the natives that he had been appointed Commissioner of Indian Affairs for Washington Territory, they gave him a demonstrative reception in front of Dr. Maynard's office near the waterfront on Main Street. The Bay swarmed with canoes and the shore was lined with a living, swaying, writhing, dusky humanity until old Chief Seattle's trumpet-toned voice rolled over the immense multitude, like the startling reveille of a brass drum, when silence became as instantaneous and perfect as that which follows a clap of thunder from a clear sky.

The scene contrasts dramatically with that of a month previous when Judge Lander held court. Then attorneys and pioneers representing the best in civilized standards were gathered in the same vicinity where now the native Duwamish assembled. This amicable gathering concluded fortunately a year that had brought many grave Indian problems.

This was to be Chief Seattle's big day. He was on his old familiar camping ground, where he was accustomed to addressing his people. He was among the white people whom he loved.

When a little brown-eyed lad of six, he had gazed with wonder upon Captain Vancouver's great "bird-ship," the *Discovery*. Someone has suggested that kindness shown the little Indian boy by Vancouver and his men won his heart for the white man for all time.

Of Chief Seattle's personal appearance and gifts of oratory, Dr. Smith has given us the following description:

Old Chief Seattle . . . . . was broad-shouldered, deep chested, and finely proportioned. His eyes were large, intelligent, expressive, and friendly when in repose and faithfully mirrored the varying moods of the great soul that looked through them. He was usually solemn, silent, and dignified, but on great occasions moved among assembled multitudes like a Titan among Lilliputians; his lightest word was law.

When rising to speak in council or to tender advice, all eyes were turned upon him, and deep-toned, sonorous and eloquent sentences rolled from his lips like the ceaseless thunders of cataracts flowing from exhaustless fountains, and his magnificent bearing was as noble as that of the most cultivated military chieftain in command of the forces of the continent. Neither his eloquence, his dignity nor his grace were acquired.

Dr. Smith explains how the chief began his address after the governor had spoken to the natives:

The governor was then introduced to the native multitude by Dr. Maynard and at once commenced in a conversational, plain, and straightforward style an explanation of his mission among them. When he sat down Chief Seattle arose and with all the dignity of a Senator who carries the responsibility of a nation on his shoulders. Placing one hand on the governor's head and slowly pointing heavenward with the index finger of the other, he commenced his memorable address in solemn and impressive tones.

Never having stooped to learn the artificial Chinook, the proud old chief spoke in his native Duwamish. Dr. Smith had learned this tongue and was able to take notes, but could not get the whole speech. The young translator may have added something of his own beauty of diction in the translation; yet other pioneers who also knew the language say that it is practically verbatim. Dr. Smith said that it "lacks all the charm lent by the grace and earnestness of the sable, old orator and the occasion."

The speech belongs not only to Seattle but to all America. It is the swan song of a vanishing race. There is in it the soul of Chief Seattle: the conflict, the sadness for his people, his love and compassion for all.

Yonder sky that has wept tears of compassion upon my people for centuries untold, and which to us appears changeless and eternal, may change. Today is fair. Tomorrow it may be overcast with clouds. My words are like the stars that never change. Whatever Seattle says the great chief at Washington can rely upon with as much certainty as he can upon the return of the sun or the seasons. The White Chief says that Big Chief at Washington sends us greetings of friendship and goodwill. This is kind of him for we know he has little need of our friendship in return. His people are many. They are like the grass that covers vast prairies. My people are few. They resemble the scattering trees of a storm-swept plain. The great, and I presume— good White Chief sends us word that he wishes to buy our lands but is willing to allow us enough to live comfortably. This indeed appears just, even generous, for the Red Man no longer has rights that he need respect, and the offer may be wise also, as we are no longer in need of an extensive country.

There was a time when our people covered the land as the waves of a wind-ruffled sea cover its shell paved floor, but that time long since passed away with the greatness of tribes that are now but a mournful memory. I will not dwell on, nor mourn over, our untimely decay, nor reproach my paleface brothers with hastening it as we too may have been somewhat to blame.

Youth is impulsive. When our young men grow angry at some real or imaginary wrong, and disfigure their faces with black paint, it denotes that their hearts are black, and that they are often cruel and relentless, and our old men and old women are unable to restrain them. Thus it has ever been. Thus it was when the white men first began to push our forefathers further westward. But let us hope that the hostilities between us may never return. We would have everything to lose and nothing to gain. Revenge by young men is considered gain, even at the cost of their own lives, but old men who stay at home in times of war, and mothers who have sons to lose, know better.

Our good father at Washington—for I presume he is now our father as well as yours, since King George has moved his boundaries further north—our great and good father, I say, sends us word that if we do as he desires he will protect us. His brave warriors will be to us a bristling wall of strength, and his wonderful ships of war will fill our harbors so that our ancient enemies far to the northward— the Hydas and Tsimpsians, will cease to frighten our women, children and old men. Then in reality will he be our father and we his children. But can that ever be? Your God is not our God! Your God loves your people and hates mine. He folds his strong protecting arms lovingly about the pale face and leads him by the hand as a father leads his infant son—but He has forsaken His red children—if they really are his. Our God, the Great Spirit, seems also to have forsaken us. Your God make your people wax strong every day. Soon they will fill all the land. Our people are ebbing away like a rapidly receding tide that will never return. The white man's God cannot love our people or He would protect them. They seem to be orphans who can look nowhere for help. How then can we be brothers? How can your God become our God and renew our prosperity and awaken in us dreams of returning greatness. If we have a common heavenly father He must be partial—for He came to His paleface children. We never saw him. He gave you laws but had no word for his red children whose teeming multitudes once filled this vast continent as stars fill the firmament. No; we are two distinct races with separate origins and separate destinies. There is little in common between us.

To us the ashes of our ancestors are sacred and their resting place is hallowed ground. You wander far from the graves of your ancestors and seemingly without regret. Your religion was written upon tables of stone by the iron finger of your God so that you could not forget. The Red Man could never comprehend nor remember it. Our religion is the traditions of our ancestors—the dreams of our old men, given them in solemn hours of night by the Great Spirit; and the visions of our sachems, and is written in the hearts of our people.

Your dead cease to love you and the land of their nativity as soon as they pass the portals of the tomb and wander way beyond the stars. They are soon forgotten and never return. Our dead never forget the beautiful world that gave them being. They still love its verdant valleys, its murmuring rivers, its magnificent mountains, sequestered vales and verdant lined lakes and bays, and ever yearn in tender, fond affection over the lonely hearted living, and often return from the Happy Hunting Ground to visit, guide, console and comfort them.

Day and night cannot dwell together. The Red Man has ever fled the approach of the White Man, as the morning mist flees before the morning sun.

However, your proposition seems fair and I think that my people will accept it and will retire to the reservation you offer them. Then we will dwell apart in peace, for the words of the Great White Chief seem to be the words of nature speaking to my people out of dense darkness.

It matters little where we pass the remnant of our days. They will not be many. The Indians' night promises to be dark. Not a single star of hope hovers above his horizon. Sad-voiced winds moan in the distance. Grim fate seems to be on the Red Man's Trail, and wherever he goes he will hear the approaching footsteps of his fell destroyer and prepare stolidly to meet his doom, as does the wounded doe that hears the approaching footsteps of the hunter.

A few more moons. A few more winters—and not one of the descendants of the mighty hosts that once moved over this broad land or lived in happy homes, protected by the Great Spirit, will remain to mourn over the graves of a people—once more powerful and hopeful than yours. But why should I mourn at the untimely fate of my people? Tribe follows tribe, and nation follows nation, like the waves of the sea. It is the order of nature, and regret is useless. Your time of decay may be distant, but it will surely come, for even the White Man whose God walked and talked with him as friend with friend, cannot be exempt from the common destiny. We may be brothers after all. We will see.

We will ponder your proposition and when we decide we will let you know. But should we accept it, I here and now make this condition that we will not be denied the privilege without molestation of visiting at any time the tombs of our ancestors, friends and children. Every part of this soil is sacred in the estimation of my people. Every hillside, every valley, every plain and grove, has been hallowed by some sad or happy event in days long vanished. Even the rocks, which seem to be dumb and dead as they swelter in the sun along the silent shore, thrill with memories of stirring events connected with the lives of my people, and the very dust upon which you now stand responds more lovingly to their footsteps than to yours, because it is rich with the blood of our ancestors and our bare feet are conscious of the sympathetic touch. Our departed braves, fond mothers, glad, happy-hearted maidens, and even the little children who lived here and rejoiced here for a brief season, will love these somber solitudes and at eventide they greet shadowy returning spirits. And when the last Red Man shall have perished, and the memory of my tribe shall have become a myth among the White Men, these shores will swarm with the invisible dead of my tribe, and when your children's children think themselves alone in the field, the store, the shop, upon the highway, or in the silence of the pathless woods, they will not be alone. In all the earth there is no place dedicated to solitude. At night when the streets of your cities and villages are silent and you think them deserted, they will throng with the returning hosts that once filled them and still love this beautiful land. The White Man will never be alone.

Let him be just and deal kindly with my people, for the dead are not powerless. Dead, did I say? There is no death, only a change of worlds.

THE INDIAN TREATIES

The story of the making of the Indian treaties is a volume in itself, in descriptions of the actual treaty councils, in their relation to the Indian War that followed soon after, and in the long controversy that has continued even to this day over the terms of the treaties and the government's part in the transactions.

Governor Stevens lost no time, after his meeting with Chief Seattle, in setting out on his difficult and delicate treaty-making mission in company with Colonel Michael T. Simmons, a brother of Mrs. Maynard, who was then Indian agent. His corps of assistants included Benjamin Franklin Shaw, an excellent interpreter of Chinook.

The first treaty was made at Medicine Creek on December 26, 1854, with the Puyallup, Nisqually, Steilacoom, and other tribes about the southern end of Puget Sound, of whom Leschi was the most powerful chief.

By the terms of this treaty the Indians gave up their title to land comprising one-half of King County and all of what are today Pierce, Thurston, and Mason Counties. In return they received three small tracts for themselves and were to be paid $32,000 in money and other benefits.

There was dissatisfaction with the terms of the treaty almost immediately. The Indians claimed that they had not realized how little they were receiving for what they had relinquished. This feeling of an injustice done helped, in some degree, to fan the flames that started the war. In the summer of '56 Governor Stevens met with these Indians again and sought to rectify the mistake, with the result that the present Muckleshoot and Puyallup reservations were given to them in place of the more undesirable lands offered at first.

The second treaty arranged by Governor Stevens—the Treaty of Point Elliott—was attended with great pomp and ceremony. It was made in January 21-23, 1855, at Mukilteo with Chief Seattle's Duwamish and Suquamish Indians and with the Snohomish, Snoqualmie, Skagits, and other tribes from northern Puget Sound.

For days hundreds of canoes came from all directions and nosed their way in along the beach. Along the trails from out of the forest came other natives. Twenty-five hundred of them in all assembled awaiting the arrival of the governor, who arrived on the 21st with his party on the *Major Tompkins*.

On the following morning the conference was called. The natives strode in in single file and in dignified silence took seats in a semicircle on the ground in front of the governor and his staff. The four chiefs—Seattle of the Duwamish tribe, Pat-Ka-nim of the Snohomish, Goliah of the Skagits, and Chow-its-hoot of the Bellingham Bay Indians—took seats in front as befitted their rank. The subchiefs occupied the second row, and the various tribes took their places behind them in separate groups.

What a spectacle of savage pageantry it was! It was a scene of great dignity—a scene that will never be enacted again. A great semicircle of savages in their gay barbaric trappings gathered about a handful of white men and listening to them in respectful silence. Back of them was the evergreen forest—in front, the wide, blue Sound—beyond, the snow-covered Olympics.

The governor addressed the gathering first, speaking a few words in English, which were then interpreted into Chinook by Mr. Shaw. Part of the address is given simply to show his method of reaching these primitive people:

My children, you are not my children because you are the fruit of my loins but because you are children for whom I have the same feeling as if you were the fruit of my loins. What will a man do for his own children? He will see that they are well cared for, that they have clothes to protect them against the cold and rain; that they have food to guard them against hunger. You understand well my purpose and you want now to know the special things we propose to do for you. We want to place you in homes where you can cultivate the soil, raising potatoes and other articles of food, and where you may be able to pass in canoes over the waters of the Sound and catch fish, and back to the mountains to get roots and berries.

He then told them that he had traveled many moons back to Washington City to see the Great Father in their behalf, and proceeded:

My children, I have simply told you the heart of the Great Father. But the lands are yours and we mean to pay you for them. The white children of the Great Father, but no more his children than you are, have come here, some to build mills, some to till the land, and others to sail ships. My children, I believe that I have got your hearts. You have my heart. We will put our hearts down on paper and then we will sign our names. I will send that paper to the Great Father and if he says it is good, it will stand forever.

Most of these Indians had been converted to the Roman Catholic faith, and after the governor's speech, the scene, already impressive, became more so when twenty-five hundred Indians sang a mass of the Church and recited a prayer.

Before the treaty was read, each chief made a brief but dignified reply to the governor. Seattle spoke first, followed by Pat-Ka-nim, Chow-its-hoot, and then Goliah. Their replies were similar, each referring with gratification to the provision made in the treaty for doctors. "My heart is very good toward Dr. Maynard," said Chief Seattle. "I want always to get medicine from him."

Then followed the reading of the treaty. By its terms the Indians ceded their title to the lands controlled by their tribes, except certain parts to be held for reservations. Those provided in this treaty were Port Madison, Lummi, Tulalip, and one on Fidalgo Island. Their land was to be paid for in thirty annual installments, and the money with which to prepare the reservations for occupancy. Certain numbers of blankets and provisions were also promised. Furthermore, the United States was to furnish a central industrial and agricultural school, supply instructors, blacksmiths, carpenters, and physicians.

The governor signed the treaty, followed by the chiefs and head men of the tribes. Then, the grand old chief, Seattle, who was always ceremonious, came forward and presented the governor with a white flag, pledging their loyalty in these simple words, "By this we make friends; we will never change our minds." And they never did.

The second day of the conference was spent in a potlatch—a ceremonial distribution of gifts—without which no Indian ceremony was complete. The presents which the governor had provided for the occasion were given out; the *Major Tompkins* fired a salute of thirty-one guns; and the Indians then returned to their camping places to await the ratification of the treaty.

Governor Stevens next made treaties at Hood Canal and at Neah Bay, thus completing his task of settling with the Puget Sound Indians, all of whom had pledged their friendship and relinquished their lands under the terms proposed by the government.

He next turned his attention to the tribes east of the Cascade Mountains. Runners were sent ahead who arranged a meeting near Fort Walla Walla. Here the governor negotiated a treaty with the Walla Wallas, the Umatillas, and the Cayuse Indians in June, 1855.

In the same month he made treaties with the Yakimas, the Klikitats, and with the Nez Perce's; later with the Flatheads and Pend d'Oreilles.

The governor then went east of the Rocky Mountains into what is now Montana where, in October, he made a treaty with the Blackfeet—his tenth treaty. In all he had extinguished the Indian title to approximately 100,000 square miles of land.

He was far from home and his presence in the Blackfoot country was the source of much anxiety on Puget Sound. Hardly had he left the Walla Walla conclave than the fierce tribes thereabouts began plotting against him; consequently his return from the Blackfoot council was under hostile and dangerous conditions. Even as they pledged their friendship, many of the leaders of the Eastern Washington tribes were secretly planning to exterminate the whites. Grant says:

Months before attending the council called by Governor Stevens to perfect the treaties, they had been assiduously collecting arms and supplies and planning to effect a combination of the various tribes to strike simultaneously at the exposed settlements, to murder isolated men, to cut off small parties, to exterminate the whites as far as practicable, or at all events to create such a terror on their part that they would leave the country and deter others from coming.

Meany writes that Governor Stevens came to realize that the Indians had been plotting for years. The Governor frankly avowed that he would not have held the Walla Walla council if he had known the real feelings of many of the Indians. He said to the legislature:

It originated in the native intelligence of restless Indians, who, foreseeing destiny against them, determined that it must be met and resisted by arms. We may sympathize with such a manly feeling but in view of it we have high duties.

Later, in the heat of the Indian War, many declared that the treaties had been the cause and blamed Governor Stevens for bringing it about. But it was not the treaty making. The cause was deep-seated. The treaties only emphasized the fact that the Indians were losing their hold on "Mother Earth," as they called the land. They could not be pushed farther West, as civilization had always pushed them heretofore, and this was their last stand.

The crash was inevitable sooner or later, for two adverse modes of life—two races, one civilized, the other barbarous —were bound to conflict. Both could not dominate; one or the other had to give way. Whether the adjustment could have been made in a happier way, we cannot judge.

THE YEAR OF '55 fairly hummed with prosperity in the little settlement. It is hard for us looking back through the vista of years to understand how the settlers could have proceeded serenly on when massacre and death were lurking near. But they were young, times were prosperous, and life was abundant all about them. The Indian troubles of the turbulent summer of '54 were now ended, as they believed, by the making of the treaties. The confidence felt after the governor had arranged with the Sound Indians is reflected in one of the Blaine letters:

Our governor has been employed some weeks past in treating with the Indians on the Sound. . . . . They seem entirely satisfied with the treaty as far as I can learn. . . . . I think we shall apprehend no more trouble from them.

The subsequent good news from east of the Cascade and Rocky Mountains that the governor was treating successfully there added to the pioneers' confidence. Supposedly having disposed of the Indian problem, they proceeded with all the assurance of the white race to plant and build and organize.

All of the stores on Commercial street were doing a thriving business, a fourth having been opened by a Jewish firm by the name of Bettman. Plummer and Chase's, which was also the post office at this time, was busier when the mail came in, than the mill itself. The firm secured a license to sell "spiritous liquors" that summer and installed a bar. Another license was granted them to run a "bowling salloon" which they set up in the basement of the store. Plummer was, like Terry, a "go-getter." His store became the center of Commercial Street activity.

The Denny-Horton-Phillips firm did so well that it was necessary for Arthur Denny to go to San Francisco to buy stock for the store. At the end of their year together, the three partners had not only paid expenses, but each had cleared $300—a very good profit in those days. Late in '55 when Arthur Denny was again elected to the legislature he sold his interest to his partners.

The busy tap of carpenters' hammers added its note of progress when builders worked on a fine, new home that Charles Plummer was building for his bride, the former Miss Ellender Smith, whom he had married in January. The house he built at the corner of what is now Jackson and Occidental was the most ambitious one in the county, quite eclipsing the Blaine house grandeur. This large, pleasant white house with the green blinds, ornately trimmed piazzas enclosed with lattice work, and its picket fence became "the show place" of the village.

At Second and Cherry Streets the new church building was nearing completion. Mr. Blaine, who had often been discouraged over the lack of growth in the church, must have felt the quickening influence of that season, for he wrote, "Pray for us. Spiritually our church is improving we think."

Another industry had its modest beginning when two shoemakers, M. D. Woodin and Seymour Wetmore, conceived the idea of setting up a tannery and making into leather the plentiful supply of deer hides furnished by the Indians. Both men were good shoemakers but, like the early doctors, did not have enough work to keep them busy at their trade. The handmade shoes of that period lasted a long time, and when they needed repair, each man was his own family cobbler.

Water power for grinding the bark necessary in the operation of tanning was obtained from a noisy little brook that tumbled down the steep hillside just east of Yesler's mill— about where the Prefontaine fountain is today.

Mr. Wetmore did not continue in the business; but Mr. Woodin, an expert at his trade, who had been employed by the Hudson's Bay Company before coming to Seattle, did, and he and his son Ira built it into a profitable business after the Indian War. Later they were the founders of the present town of Woodinville.

The lumber industry had now grown until Yesler's mill had many equals. There was more than enough work for all. Not only San Francisco but world markets were looking to Puget Sound for lumber. In all there were about twenty-four sawmills on the Sound, mostly steam mills. Meig's mill at Port Madison, Captain William Renton's at Port Orchard, one at Port Gamble built by a number of Maine lumbermen, one at Utsalady were all well known. The water power mill on Black River belonging to Eaton, Fanjoy, and Talbot, had also done well except for unusually high water during the previous summer which caused disastrous floods all along the river.

As the mills prospered, individuals prospered in logging off their claims. North of town David Denny cleared the acres that are today the busy city blocks north of Denny Way. As he paused in his work he could hear the axe of his neighbor, Thomas Mercer. By ox team and by raft the timber came in to the mill, from the young men logging around Salmon Bay, from the Hanford and Holgate claims, and from up the Duwamish.

Grant tells us that Van Asselt and his partner, Samuel Maple, made four and five dollars a day hewing timbers. When they squared their accounts at the close of '55, they had $3,600 besides improvements on their property worth over two thousand dollars. It is written that Samuel Maple "was a good hand with oxen."

The settlement had not received the large accession to its population that the founders had hoped for, but those who did come made up in quality for what was wanting in quantity. Among the new arrivals was Seattle's second attorney, Christopher C. Hewitt, whom Grant describes as a young man of character and refinement. Like the pioneer doctors

and shoemakers he was obliged to supplement his practice
with other work, and although his shingle read imposingly,
"Chancellor in proctor and admiralty," he earned his livelihood making ox-bows. Good wages were paid for these
hand-made bows, which required quite a knack.

As a seaport Seattle had already made a good beginning.
In the fall of '54 one of the Blaine letters reads:

We have had eight or ten different vessels in here within two or
three weeks. Last Saturday was a lively day, there being five vessels
in, and two came and went. This is encouraging for a place which
two years ago scarcely had a vessel in for months together. . . . . One
is now loading for Australia.

Then in January '55, we read, "Two vessels are in the
harbor, a slip loading with fish and lumber for the Sandwich Islands, a brig loading with coal for San Francisco."

The farmers along the rivers were prospering splendidly.
Their prosperity became a part of Seattle's. The Puget
Sound country was entirely new to all of them, and they
were amazed and delighted at the size of the vegetables
and fruits that were grown here and at the rapidity with
which they developed. "Like Jonah's gourd" was the way
Mrs. Blaine described their growth. In the rich land along
the Duwamish, Collins grew turnips that weighed as much
as thirty-five pounds, potatoes four pounds, and onions two.

Already his orchard, planted in the fall of '51, was in its
second year of production. Mrs. Blaine wrote after a trip
up the river that "they took us into the peach orchard and
we all had all we could eat and Mr. Collins gave us some to
bring home. I preserved mine and they were very good."

Collins, who seems to have had modern ideas of publicity, took some of his product into the office of the Puget
Sound *Courier* in Steilacoom and received the following
notice:

L. M. Collins of Duwamish river paid us a visit yesterday morning and deposited for our table a half bushel of fine, luscious peaches
raised on his farm. He estimates his present crop of this excellent

fruit at three hundred bushels—a nice yield certainly for trees on the second bearing. His large nursery and orchard containing a thousand trees or more of all kinds, will, in a few years, handsomely repay the cost and trouble of planting. The trees were planted in the fall of '51.

Orchards planted even later were showing the remarkable growth of a "Jonah's gourd," among them the Blaine's orchard grown from seeds brought from New York, Dr. Smith's at Smith's Cove, and Hanford's on the steep sides of Beacon Hill. On White River, George King already had a good nursery started.

The development of the farms was reflected in lower prices. Mrs. Blaine wrote:

It is much cheaper living now than when we came. . . . . The last flour we got we paid $12 a barrel, potatoes will hardly bring 50 or even 25 cts. a bushel and other vegetables alike cheap. Beef, pork and such things that are imported are still up, but fresh beef sells for 8 to 18 cts. a pound. There is no doubt but that another year there will be nearly as much of everything produced here as will be required for the support of the inhabitants. There has been almost enough this year.

Their development in dairying was not so marked. Here again we get from Mrs. Blaine a very good idea of their methods, which show us why the Indians were able to capture so many cows a few months later. David Blaine had bought these cows while at a conference in Oregon. She wrote:

David bought two very good cows with heifer calves about six months old for $105 which is much cheaper than they could be bought about here even if there had been any sale as those who own cows here ask about $75 to $100 for cow and calf. The folks here do not take the calves from the cows but let them suck as long as the cows give milk. There are no pastures here and the cows run in the woods and would not come up to be milked if their calves were weaned. The calves are kept in a pen or yard and the cows turned in to them till they get a part of the milk and then they are tied whilst the rest of the milk is taken.

Under such adverse circumstances milk and butter continued to be luxuries. A quaint memory of Thomas Mercer furnished by his daughter Susan (Mrs. David Graham) is that when a sailing vessel arrived with firkins of butter, her father would say to Dexter Horton, "Come on up to supper tonight. We are going to have butter."

In early summer every sailing vessel, every scow, and every canoe that came into the harbor brought the magic news that gold had been discovered east of the Cascade Mountains near Fort Colville.

As weeks went by reports were brought in that prospectors were pouring into the gold fields from their own Territory, from Oregon, and from California. Mr. Blaine wrote from Oregon, where he had gone to attend conference, "Hundreds are going over there to mine, leaving claims and crops and all their improvements. Should the mines be as extensive as reports state, we shall go ahead of California in a short time."

This news of gold gave impetus to every activity on the Sound. It made the settlers deaf to mutterings of discontent among the Indians. The pioneers of Seattle began to plan to "go ahead of California in a short time," and saw their city as a second San Francisco.

But the news did not send the settlers of Seattle hurrying over to the gold mines. Joseph Fanjoy and O. M. Eaton, who sold their sawmill on Black River to Charles Plummer and started over the mountains, were the exception. To most of the settlers gold east of the Cascades meant that they must renew their efforts to make their city the seaport and trade center for the prosperous country back of them.

GLEANINGS FROM OLD RECORDS

One wonders who or what it was that "sold" Seattle to Chief Justice Edward Lander that he should have returned in the spring of '55 to invest in real estate. Did those young pioneers gather about him when he came to hold court and convince him of the inevitable greatness of their city? Did

they point to wealth still unexplored? To the value of
Seattle as a seaport, which value had been recognized by the
founders of the city and later by Governor Stevens and by
Captain McClellan? Did the "irrepressible Terry"—as
Meeker called him—show Mr. Lander a bargain in land
which the two of them could buy?

Whatever the reason, he and Charles Terry bought the
west half of Carson Boren's claim in April '55, in one of
the most remarkable real estate transactions that has ever
been made in the city. The record of this transaction is found
in the first volume of King County deeds and reads as
follows:

To all to whom these presents shall come, greeting: Know ye that
Carson T. Boren and Mary Boren his wife of the Town of Seattle
in the County of King and Territory of Washington for the consideration of Five hundred dollars received to our full satisfaction of
Edward Lander of the County of Thurston and Charles Terry of
the County of King in said Territory of Washington do grant, bargain, sell and convey to the said Edward Lander and Charles Terry
their heirs and assignees All the west half of the land claim of the
said Carson T. Boren and lying between the land claims of Henry
L. Yesler and Arthur Denny containing three hundred twenty acres.

Arthur and David Denny witnessed this deed, no doubt
with many regrets at seeing their kinsman giving up his land.

Boren's property extended from the historic corner of
First and Marion Streets, marked today by the Exchange
Building, along the water front to James Street. It ran back
including the present financial section of Cherry and Columbia Streets until it ascended the hill it broadened out to
include three hundred and twenty acres. Half of this present immensely valuable land he sold for a little over three
dollars an acre.

From the first we have seen that Carson Boren did not
care for land. He was young and a conscientious worker.
but unfortunately, unhappiness in his home life robbed him
of that ambition that actuated the others. It sent him to the
woods and away from the habitations of men. He loved the

woods, and as the years went on, he became a dreamer and hunter, content with very little of this world's goods.

In commenting on this real estate transaction Mrs. Blaine wrote pertinently:

The man that owns the part of town in which we live has sold out to-day to two men, both shrewd and well posted up in regard to matters. One is the circuit judge of the Territory and the other a real business man. They would not have bought unless they had good reason to know that they would not lose anything. Judge Lander is in communication with all our public men and knows as well as anyone the prospects of the different towns on the Sound.

Some historians give $2,000 as the price paid for the land. but this is a mistake, which arises from the fact that Boren bonded himself to that amount until he could give a clear title after the government had extinguished the Indian title by treaty. The record of the bond is dated '55, but the actual deed was not given until '56. A bond was given in most of the real estate transactions of '55, some for $500, others for $1,000 or more, to be paid usually "by 1st day of June, 1856, or so soon thereafter as corresponding title may be obtained from the government."

Volume I of King County deeds contains many records of lands sold by Carson Boren. Lot by lot he sold the remainder of his property. David Maynard also continued to sell a number of lots.

A good idea of real estate conditions at that time is obtained from one of Mr. Blaine's letters:

If you wish to make an investment here and will send $25 or $50 I will lay it out for you to good advantage and it would be a fine thing if each of the girls, Eleanor, Matilda, Martha, Darinda, and Seraphina could get one or two town lots each in Seattle. They could be purchased now for $15 or $20 a lot and in a few years will be worth as much per foot. The lots are 120 feet long and 60 feet wide.

In the same Volume I that records these early land sales are to be found records of chattel mortgages that are highly entertaining. In one there was "sold and delivered to Mary Ann Boyer one scow fourteen feet in width, by 45 feet in

length for the sum of one hundred and ten dollars." This
entry becomes more interesting when we learn that Mary
Ann Boyer [Mother Damnable] received the scow in payment for a delinquent board bill.

Another transaction is recorded by which " for a valuable
consideration" there was sold "one yoke of cattle described
as follows: One Brindle short horns, one red and with white
spots and a short tail."

In another record book, a battered little notebook, are
found the first King County treasurer's records beginning in
the latter part of '54. Lewis Wyckoff, the first assessor, had
assessed the property and William A. Smith set down the
taxes as they were collected by the sheriff, Thomas Russell.
At the end of the first fiscal year the King County tax collection amounted to $646.08. In striking contrast is the
statement of the King County, Seattle taxes due February
2, 1931—$28,405,898.

In July of '55 the second general territorial election was
held. According to the provisions made by the legislature.
King County was now allowed three members in the lower
house. David Phillips, A. B. Webster, and Arthur Denny
were elected. J. Patton Anderson succeeded Columbia Lancaster as delegate to Congress.

At this time the pioneers voted on the Maine liquor law.
which had been passed at the second session of the legislature. The measure passed in King County by a vote of
81 to 44; in the Territory, however, it lost with 564 to 650.

Volume I of the King County commissioner's books records a busy year and fills ten closely written pages. Road
building items and bills paid to the new sheriff, constables.
election officers, and other county officials show how active
the settlers were during the year preceding the Indian War.

One item in this prosperous year is for three dollars,
which they voted to spend for a book in which to keep their
minutes. Later they paid a village scribe to copy their notes,

which he did with a flourish of shaded capitals, very fancy, but difficult to read. The wage of three dollars a day appears to have been the standard paid for all types of work from road workers to court witnesses.

Dr. Maynard, who had served as clerk of the district court, was paid for his services, but the commissioners felt that they could not afford to buy a seal for the doctor. This matter came up several times, and one senses a coolness between the commissioners and the clerk over the matter. At the next session of court the doctor affixed this reproachful note to the public papers, "I have hereunto fixed my own private seal, no official seal having been furnished."

Trifling economies, small matters, and petty accounts, those first records appear to us who think of the treasurer's and commissioners' reports in terms of millions, but it is well that the pioneers made those serious beginnings just when they did. If they had realized how close they were to danger and annihilation they would never have had the courage to lay the town and county foundations so securely.

The "mania for roads" gained new impetus in the prosperous summer of '55. Work was continued on the road from Van Asselt's claim south, with Collins prosecuting those who did not volunteer their quota of work.

The only record of wages paid for road work is for the work of three men from Mox La Push, who worked on a road to "Tobin's Mill." Each worked five days in Pierce County and five in King for which they were paid three dollars a day.

Nothing speaks more eloquently of the pioneers' road-building energy than the ten full pages of the commissioners' records for '55. In sad contrast are the four and a half pages for the following year, loosely written as if the scribes were discouraged even in their penmanship. Nothing illustrates better than these contrasting pages how sanguine the pioneers were in the summer of '55, proceeding as if noth-

ing were about to happen, secure in their faith that the
treaties were settling any trouble with the Indians.

HOW COULD THE PROSPECTS BE BRIGHTER?

The discovery of gold east of the Cascades early in the
summer of '55 accented anew the pioneers need of a road
through the mountains. Here they were, the logical seaport
and supply station for the gold fields, but barricaded by the
mountains.

By this time they were persuaded that the Naches Pass
was not feasible, and their thoughts turned toward the one
nearer home that Tinkham had demonstrated as practicable
in the winter of '54. Arthur Denny wrote, "It was found
that the military road was not a success as a wagon road
across the mountains. We next turned in the direction of the
Snoqualmie Pass, so-called at that time."

An important exploring expedition set out from the vil-
lage on July 23, 1855, led by Judge Edward Lander.
Others known to have been in the party were: Carson Boren,
Franklin Matthias, Charles Plummer, John Nagle, A. F
Bryant, Dr. Bigelow, Charles Walker, and Dexter Horton.

Grant speaks of this expedition as "showing as much as
any one thing the independent energy of the place." Arthur
Denny, although he was in San Francisco at the time it took
place, devotes several pages of *Pioneer Days on Puget
Sound* to a description of the expedition, speaking of it as
if it was one of the most important moves the pioneers
made. It marked the beginning of an undertaking that they
pursued persistently all through succeeding early history—
the building of the famous Snoqualmie wagon road.

The party went out by way of Squak—now Issaquah—
and Snoqualmie Falls where they divided into two groups,
one going by way of a pack trail used by the Hudson's Bay
Company, and the other by an old Indian trail. The two
groups met at Lake Keechelus and again separated, one party

returning by the Green River, and the other by the Cedar.

Their plan was to determine upon the best of the old trails to widen into a wagon road. If they could establish a practical route, they hoped to get government aid in addition to the appropriation that Congress had already made toward building a road through the mountains.

Always they had in mind, not only the wagon road, but the Pacific railroad. If they could make a beginning and establish the most suitable pass, it would pave the way for the railroad

But the city founders were intensely practical. Their immediate purpose was to take advantage of the gold rush not by going to the mines but by bringing the riches of the mines to Seattle. The Olympia *Pioneer and Democrat*—the successor to the *Columbian*—wrote of this expedition of the "23d ultimo" that:

The company was composed of some of the best practical business men of Seattle—farmers etc. of that vicinity who feeling assured that the road contemplated to reach the other side of the mountains, will be best adapted for the transportation to the mining regions, have determined not to return until at least a pack trail has been procured eastward for public accommodation.

Mr. Denny wrote of this road building, which was in addition to the county road work, "As a result of this exploration we proceeded to cut a trail out by way of Meridian prairie and thence crossing Cedar river at the old Green river trail and out by Rattlesnake prairie."

Rattlesnake Prairie was so named by the members of the exploring expedition because of a joke on themselves—a story much relished afterward in the cookhouse. The explorers heard what they thought was the dread rattle. Investigating cautiously, they discovered that it was the seed in the dried pod of the camas plant, which grew on this prairie. When brushed by passersby the pod produces a rattling sound similar to the rattle of a snake. Clarence Bagley tells how he often jumped instinctively when, as a barefoot boy in Oregon, he heard this rattle.

The settlers of Seattle not only needed a wagon road through the mountains but they also needed steamboats as a faster means of transportation than the sailing vessels, which depended upon the caprice of the wind.

The wreck of the *Major Tompkins* in January of '55 had been keenly disappointing. It had meant much to have this steamer arrive even if she was exasperating as a mail carrier. To be left again without an adequate steamboat was a decided setback. The *Water Lily* was put on the run to Olympia, with Charles Terry, the gallant skipper for a time. But she was frail and small, like the *Fairy*, which was still used to some extent.

All during that busy summer of '55, Puget Sound settlements fretted for want of a steamboat. When in October another reliable one, the *Traveller*, arrived, the *Pioneer and Democrat* of Olympia wrote:

Through the enterprise of Mr. John G. Parker of this place a small but neat and comfortable steamer has been placed on the waters of the Sound to ply between this point and Seattle, also to carry the U. S. Mail.

But the new steamboat soon served another purpose. She was mobilized and did good service in the Indian War. Subsequently she was the first steamboat to navigate the Snohomish, White, and Nooksack Rivers.

Something fatal seemed to pursue these early steamboats, for they all came to "some bad end"; The *Major Tompkins* was wrecked, as we know; the *Traveller* sprang a leak after three years' service and sank; the boiler of the *Fairy* exploded in '57, and she sank in the Steilacoom harbor as she was leaving for Olympia; and, while the end of the *Water Lily* was not so tragic, early King County records show that she was auctioned off at a public sale.

Seattle had grown until there were about forty houses and two hundred and fifty people in the settlement in '55. Alki was practically abandoned. The county commissioners' notes read that "the precinct of Alki be annulled." After Terry had given up his dream of Alki, he left for New York for a visit, but he returned later and helped carry on at Seattle.

Forty houses and two hundred and fifty people do not sound like much of a village, especially one described as "stumpy" and "with miserable Indian shanties all about and Indians meeting you at every step." But it was not to be measured by houses, or stumps, or population. It was a crude but pert little village to be measured by its potentiality for growth; it was full of vitality, and fully expected to become. just what it did in later years, a great seaport and railway terminus.

Speaking of this period Grant says:

Much of the talk of the day was of the coming growth and grandeur of Seattle and these matters of oratory would work their hearers up by descriptions of what the near future was to bring, which we fear may have bordered on bombast.

David Blaine was one of the earliest Seattle "Boosters." After an article of his had appeared in an Eastern paper, his wife wrote to her people:

I have shown it to two or three asking them if it partakes of the gaseous character peculiar to many communications from this coast. They all agree it is quite within bounds and that more wonderful stories might be truthfully told.

A letter written by Mr. Blaine to his brother expresses better than anything else this spirit that actuated the young pioneers who founded Seattle. It is quoted at some length, not because it was the sentiment of a single man, but because it was the ambition and vision of the town made articulate. Only by understanding their extravagant aspirations for a railroad and maritime trade can we understand their supreme endeavor after the Indian War had well night annihilated them. The young minister wrote:

There is only beginning enough to indicate the certainty of a future here not unlike New York or London in commercial importance. This may sound like castle building and it may be years ere such a state of things is realized, but it is conceived in the womb of the future beyond a reasonable doubt.

This prophecy the writer proceeded to justify by enumerating the reasons for it, the first of which was the building of a Pacific railroad by the northern route. Although Jefferson Davis had opposed such a route, Seattle had by no means given up the idea. Referring his brother to articles in the "public prints" about the proposed Pacific railroad, Mr. Blaine says that although "Southern wealth and influence, San Francisco capital, and much governmental influence will give some southern route the first start," a railroad by the northern route must soon follow because of its greater advantages, which he points out:

If the connection with the Pacific be made here at this place the distance to China is several hundred miles less than to San Francisco. . . . . . Now, why will the R. R. by the northern route terminate at this place? My answer is this, there is no possibility to making the Columbia river a safe and convenient channel for shipping in all kinds of weather. It cannot become the outlet to the Pacific R. R. even though it should come through on the south pass on account of the dangerous bar at its mouth.

Then the Northern Pacific R. R. will have its terminus at some point on Puget Sound. There are said to be but two passes through the Cascade range of mountains, the Snoqualmie pass and a pass just south of Mt. Rainier where a road can be built with the greatest ease, while there are difficulties more or less insuperable in the face of the country lying between these mountain passes and the other towns on the Sound.

We have here at Seattle also one of the finest natural harbors for vessels of all sizes to be found in the world, and large enough to contain all the shipping of England and America at the same time. In addition to this, Nature has deposited within ten miles of town, hundreds and perhaps thousands of acres of stone coal for the supply of steamships and steam cars innumerable.

With these advantages together with one of the finest and most healthy of climates, and a most charming surrounding of natural scenery, how could the prospects of a future growth at once healthy, permanent, and unexampled be brighter?

In our modern vernacular, truly, the preacher was "some booster."

CHAPTER XIII

THE INDIAN WAR

THE PROSPERITY of the summer of '55 unquestionably helped to precipitate the Indian War. The buoyancy and confidence of the whites, their spirit of conquest and of racial supremacy incited the Indians to make their last stand against them. In speaking of those months of prosperity, Bagley says:

All these incidents served to convince the more restless spirits among the native tribes that if ever attempt was to be made to stay the increasing tide of white immigration, this was the time to begin.

The Yakima and Klikitats, a band of the Yakima tribe who with promise and great show of friendliness had signed the treaty in June, began almost immediately to plot against "the Bostons." These two tribes, known as "horse Indians," were far more fierce than the "canoe Indians" of Puget Sound. Owhi of the Yakimas, and Quilchen of the Klikitats now became the leaders in the proposed uprising.

During the summer they plotted to join the Nisqually Indians under the leadership of Leschi, whose mother was a Yakima. Leschi and his half brother, Quiemuth, with Kitsap and Kanasket of the Muckleshoots and Puyallups, respectively, entered into the plot, and while the white people were absorbed in their own prosperity, began agitating and organizing for the war that was to follow.

After the gold rush had started, and the Indians saw more white men pouring in to take possession of their country, their hostility was aroused to even greater hatred. Here was their opportunity, for the miners, traveling in small, unprotected bands through an unfamiliar country, were easily ambushed. Long before it was discovered by the whites in the settlements the Indians were killing white men on their way to the gold fields.

Leschi was an intelligent, race-conscious Indian, who became the rebel agitator and leader west of the Cascade

Mountains. He owned land and was very much dissatisfied with the Nisqually Treaty.

Lieutenant Phelps, of the *Decatur*, wrote of him afterward:

Leschi the famous Nisqually chief made speeches throughout the country and went as far south as Rogue river to gain adherents. He it was who invented the terrible story of the Polakly Illehe or the Land of Darkness—a fearful place where he said the white men were going to send all Indians, where the sun never shone, and where the mosquitoes were so big that a single bite would kill the strongest man.

Although the real plotting that was going on among the Indians was not discovered by the settlers, there were hints of it and even warnings all through the summer. But the pioneers had grown used to this undercurrent of fear and that was one reason why they were not more alert to the imminent danger at this time.

This sense of danger had become a part of the very life on the frontier—a nameless dread of something unseen and lurking in the shadows. Referring to the hardships of that period, the sweetbriar bride said in after years, "I wouldn't go through it again if you were to give me the whole state of Washington."

I have described the town as it clustered about the mill that summer of '55 with its feeling of protection, but there is another picture of pioneer life as it was lived in the forest, equally typical of those days—life such as the sweetbriar bride was living. No one knew better than she what this fear of Indians meant to the pioneer woman. Alone in her cabin with little Inez while David was away cutting logs, she never knew what a shadow across the door or the rustling of a leaf might mean.

Late that summer of '55 a number of Indians visited her and insolently demanded, "Klosh mika potlatch wapatoes!" which meant, "Give us some potatoes!" They were so ugly and menacing that she hurried out and dug the potatoes quickly so that they might have no cause for displeasure. One can understand her relief when she saw them depart.

Even on this occasion one of the Indians lingered as if something were troubling him and he wished to tell Louisa about it. It was thought afterward that he wanted to warn her of the attack that was being planned.

Grant gives an excellent description of another pioneer woman's experience:

Among the motley squads of Indians who passed to and fro in the streets was one old woman who came from the Old Man House, and who was understood to be a relative, perhaps a sister, of Seattle. She was called Sally. She wore a bonnet and came to the Methodist Church and no worshiper was more devout. She had her favorites among the housekeepers of the village and one of these was Mrs. Hanford. She would come and ask for a bright new tin pail and after a time would return with it filled with huckleberries or blackberries from the forest or with cranberries from the marsh. Once, in the summer of 1855 she came and after wearily bringing in her customary present sat down on the floor and began to sob and weep.

"What is it, Sally?"

"It was all very bad."

She had learned, she said, of the great Socalee Tyee, the white man's God. But her heart was also toward her people, yet the heart of her people was against the white man; and the white man would be against her people and kill them. Her heart was very sick.

This conflict that went on in the hearts of some of these primitive people, torn between loyalty to their own race and love of their white friends, is one of the touching phases of the history of this period.

The plaint of old Indian Sally that her heart was toward the white man and also toward her people, expressed much that we must realize if we are to read the story of the Indian War understandingly. For the first few years after settlements had been made on the Sound, the Indians had been friendly, gladly working for the pioneers and trading with them, partly because of the feeling that the white man was protection against the savage northern tribes. On the other hand the natives had been invaluable help to the settlers during their first hard years, supplying them with food, teaching them woods lore, showing them trails, and carrying them from place to place in their canoes.

In a few instances this mutual helpfulness developed a real affection between the two races, which affection brightens the pages of local history. The friendship between Chief Seattle and Dr. Maynard, who had much influence with the natives as a doctor and friend; that of Henry Yesler, much respected through his contacts as employer in the mill; David Denny's and Thomas Mercer's, the former's strengthened by his knowledge of the native language; Arthur Denny's with Pat-ka-nim, were all bonds that endured even through the Indian war on the part of the Indians about the town of Seattle.

Pat-ka-nim warned Arthur Denny several times during the summer of '55 that there was going to be trouble. One night in the early fall he called Mr. Denny outside his cabin again and told him that he was on his way up the Steilaguamish River to hunt for mountain sheep, but wanted to warn his friend before he left that there was going to be trouble.

In all of the outlying and less protected districts there was a growing fear of the Indians. A story, humorous in a way, is told of Luther Collins' daughter Lucinda. Lucinda had by this time learned not only Chinook but the Indian ways of thinking and acting. When Henry Van Asselt, a very good shot, killed an Indian's dog which was bothering his calf, Lucinda knew that it meant trouble, for one might as well kill an Indian as to kill his dog.

The next day, while she was among the natives, she heard them threaten to kill the man who had shot the dog.

"But you can't kill him because he has lead in his body," she told them, knowing their superstition that a man with lead in his body was invulnerable.

"More than that," continued Lucinda, "he is sure with his gun. Day or night he can shoot and kill."

Van Asselt took pains to show the Indians the mark of the bullet charm, and also to exhibit his markmanship by casually bringing down a few crows one after another. It is said that he depended on their awe of his charmed life during the dangerous months before the outbreak. One story was told of his encountering a gang of hostile savages and saving his own life and that of others by his talisman.

When Arthur Denny was returning from Olympia in the fall of '55, his canoe, paddled by two Indians, was pursued by Indians in another canoe, who kept up a steady fire of threats in their native language—not Chinook—while his men paddled furiously to get out of their reach. Mr. Denny learned afterward from his canoemen that the savages had demanded that he be given to them in revenge for the killing of some of their own tribe, saying he was a "hyas tyee" —a great man—and therefore suitable for their purpose. His Indians had answered with both cunning and faithfulness that he was not nearly so great a man as some others. and that he was also a very good friend to the Indians. Save for the craftiness of those faithful canoemen, the career of Arthur Denny would have ended right there.

Knowing as he did the danger of an Indian outbreak, Mr. Denny had worked in the legislature for the enactment of a law to organize the militia for protection in case of trouble. without realizing, of course, how actual and close it was.

None of the pioneers seem to have realized it. Apparently their minds were on roads. Meany says:

*Nothwithstanding the evidences of savage unrest, the rumor of impending war, the settlers of Puget Sound were enterprising and ambitious. In the summer of 1855 Judge Edward Lander. Arthur A. Denny and Hillory Butler left Seattle to inspect the wagon road over the Cascade Mountains, hoping to find ways or improving it.

These three men had gone as far as the Black River, where they camped waiting to be joined in their mission by

Dr. Bigelow, when they were surprised by a messenger, who had paddled swiftly after them, calling them back as quickly as possible to Seattle.

This is what had happened. That morning after they had started out, three prospectors who had started for the gold fields, came staggering into the settlement. They were torn and scratched and famished for food after traveling through the thick forest by night and hiding by day. Five of them had left the village together and had reached the Yakima Valley when two of their party, ahead of the others, were shot down by the Indians. Their companions became aware of the tragedy in time to retreat hastily and escape to Seattle.

As the townsfolk crowded about them and heard their story, quickly the word went round, "We must stop our men before they start over the mountains. Send someone quick." There was consternation in the village until their safe return.

Now the pioneers knew! This was more than a warning. The Indian War had begun. As they discussed it, they realized what must have been the fate of Fanjoy and Eaton, who had started for the gold mines early in the summer. No one had heard from them, and the settlers had thought it was because of the distance and lack of communication. No one ever did hear from them. It was never known how many lone miners were killed by the Indians.

After the escape of the three miners to Seattle in early September, events occurred in rapid and tragic succession. Sinister rumblings like slow approaches of a storm now burst into decided bolts of thunder and flashes of treacherous lightning.

THE WHITE RIVER MASSACRE

All accounts of Seattle's part in the Indian War begin with the experience of Allen L. Porter of White River. Mr. Porter had been one of the Biles train that had cut its way through the Naches Pass in the summer of '53. By this time he had cleared his land so that his ranch was beginning to repay him for his labor.

When he heard the terrifying word that the Yakimas had murdered two Seattle men on their way to the gold fields and that his neighbors down the valley, Fanjoy and Eaton. had doubtless met the same fate, he began to fear for his own safety since he was alone in the upper valley. Not wishing to abandon his ranch he took the precaution of sleeping outside in the bushes, as the Indians frequently attacked under cover of darkness. He had done this several times, when, on the night of September 27, 1855, he saw some men stop at his house. Thinking they were white men needing shelter he hurried forward, and was nearly on them when he discovered that they were Indians. It did not take him long to realize that they had come to murder him. Not finding him they attacked his house.

Then, like another **Paul Revere**, he hurried down the river, his steed a swift canoe, warning the settlers as he fled toward Seattle. All of them soon followed and came into the village, frightened refugees, forced to leave their homes and gardens, all the fruit of their toil to the Indians. It was sickening news to the settlers in Seattle.

A few weeks previous, three men had struggled in with tragic news from over the mountains, but this experience had happened close to home. There were many anxious consultations in the cookhouse. The pioneers began to make preparations to build a blockhouse on a bluff overlooking the Sound near what is now the southwest corner at First Avenue and Cherry Street, where all might retreat in case of an attack, and to organize a volunteer company of soldiers. They were perilously unguarded, back of them the forest that might hide an Indian horde, and in front of them the Bay. And they were few in number—only a little over two hundred souls in all—compared with thousands of Indians. The situation was indeed serious.

But once again white sails appeared in their hour of need. One week after the attack on Porter's house the sloop of war, *Decatur*, Captain Isaac S. Sterrett, came sailing into the Bay. She had been ordered to Puget Sound from the Sandwich Islands in July in response to the territorial legislature's memorial to Congress the preceding winter for protection by water. Compared to the mighty men-of-war that anchor in Seattle harbor today, the *Decatur* was an insignificant little ship, but when she fired a salute and the sound of her guns echoed against the hills back of the town, it carried with it the reassurance of the United States Navy.

In writing of this timely arrival of the *Decatur* in a historical paper later, Abbie Holgate Hanford told how a little group of pioneer mothers gathered together after Porter's alarm and prayed together that the Lord would send them protection. Snowden wrote in his *History of Washington.* "When the *Decatur* arrived in the harbor a few weeks later, her coming was regarded by these people as an answer to prayer." My mother remembered how her mother, Mary Denny, looked out from their cabin door and exclaimed through tears of gratitude, "Thank God. Our prayers are answered."

Governor Stevens was still in the Bitter Root country and Secretary of State Charles H. Mason was Acting Governor. Hearing that the settlers of the White River Valley had fled to Seattle, Mason took a squad of soldiers, went to Porter's Prairie and conferred with the Indians. Perhaps due to the fact that Mason was accompanied by soldiers, the Indians were more than friendly and assured him that it was all a mistake, that the settlers were frightened without cause, that they had not attacked Porter's house, and never would.

Being thoroughly deceived, Mason came back feeling that the settlers were timid and easily alarmed, and that they had been foolish to leave their homes. He told them to go back; they would be safe, for there was no danger. He also went on board the *Decatur* and told Captain Sterrett that the alarm was false; the Indians were not hostile; his protection was not needed, for they had no intention of attacking; it was simply an excuse on the part of the settlers to keep the *Decatur* in the harbor for the sake of trade from the ship.

This made Captain Sterrett angry. He went ashore and singled out Arthur Denny upon whom to vent his wrath. He told Mr. Denny that the settlers were a lot of cowards. squatters, and land sharks; he did not propose to be hoodwinked in any such manner, but would weigh anchor and set sail immediately.

With bowed head Mr. Denny patiently listened to the end, and then quietly and sadly replied, "If you, to whom we have a right to look for protection, choose to desert us in our extreme danger, I have no power to stop you, and, if the White River settlers return to their homes as Mason advises them to do, all will be murdered within a fortnight."

Mr. Denny's quiet and earnest manner so impressed the captain that in great perplexity he said, "You seem so earnest, how can I tell whom to believe? I shall stay and find out for myself."

For four years Arthur Denny had lived among the Indians and he knew their methods. Acting Governor Mason was undoubtedly sincere in his decision, but he had met the Indians in council and not intimately in everyday life as the settlers had.

Reassured by the advice of Mason and his squad of soldiers, most of the settlers returned to their ranches on the White River. It was the fall of the year and much was to be done; they were happy to find their homes undisturbed and the Indians friendly. Porter, they decided, had been unduly alarmed.

Some of the people in Seattle felt the same way and scoffed at those who expressed fear. The presence of the *Decatur* undoubtedly did much to reassure them. Work on the blockhouse proceeded slowly because of deterrent ones who saw no need of it. Louisa Denny remarked in her pert way, "Yes, and there were those who scoffed at Noah when he built the Ark."

Many of the people, however, were coming to realize that this was much more than a local thing; it was a general uprising of the Indians throughout the Northwest. After the murder of the men on their way to the mines, an Indian Agent, A. J. Bolon, had gone over trustingly to investigate and had been murdered in a most cruel and treacherous manner. Major Granville O. Haller then went over in pursuit of the murderers with a company of soldiers, but was overwhelmed by great numbers of Indians and forced to go back. This was the actual opening of the Indian War.

All over the Territory the different settlements prepared to defend themselves against what was to be the last stand of the red men and their final effort to exterminate the whites. Companies of volunteers were formed, one in Olympia under Captain Gilmore Hays, one under Captain William Wallace of Steilacoom, a prominent territorial lawyer, and a group known as the Eaton Rangers under Captain Charles Eaton of Olympia. James Tilton, who had been sent to the territory as Surveyor-General, was made Adjutant General in charge of the volunteers.

Many of the men of Seattle, together with some who had been driven in recently from outside, volunteered for three months' service on October 25th, and organized themselves into a company for defense. Christopher C. Hewitt was made captain; D. A. Neely from White River, first lieutenant; John Henning, sergeant; and Dr. Smith, surgeon. They began training at once.

Toward the last of October a company of regulars under Lieutenant W. A. Slaughter of Fort Steilacoom was sent out along the military road toward the Naches Pass with volunteer companies under Hays and Wallace, and with the Eaton

Rangers. They had a number of encounters, enough to prove again that the Indians meant business.

While the settlers were confident that the volunteers and regulars could protect them, they realized that it was not going to be a simple matter. The sense of lurking danger increased. Out in their cabin north of Seattle, David and Louisa Denny stayed as long as they dared. One evening they became frightened and went down to the Bell cabin for the night and moved into the village the next day.

To the south of town the Hanfords were warned by "Salmon Bay Curley." Cornelius Hanford, then a small boy, wrote afterward, "I remember well his coming to my father's log cabin and strongly urging hasty removal of the family to the village." After having been frightened one night when dark faces peered in at the windows, they hastily prepared to follow his injunction, and loaded their goods onto a scow the following day. But by the time the scow was loaded they were dismayed to find that the tide had gone out, leaving the scow fast in the mud, and leaving them there to spend another unhappy night.

And yet with all this imminent danger there was nothing warlike in the appearance of the town on the evening of the 28th at the close of a quiet October Sabbath. Some of the settlers were attending evening worship in the little white meetinghouse; others were lounging about the cookhouse; the *Decatur* lay idly at anchor—when a canoe sped from the mouth of the Duwamish. When it touched shore a group of frightened people sprang out: Mr. and Mrs. William Cox, Moses Kirkland and his daughters, and Joe Lake, settlers who had returned to their farms less than a fortnight before. Breathlessly the crowd that had gathered round listened while they told how they had just escaped from the Indians.

At about seven o'clock that morning Joe Lake had been shot at while standing in the door of the Cox home. He showed their listeners the bullet hole in his coat. Then he told of hearing gunfire and screams in the direction of the other neighbors. Immediately they had fled and paddled furiously all day warning the settlers along the river as they passed.

They had escaped, but what of their neighbors? The pioneers were stunned at the news, for they had a dreadful realization of what had happened. White-faced, they looked at one another. There was little talking. More settlers from up the Duwamish began to arrive. The news spread rapidly. The volunteers, who had enlisted only three days previous. made preparations to move. Men and women in Seattle slept little that night. Fathers and mothers shuddered at what might happen to their little ones.

The next morning another canoe arrived from the Duwamish paddled by an Indian known as "Indian Dave," who appeared to be alone until three children were discovered huddled in the bottom of the canoe. The children had been orphaned in the massacre of the previous day. Stealthily through the night an Indian named "Tom" had paddled down the White River with them hidden under a bear skin. until he came to the mouth of the Duwamish when he transferred them to Indian Dave.

The oldest of the children, little John King, almost seven years of age, told the settlers enough to convince them that a hideous massacre had taken place. The gruesome details they discovered later.

Immediately Captain Hewitt and his newly formed company started for the scene of the murders to bury the dead and rescue any settlers that might remain alive. After two days' marching over the rough trails they reached the place near the present town of Auburn.

It was a grim experience for these volunteers to come upon, one by one, the mutilated bodies of their neighbors and friends whom they had sheltered so shortly before. An

account of what they discovered is quoted from a letter
written by Captain Hewitt:

After two days' hard work we reached the house of Mr. Cox
which we found robbed. . . . . We then proceeded to Mr. Jones' place
where we found our worst fears more than realized. The house was
burned to ashes and Mr. Jones, who was sick at the time, was burned
in it. Mrs. Jones was found lying near the house shot through the
lower part of the lungs, face and jaw horribly broken and mutilated
apparently with the head of an ax. We found Mr. Cooper who was
living with Mr. Jones at the time, about 150 yards from the house
shot through the lungs, the ball entering the left breast. We buried
the bodies and proceeded to the house of W. H. Brannan a mile
distant.

Mrs. Brannan and child we found in the well, her head down-
wards. The mother was stabbed to the heart. . . . . She had apparently
started to run with her child, an infant ten months old. . . . . Mr.
Brannan was found in the house literally cut to pieces. . . . . After
burying them as circumstances would permit we proceeded to the
house of Mr. King, or rather where his house was, which we found
burned to ashes and where the most horrible spectacle of all
awaited us.

The bodies of both Mr. and Mrs. King had been roasted
in the fire and partially devoured by the hogs. The Kings
had two children, a boy five years old, who had been taken
away by the Indians and returned months later, and a baby
that was never accounted for in any way.

A sequel to Captain Hewitt's account is the story that was
supplied years later by Mrs. Jones' oldest child—the step-
son of Mr. Harvey Jones—"Little Johnnie King," whom
Indian Tom and Indian Dave had rescued. His younger
half brother and half sister were with him during the tragedy. When he became Dr. John King of Burgh Hill, Ohio,
he told the story as it had been stamped indelibly on his
mind.

A few days before the massacre, Nelson of the Muckleshoot Indians—the same Nelson who had been in the shoot-
ing affair in front of Low's cabin the first winter at Alki—
had visited the Jones' cabin one afternoon and acted very
moody. At this time, he was friendly with the whites and

was employed in doing errands between White River and Seattle. On this visit he made the remark that pretty soon the white people would own the whole country and the Indians would be driven away. Whether Nelson was trying to warn them, no one knows. Those who knew him well believed that he, like other Indians at this time, was struggling between his friendship with the whites and loyalty to his race.

On Sunday morning, October 28th, Mrs. Jones and the three children and Enos Cooper, who worked for them were eating breakfast. Mr. Jones was ill and in bed. There was a knock at the door. On opening it Mrs. Jones found herself face to face with armed Indians. Quickly bolting the door she prepared for defense.

The children were hidden under a feather bed, and it was from this hiding place that little Johnnie heard and saw much that happened. After the adults had been killed, the Indians discovered Johnnie peeping out from the feather bed and pulled the trembling children out.

Outside the cabin Nelson was directing the attack. The children knew him and trusted him. He told Johnnie to take the younger ones and go to the John M. Thomas place two miles away, for the child had gone to school in the Thomas home and knew the way. The Brannan home was nearer and Johnnie went there instead, but finding it deserted returned to his own home, which the Indians had burned. What the children found on their return is told in Dr. King's own words:

We were hungry. We had been driven from the breakfast table. In the log building had been stored some potatoes and firkins of butter. The potatoes were nicely roasted and there were streams of butter from the charred firkins. I dug some potatoes from the pile and spread some butter upon them and thus made a satisfactory meal for all of us.

I now thought of making my way to Mr. Thomas. I went somewhat circuitously past the barn and woodshed. While here a half-grown pup, a great favorite and a very noisy fellow too, came bounding to me. The children played with him and I was at first disposed to comply with their wishes that we take him with us. On second thought I knew that it would not do as he would betray our presence should we see an Indian. I did what was very hard to do—took a stick and frightened him away. I shall never forget the expression on the poor brute's face at such unexpected and unusual treatment. Going further I again called, "Cooper, Cooper," but the only answer was a pitiful echo from the woods.

As I was passing along I unexpectedly came upon my mother prostrate upon the ground a hundred feet or so southwest from the remains of our dwelling. She was yet alive. I do not know how or when she came there nor what was the nature of her injuries. She was pleased to know that we were safe but chided me for my delay in making my escape. She told me I must take the children and go to Mr. Thomas (the same man that Nelson had named a few hours before). I did not want to leave her but she told me it was best, that she could not live and that I might save the children and myself. I wanted to remain. She explained that if the Indians came back they would probably kill us all and that I must go. With a sad heart and with a courage inspired by mother's charge of responsibility I made the attempt to do as she bid me. I never saw her again.

From there the little fellow took the children two miles to the Thomas' home but the family had fled to Seattle. He then returned toward his own home again:

Mechanically I began retracing my steps to my home. The children were a constant source of danger to me and to themselves. My little brother was inconsolable. He wanted to go home to see his mother. He seemed to think I was out upon an expedition of my own and would not go home. I could keep my sister quiet by saying, "Indians kill," but my brother did not understand the meaning of this nor how his cry might attract the attention of the Indians should any be near. I was becoming tired as I had carried my brother the greater part of the trip over three miles or so. I lacked about two weeks of being seven years of age. It was getting late of the afternoon of a day late in the fall. They and I too were getting hungry and I had nothing to give them or eat myself except bark and edible root which mother at one time had showed me. I was in danger from Indians and wild animals and as far as I knew some thirty miles from a white settlement. An almost overwhelming sense of my danger and helplessness came over me as I thought of the coming night. But I trudged on.

At this time the child met an Indian who turned out to be the friendly Indian Tom, who took the children to his wigwam where they were cared for by his squaw until the moon was up. Then Indian Tom took them down the river to Seattle.

Here they were kept on the *Decatur* for a while and then sent to relatives in the East, who brought them up. The King boy deservedly became a hero, and on his way East was made much of in San Francisco. His appearance there on a public platform called for a shower of gold from the sympathetic audience of the generous mining city of that period. The story of "Little Johnnie King" appeared in the papers of the time, and was the inspiration for editorials and poems.

Another dramatic story of the White River massacre was that of another child named King, the five-year-old son of George E. King, who was carried away by the Indians at the time his parents were murdered. In *Pioneer Reminiscenses*, Ezra Meeker tells the story of how this child was kept all that succeeding winter by an Indian who became very fond of him and wanted to adopt him. In the spring when the child's presence was discovered by the white people and he was returned to them, he had forgotten his native tongue and could speak only the Indian language. The King baby, who was never found, was numbered with the slain.

The names of those massacred were: Mr. Harvey H. Jones and his wife, Eliza J. Jones, Enos Cooper, Mr. and Mrs. W. H. Brannan and infant child, and Mr. and Mrs. George E. King and baby.

THE PIONEERS PREPARE FOR WAR

After the sickening details of the White River massacre became known the whole Territory was aflame. There was no question in the minds of any one as to the enmity of the Indians. Indifference went to the opposite extreme, as expressed by Arthur Denny, "Those who, a short time before, insisted that the Indians were all friendly, would now declare most vehemently that all were hostile, and must all be treated as enemies."

The blockhouse was speedily finished, with some of the doubters working the hardest of all. Twelve-inch piles. which David Denny had prepared for shipment to San Francisco, were hauled up the embankment by ox-team and used for this 40-foot-square fortification which was named Decatur after the sloop-of-war. Marines from the *Decatur* helped the villagers, and those who had come in for protection, in the building.

Settlers throughout the Territory crowded into blockhouses which were speedily built. About sixty in all were built, some smaller ones in the outlying districts in which settlers too far to reach the towns fortified themselves, and larger ones, surrounded by stockades, in the settlements. The stockade at Olympia enclosed two squares. Ezra Meeker describes the flight of the people of the Puyallup Valley in this way, " 'The Indians have broken out,' was passed from one settler's cabin to another by rumors so quickly that by the morning of the 29th all were on the move towards the fort." He further describes how they left their homes in such haste that "they were almost absolutely destitute of clothing, bedding, and food as well as shelter."

Many of the women of the valley had been alone at the time, their husbands serving in Wallace's volunteer company. Some found shelter in the Hudson's Bay post at Nisqually, others at Fort Steilacoom.

When the news of the massacre reached Seattle on that memorable Sunday evening of the 28th, Thomas Mercer was still on his place north of the village. Dexter Horton and William (Bill) Gilliam went out quickly to warn him. Mrs. Susan Mercer Graham remembers how her father talked in low tones to the men outside the cabin; how, stepping inside, he told his daughters not to be frightened but to pack some clothes and bedding, for there was danger from Indians and they must get into town at once.

Stumbling along the dark trail, her hand in Dexter Horton's, Susie began to cry. Mr. Horton told her not to cry; there might not be any Indians lurking about, but then again there might. They must be very quiet.

Someone hurried out to warn Dr. Smith and he came paddling in with muffled oars, bringing his mother to safety. From all sides settlers came hurrying in to the settlement. Its accommodations were taxed to the limit.

This influx into the towns meant an extreme hardship for the farmers, for in this climate the fall harvesting had not been completed. Henry Van Asselt told in after years how he and Sam Maple and Dr. S. L. Grow cared for their crops and stock and slept in the woods at night. Dr. Smith hired two sailors to go out to his claim with him. They barred the doors and slept in the attic, hauling the ladder up after them. Mr. Mercer remained in a little house in town, but drove out to his farm by day. As one account reads, "In this way the crops were all saved, cellared, and stacked only to be destroyed afterward by the torch of a common enemy."

One good effect of this gathering in the town is recorded by Mrs. Blaine:

Prayer meeting had just closed. It was here at our house. Until recently the people have been so scattered we have found it impossible to sustain evening meetings but now as they are driven together we are reviving them, have them at private houses. There were 16 here to-night and we had a good time. Good may grow out of these troubles. Oh, that it may.

Lieutenant Slaughter with his regular and volunteer companies continued in the White and Green River valleys. their object being to keep the hostile Indians of that section from joining the friendly Indians around Seattle, and to guard the Naches Pass against the Klikitats.

The Klikitats, warlike in appearance as well as in practice. were the most dreaded of the enemy. They wore their hair cut straight across just over the eyes and at the back. "You look like a Klikitat," was for many years afterward enough to keep young women from wearing their hair in bangs.

The name "Klikitat" was a word of dread to the weaker tribes around the Sound, the despised "fish eaters," who had so often been attacked by the stronger bands east of the mountains. This dread kept some of the Sound Indians from joining in the attack on the white man.

The line of defense from Fort Steilacoom toward the Naches Pass could have been made more efficient at this time if there had been more aid from the regular army. But General John E. Wood, stationed in California, who was in charge of the army on the Pacific Coast, was influenced by pettiness and a lack of understanding of the case; consequently, only a few companies of infantry were sent to supply the government forts at The Dalles, Fort Vancouver. and Steilacoom.

One of the regulars stationed at Fort Vancouver during this period was Lieutenant "Phil" Sheridan, later of Civil War fame. Lieutenant Ulysses S. Grant had also been at this fort previously, but was in the East at this time.

The "Bostons" were greatly encouraged when Sir James Douglas of the Hudson's Bay Company at Victoria sent the steamer *Beaver* to help, and also supplied the pioneers with much-needed muskets. This was an unhappy surprise to the Indians, who had not expected the "King Georges" to help the "Bostons."

The natives remembered very well the ill feeling that had existed between the two white nations and the threats of warfare that had accompanied the "fifty-four forty or fight" dispute of ten years previous. They remembered how the "King Georges" had withdrawn to the north and how the "Bostons" had continued in this vicinity. Certain it is that they never counted on the strong, racial loyalty that made Douglas send the stout ship *Beaver* to the aid of the American settlers.

The Indians were warring on the "Bostons" alone. The "King Georges" were present in the Indian territory only to trade; the "Bostons" were here to stay. Besides, many of the "King Georges" had married squaws—a practice encouraged by the Hudson's Bay Company—and so had become interconnected with their own people.

It is said that the Indians had proposed to spare the life of Mrs. Brannan because she was a "King George," but changed their minds because her husband, "a Boston," angered them by his desperate resistance.

Lieutenant Slaughter in the Green River Valley sent word to Acting Governor Mason that Pat-ka-nim was trailing him and was skulking around his camp every night. Mason ordered Captain Sterrett to arrest two of Pat-ka-nim's brothers and all members of his tribe who were then camping in Seattle, and place them in irons.

Again Captain Sterrett went to Arthur Denny and told him that he intended to arrest these Snoqualmies at once. Mr. Denny insisted that Pat-ka-nim was friendly; that he was at that time up the Steilaguamish River hunting; and that they had trouble enough with enemy Indians without attacking the friendly ones. He offered to prove that Slaughter was mistaken by going himself out to Pat-ka-nim's camp and bringing him in. The captain refused his taking such a risk, but consented to his sending an express for the Indian chief. Mr. Denny agreed to be responsible for him until his return. Mr. Denny wrote:

Very fortunately for me and probably for Pat-ka-nim too, he was on hand within the time agreed upon. He had his women and children with him. He also brought a cargo of mountain sheep, venison, horns and hides, specimens of which he took on board and presented to the Captain.

Not long after this proof of his loyalty, Pat-ka-nim and a party of his tribe were employed by the governor as scouts, and did good service during the remainder of the war.

After returning from the scene of the White River massacre Hewitt's company of volunteers was completely organized and provided with guns, some of which were supplied by Captain Sterrett. All through November the company drilled faithfully. Mrs. Blaine wrote to her relatives in the East:

> I can assure you our little town has something of a martial appearance. Twice a day the Co. of volunteers are assembled at the fort (which I think I told you was close by our house) and answer to the roll and go through their drill. Then almost every man carries his gun.

As the general plan of campaign at this time was to keep the hostile Indians from influencing the peaceful ones, it was proposed to segregate the latter by gathering them together on the reservation near Port Madison. Early in November, Dr. Maynard was engaged by Michael Simmons. the Indian agent—Mrs. Maynard's brother—to gather them together and take them across the Sound.

The task required tact and patience, for the Indians were uneasy and reluctant to go. Chief Seattle, it is said, was restless and very much disturbed.

While the settlers were preparing defenses, the Maynards were building shelters on the reservation, and pacifying and reassuring the restless Indians who might otherwise have been persuaded to join the enemy.

Toward the latter part of November, Captain Hewitt's company was ordered to establish a post at the forks of the White and Green Rivers and there await orders from Lieutenant Slaughter of the regular army. The women of the village gave a supper for the volunteers the night before they left and presented them with a handsome flag. Whether this flag was homemade or not, we do not know. We know that later the women made a flag while in the fort. Our only knowledge of this flag is that according to Mrs. Blaine it was a "handsome" one.

It was an anxious day in the life of the village when the volunteers left for what, as everyone thought, would be their quarters for the winter. Adjutant General Tilton sent the steamer *Traveller* to transport them up the river. One can picture the little stern-wheeler chugging noisily away from Yesler's wharf where the pioneer men had gathered to see them off while anxious women watched from every hillside cabin.

The pioneers were much disturbed that Captain Sterrett was relieved of command of the *Decatur* by Captain Gansevoort. They sent their remonstrance to the Navy Department, and later Sterrett was restored to command but Gansevoort served during the siege.

As long as the *Decatur* was in the harbor the town felt very well protected even with the volunteers away; but there were anxious days when the ship was obliged to be away, once on an errand to Steilacoom, once at Port Madison in response to a report that there was to be an attack from northern Indians, and for a short time when she was laid up for repairs.

After describing one of these anxious periods in a letter. Catherine Blaine added this exclamation, "The *Decatur* has just fired her gun. She is coming into harbor!" With Mrs. Blaine one is relieved to hear the welcome sound of that gun.

The volunteers had been gone only a few days when the townsfolk received an express from Steilacoom saying that they were to get word immediately to their men to remain in a place of security until further orders; that Lieutenant Slaughter's company had been attacked by Indians with one white killed, others wounded, and thirty head of horses and mules driven away.

There were sleepless nights until messengers returned from Hewitt's camp with news that all was well and that the volunteers had started to fortify themselves.

Early in December Mrs. Blaine made a comment which becomes significant when we realize that this was shortly before her first child was born:

I try to keep as cool as I can about the whole matter and I think I succeeded pretty well considering everything but I can't help thinking about these matters much more than I want to. I hope the consequences will not be bad.

By the end of November—a month after the massacre—much had been accomplished for the winter's defense. Arthur Denny said afterward that when he left at this time for his third term as representative at Olympia, the town seemed well protected. The blockhouse of hewn logs stood on the hill. Close in lay the good ship *Decatur*. Every man was armed and most of the outlying settlers were now in Seattle close about the blockhouse fort. Marines and citizen soldiers guarded the outposts. Lieutenant Slaughter and the volunteer companies guarded them in the direction of Naches pass. The friendly Indians were either in town or on the reservation across the Sound where they could not be persuaded to join the enemy. The trail over the mountains would soon be snow-blocked, hindering the Indians from east of the mountains from crossing. It was not a cheerful prospect but it was not hopeless.

THE DEATH OF LIEUTENANT SLAUGHTER

Whatever sense of security the villagers may have had in feeling that they were fortified for winter was shattered when, on December 4th, swift messengers again came paddling hurriedly down from the White River, this time with the news, "Lieutenant Slaughter has been killed!"

The tragedy had occurred on the site of the White River massacre in a deserted cabin. Now the settlers feared that not even the presence of the regular army would check the savages in warfare.

Hewitt's company had been securely fortified at the junction of the White and Green Rivers awaiting orders from Lieutenant Slaughter. Toward evening on December 3rd word came that Slaughter had arrived and camped for the night about four miles distant. With a guard of several men Hewitt went down at once to confer with him.

Slaughter and his company of about sixty men of regulars and volunteers from Captain Wallace's company had been marching all day in the rain, and were wet through, chilled and tired. They had covered only eight miles but that was a long march through the unbroken forest. After supper they proceeded to dry their clothes and rest about the fires. Mrs. Blaine's letter and other contemporary accounts agree that Slaughter was urged to take his men to the better fortified camp of the Seattle company, but replied that his men were too tired to make another move that night.

The following account of what happened was furnished in after years by David Denny, a member of Hewitt's company of volunteers:

An Indian guide named Puyallup Tom accompanied Lieut. Slaughter through the Green River country where he was to meet with the company of volunteers of which I was a member. It was cold and raining nearly all day. When near the spot where they camped they saw an Indian dog skulking along in the under brush. Puyallup Tom said that the dog's master was not far off and to "Closhe nanatch" (look out).

Darkness came on before they reached the camp of the volunteers who were on the west side of the river. The Lieutenant found a small cabin in the opening in the woods and here he made camp for the night. They were all drenched to the skin so they stacked their arms and built large fires of fence rails around which the soldiers stood to dry. The Lieutenant did not put out any guards as he had not seen any Indians that day.

He made his quarters in the cabin with his officers where they had a fire on the earth floor. As the night drew on the hooting of owls was heard. The guide told him that it was the Indians signaling to each other but he said, "No, you're mistaken." Puyallup Tom begged that the fire be extinguished but the Lieut. refused.

He sent a courier to the camp of volunteers and three of their officers came to confer. The soldiers were around the bright fire and the Lieut was sitting in the cabin when the Indians fired a volley into their midst killing Lieut. Slaughter instantly. The bullet came in between logs striking him in the heart. He made no sound save the sharp intaking of his breath and fell over dead.

Two of the soldiers were killed and several wounded. The men crowded into the little cabin and Puyallup Tom ran out and kicked the fires apart.

The Indians withdrew for a time. Finally two men who were in a fence corner heard them creeping back and fired on them.

Those men who fired from the fence corner were soldiers who had fought in the Seminole War in Florida and knew Indian methods. By such tactics they gave the impression of large numbers being on the defensive.

The Seattle volunteers heard the firing and started at once, only to meet the regulars hurrying down to their camp carrying the wounded on litters and the body of Slaughter. On the following day a detachment of soldiers was sent back to bury the bodies of the two soldiers.

It was a sad little canoe-procession that brought the body of Slaughter and the wounded soldiers down to Seattle the day after the tragedy. One of the men died on the way. Until the bodies of the dead could be transferred to Steila-coom, they lay in the new blockhouse fort, which was taking on the grim usages of war. One of my mother's most vivid memories was that of Lieutenant Slaughter's body lying under the stairs in the blockhouse.

Grant says:

No single event cast a gloom over the community as the death of Lieut. Slaughter. He was a graduate of West Point, a brave and efficient soldier and had been actively in the field from the beginning of Indian hostilities until his death.

A granite monument in Auburn beside the much-traveled Pacific Highway honors the spot where this gallant young soldier died, and not far distant a second one commemorates the White River massacre.

How close and personal this encounter brought the war to the Seattle volunteers is illustrated by a story that I have heard my father, George Frye, tell. He told of going with others to bury the dead at Slaughter's camp and taking a vote whether they would stand by the wounded in case of an attack, or whether each would look to his own safety. They voted to stay with the wounded to the last man. He had known no fear until then, he said, but the thought of being left wounded to the mercy of the Indians filled him with horror.

Lieutenant David Denny told how, when they took the body of Slaughter away from the cabin in which he had been killed and left the other dead behind, they could hear as they moved away the victorious yells of the savages as they took possession of Slaughter's camp, and how they found the bodies robbed and scalped when they returned the following day to bury them.

The settlers' fear that not even the army would be able to protect them increased. Captain Hewitt's company was ordered to Seattle shortly after the death of Slaughter. Other companies were ordered to the different settlements. leaving the field to the Indians, who thus far had come off victorious in every encounter. The best the whites could do now was to defend themselves in the blockhouses against the offensive of the enemy—an enemy well armed and perfectly familiar with the forest, which the white man found almost impenetrable.

CHAPTER XIV

THE BATTLE OF SEATTLE

ON THEIR RETURN from the White River Valley after the death of Slaughter, the Seattle company of volunteers built a blockhouse on the Duwamish where they remained until their three months' enlistment was up on January 25th. They then returned to Seattle. Dr. Smith says of this fortification on the river:

This company built a hewed-log blockhouse and surrounded it with a stockade on Henry Van Asselt's farm on Duwamish river about six miles from Seattle. The object being to prevent the Indians from coming down the river in large force and to give us easier access to Lake Washington, a trail leading from Van Asselt's being the only means of reaching it except by way of the rivers and through the dense woods. Several families lived in the blockhouse with the volunteers for protection. Scouts prospected the woods in different directions but so wary was the enemy that not much was accomplished in discovering their movements.

The young volunteers crowded in the blockhouse found this period of waiting and dreading, an irksome one. One of their means of recreation during the long winter evenings of the two months they were quartered there was to get David Graham to intone the psalms as he had learned to do in boyhood.

They even had their bit of fun, according to David Graham:

One of the men did not like to stay at the fort much of the time and was always getting leave to go to town with the understanding that he must return in case of trouble. We were about six miles from Seattle and one evening we waited until he was well on his way and then fired a volley from our rifles and yelled at the top of our lungs. After a while here he came, bent over, slipping along, craning his neck around first one way and then another, looking for Indians. We greeted him with whoops of laughter.

While the volunteers were spending tedious days in the fort, Arthur Denny was in Olympia where he was elected Speaker of the House of Representatives. Commenting on his election, the *Pioneer and Democrat* remarked editorially:

Hon. A. A. Denny has been elected Speaker, and if a Democratic House *must* require the election of a Whig Speaker, we do not think they could have done better. If the Democratic House can stand it, we can.

How this Whig Speaker of a Democratic House saw the situation in the Territory is expressed in his opening speech made on December 3, 1855:

We are assembled under the most discouraging circumstances. Our infant territory is now surrounded by hostile savages; our citizens murdered in our midst and our constituents looking to us in this hour of gloom to render every exertion, to make every effort in our power to secure assistance and insure protection.

The weather that winter of '55 was ironically beautiful. The Settlers remembered afterward the lingering Indian summer days; the soft, warm rains that kept things green. David Denny remembered how they worked on the blockhouse in their shirt sleeves. Just before Christmas Mrs. Blaine wrote, "Our little peach and apple trees are not stripped of their leaves yet."

How this good weather mocked the farmers who had been obliged to come into the village and leave their farms to the Indians. How powerless they felt to be gathered in Seattle, waiting—waiting for the forest to give up its secret.

As December drew to a close the settlers were very anxious for the safety of Governor Stevens, who had not returned from the Blackfoot country. Mrs. Blaine wrote:

No news yet from Governor Stevens and his party. Companies have been raised to go out and escort him in. He was near the western slope of the Rocky Mountains when last heard from. It is thought to be quite doubtful if he ever comes back—but he may.

Then she adds in the same paragraph, a sentence equally poignant with the atmosphere of those weeks before the outbreak. "Our cows do not come home and I have not been able to find them."

It was a dark Christmas for Seattle and for the whole Territory. Of the gloom of those weeks Professor Meany writes:

*The year 1855, as it drew to a close, saw the Territory of Washington enshrouded in gloom. It was not known how many Indians had suffered. They always managed to conceal their dead and rescue their wounded. But it was known that a considerable number of white people had lost their lives, many others had lost their homes. The survivors collected into blockhouses for mutual protection. The Indians gave continuous evidence of their presence. . . . . Food was growing scarce—ordinary business was out of the question—starvation, flight, or the tomahawk seems the only alternatives.

Only by a stretch of the imagination can we faintly realize the situation in the village. From Second Avenue to Lake Washington towered the forest. No one, except well-armed scouts, dared penetrate that formidable wood; no one knew just when it would send forth a horde of yelling savages. The suspense of those weeks was indescribable. Something was going to happen, but when and how, no one knew. The forest told no tales.

When darkness shut down upon the settlement, the forest grew blacker than the night. At the least sound of anything unusual, the settlers were alert and ready to run for the fort. Burning candles were quickly snuffed out lest they be targets for the enemy. Many were the false alarms. Mrs. Blaine wrote, "There were three false alarms last night."

One night a shot was fired by someone in the village that so frightened the settlers that they ran for the fort in their night clothes. They had many hearty laughs over this in the sunshine of the following years when danger was not so near. One laugh was on Hillory Butler who, they said, called out to the Widow McConaha to wait for him, but the widow kept on running. Another joke was on a family who up to this time had ridiculed the need of a blockhouse, but came panting into its shelter and sank down exhausted from fear and hurry. Thereafter they were ardent exponents of preparedness.

January of the new year was brightened by the news of

---

*From *History of the State of Washington* by Edmond S. Meany. By permission of Macmillan Company, publishers.

the governor's safe return. The *Pioneer and Democrat* announced his arrival in these joyous headlines: "GLORIOUS NEWS FOR WASHINGTON TERRITORY. GOVERNOR STEVENS RETURNED FROM BLACKFOOT COUNCIL. LITTLE BANDY-LEGGED 'ROUGH AND READY' IN THE FIELD."

The suspense and ominous quiet in the village increased as the days passed. Where was Leschi? What move was he planning to make? Would the deep snows in the passes keep the warlike Owhi from crossing with his fierce Yakimas? Some pioneers felt confident that with the *Decatur* and their own armed volunteers they were well protected; others were afraid they would be overwhelmed by the greater number of the enemy.

In this interval of watching and waiting, a son was born to David and Catherine Blaine on the 20th of January, the Sunday before the battle.

On the 25th, Captain Hewitt's volunteers returned from the Duwamish blockhouse and were disbanded. It was not a coincidence that the Indians attacked the village the following day. They had a thorough respect for the volunteers although the regulars belittled volunteer methods. The Indians said of the latter, "They walk straight, gun on shoulder. Injun shoot easy"; but of the volunteer, "All same Injun; bend over; sneak through bush; shoot behind tree."

No one though of it at the time, but the pioneers realized afterward that the Indians were doubtless watching the movements of the volunteers and timed their attack accordingly.

In that week preceding the battle rumors of an attack were brought by friendly Indians, one of whom was Curley. Curley's loyalty to the whites has been questioned by many. and undoubtedly the truth of the matter was that he was friendly to both sides. He would get a little ammunition and tobacco from Mr. Yesler, whom he knew very well since he had worked in the mill, and trade it for information

THE BATTLE OF SEATTLE

which he would in turn bring back to Mr. Yesler. Indian
Jim, whose sincerity was never questioned, also brought
news to the whites; likewise the "klootchmen," and other
Indians who had worked in Yesler's mill and were his
"tillicums."

Rumors that the Indians were assembling on the western
shore of Lake Washington, and that "hi hu" (many) Klikitats were preparing to advance on Seattle became more frequent. These rumors were strengthened on Friday afternoon.
the 25th, when Tecumseh, a friendly chief from Cedar
River, came in bringing his tribe and asking protection. The
settlers felt that he must know that hostilities were close.
They assigned him a camp in the south end of the settlement.

On this same day Governor Stevens stopped at Seattle on
a tour of the Sound he was making on the United States
steamer *Active*. He assured the pioneers that there was no
danger and expressed the belief that New York and San
Francisco were not safer from attack than Seattle was at
that very moment.

Fortunately Captain Gansevoort had been in closer touch
and knew local conditions better. A few days previous he
had sent an Indian scout over to Lake Washington to find
out what was going on. The scout returned on the afternoon
of the 25th, shortly after the *Active* with Governor Stevens
aboard had sailed away, with the startling news that one
thousand Klikitats had crossed the mountains, and that for
two days the local Indians had been bringing them across
the lake in canoes.

The defenses were hurriedly strengthened. The disbanded volunteers took up their guns and were put on watch.
Four divisions of soldiers and marines were posted by Captain Gansevoort to guard the town: one at the south end;
another in a store; a third in Mr. Plummer's house at the
extreme southeast part of town (at Jackson Street); and a
fourth in front of Yesler's home. A howitzer, designed to

fire over and beyond the range of the smaller guns, was placed toward the south of the settlement with nine men and a number of marines to guard it. The remainder of the marines were sent to help guard the blockhouse. This description is taken from a valuable account of the defense found in Captain Gansevoort's official report to the Navy Department.

The cookhouse was now like a barracks; soldiers were quartered there, and guards came there for warmth and rest when they changed watches.

The only vessel in the harbor besides the *Decatur* was a lumber bark, *Brontes,* which proved a faithful friend by sheltering some of the women and children. Fear for the women and children filled with terror the hearts of those brave defenders. Three little orphans in the blockhouse reminded them of what might happen.

Early on the evening of the 25th two strange Indians wrapped in blankets, loomed out of the fog and were seen skulking through the town. When stopped by the guard they said they were "tillicums" and had been to see Curley. They were allowed to pass and disappeared in the darkness. Afterward it was learned that these "tillicums" had been the enemy Owhi and another chief, called Coquilton who were on their way to a council of war with other hostile chiefs to decide upon the method of attack.

At this conference it was first planned to attack and massacre the settlers at two o'clock in the morning. But in order to have time to warn the whites, Indian Jim cunningly proposed waiting until later when the marines would have returned to the *Decatur* for breakfast after the night watch. leaving the town unguarded. This plan pleased the council and was decided upon. Curley, who, according to one account, was also present, wanted to spare Mr. Yesler, who had given many of the Indians work in his mill, but the others insisted that everyone must be killed.

The night was dark and misty. As the guards paced back and forth, they could hear sounds along the beach and in the village. About ten o'clock from the forest back of them came the hoot of an owl, soon answered by another, and then others from various points around the edges of the town. These, as they suspected, were the signals of one Indian to another.

Early the next morning, January 26, 1856, the Indians crept in close to the village and lined up along what is now Third Avenue, prepared to make a sudden attack on the cabins. They were massed where the County-City Building now stands. Close as they were, however, the forest was dense enough to hide them from sight.

Just at daybreak Indian Jim managed somehow in his native fashion to elude the others and slip in the back door of Dr. Williamson's store with the whispered word that *the Indians were upon them*. The attack had come. Word was sent to Yesler at once.

The night watch had reached the *Decatur*. The men were just beginning to eat breakfast when a canoe shot out from land carrying Mr. Yesler. Immediately the roll was sounded and the marines rushed ashore, back to the stations they had occupied the night before. The opportune moment for the Indians to rush on the cabins had passed.

The howitzer was quickly trained on the opposite side of "the marsh"—the swampy strip that separated "the Point" from the hillside to the east—where the Indians were reported to be congregated about the house of an Indian. Tom Pepper.

This information came from a squaw on the beach—Curley's sister Nancy, a very fat squaw, who came waddling along and calling excitedly, "Hiu Kliktat copa Tom Pepper's house! Hiu Kliktat copa Tom Pepper's House!" which means, a lot of Klikitats around Tom Pepper's House!

It was now eight o'clock. Candles in some of the cabins

were still burning. Many of the men had just come in from the night watch. Some were eating breakfast when suddenly came the shattering, deep-throated report of the howitzer; the savage, fiendish yell of the natives; and the quick fusillade of shots. The battle of Seattle had begun! No one mistook this for a false alarm.

Such a running for the fort! Louisa Denny grabbed Baby Inez with one hand and tumbled a pan of biscuits just from the oven into her apron with the other and ran. David, who was on guard at the blockhouse, ran to meet her and helped her in. Mrs. Blaine and her new baby were bundled into a rocking chair and taken to the shelter of the *Decatur*. Virginia Bell, running for shelter, darted like a little scared rabbit between the legs of a marine who was in her path as she entered the blockhouse, knocking him to the floor with a scramble that added to the panic.

Hillory Butler, not yet dressed, jumped into his wife's red flannel petticoat and ran—so the story goes. It may have been made up afterwards as a joke on the popular Mr. Butler, but it has come down to us as one of the typical events of that hurried flight.

Cornelius Hanford, who later became one of Washington's most distinguished jurists, then a little boy of seven, ran after his father, who carried two of the younger children. As the little chap turned conscientiously to close the door of their cabin, he was terrified by seeing a hostile Indian peeking over a fir log not far from the house.

Had it not been that the rifles in the hands of the Indians had been generally emptied by the first volley, many of the settlers would have fallen by the way in this stampede. Fortunately all escaped.

The first shot from the howitzer was followed by firing from the ship's battery and an exchange of gunfire between the Indians and the volunteers and marines. For two hours there was a steady booming and hammering of firearms while the white-faced women and children, huddled in the fort, prayed for the safety of their loved ones.

Milton Holgate, an adventurous lad of fifteen, wishing to be outside the fort with the soldiers, started out and was shot and instantly killed as he was passing through the door. This tragedy added to the horror of the day to those waiting in the fort.

It was the general belief afterward that the bullet that killed the lad was from the rifle that the Indians had stolen from Mr. Brannan at the time of the massacre; because the guns used by the Indians were made for trade, and would not carry as far as this one had.

A young man named Robert Wilson was also killed when standing on the porch of the Felker House. These were the only casualties of the day among the whites; they never knew how many Indians were killed. The two white victims were buried a few days later, close to the church.

The Indians had never engaged in such warfare before but stood their ground remarkably well. The cries of the squaws were heard urging their men on toward the blockhouse. The *Decatur's* guns rained cannon balls, shell, and grapeshot upon the forest beyond Third Avenue. This cannonading was supplemented by volleys from rifles and musketry of sailors and civilians. For years afterward shells from the *Decatur* were found embedded in the ground. Huge trunks of trees were splintered. The patter of grapeshot upon the trees sounded like hail. Once the Indians moved north of the town and attacked from that quarter, but fire from the *Decatur* forced them out of range; consequently they were unable to do much harm.

Inside the fort the frightened women comforted the children and prayed for protection. One of the men accidentally discharged a gun and the bullet went through the heavy coiled hair of Miss Kirkland, daughter of Moses Kirkland.

She fainted from fright, but the other women thought she had been killed.

Little Johnnie King was so terrified by the firing, which reminded him of the experience at White River, that marines took him to the *Decatur* during the battle.

About noon Sheriff Thomas Russell, who had been across the Sound, came paddling to the rescue bringing with him some men from Meig's Mill. In the afternoon the firing continued intermittently until about three o'clock. Once there was a prolonged lull. It was learned afterward that the Indians had stopped to feast on beef prepared by their squaws from the cattle of the settlers.

During this lull in the fight many of the women and children were hurried to the *Decatur* where, according to Captain Gansevoort's report, "they were accommodated, as far as possible, in the cabin and ward room, the officers giving up their apartments and making them as comfortable as circumstances would permit."

Some of the pioneers made further use of this lull in the fighting, while the Indians feasted on their cattle, in making a quick dash for their homes close to the fort to get provisions, guns, and valuables left in their hasty flight, before the Indians would come after dark and rob and plunder the cabins. Seeing them, the enemy immediately opened fire, but they were answered by shots from the good ship in the harbor.

The townsfolk were also hungry by this time, for not many had finished their breakfast. As the story came down to me, David Graham crept out to a nearby cabin, and baked some biscuits, and then ran back quickly to the hungry people in the fort.

The Boren house, which stood about a hundred yards from the fort, was well stocked with sugar, flour, pork, and potatoes. I have heard the pioneers tell how they crept out to Uncle Dobbins' house for these supplies, and how close the guns of the Indians seemed until they could make the shelter of the fort again.

Walter Graham told of an exploit of the young soldiers. which probably happened in the afternoon:

> In company with two or three others I went down to the beach below the fort where the bank screened us from the red men, for they were on the east of town. We went to Arthur Denny's house, north of the fort, thinking we could get a shot at them from there. We crawled through the floor from the front and going upstairs we knocked off a board from the peak of the roof on the east side. The minute the board came down a shower of bullets struck around us and we got down and out considerably faster than we went up.

Toward evening, scouts were sent out who reported that the enemy were placing inflammable material under and around the deserted cabins preparatory to burning them. Shells from the *Decatur* scattered the incendiaries, but not before they had robbed some of the cabins of food and clothing.

Mary Denny's wedding gown was taken and she often wondered which squaw it was that went trailing her treasured dress through the woods.

Woodin's tannery just outside the village near the present County-City Building was burned. When darkness came the flames against the sky told the pioneers in the fort that to the south the Holgate and Hanford homes were being destroyed, and to the north the home of William Bell.

According to Grant this conflagration, planned for the evening after the battle, was believed "to have been the signal for all Indians on the beach and across the Sound to join in the attack." Elwood Evans says in his *History of the Northwest*, the attack on Seattle was to have been so bold and successful that Indians on the reservations who were either neutral or friendly to the white men would be won over to their side.

By ten o'clock that night both sides had ceased firing and all was quiet. But it was an ominous quiet. It was not peace.

The men partitioned off the upper part of the blockhouse with blankets for the different families staying there. Those not on guard lay down to rest on beds made upon the floor; but only the children slept, for it was a sad little group, with two of their number dead and with grave misgivings as to their own future.

When the morning of the 27th dawned, the Indians had disappeared, taking many of the cattle with them. Chief Leschi sent back a boastful message that he would be back in another month and destroy the town. But he never came.

As Leschi left he burned and destroyed all that he passed —the buildings of the Duwamish group; Plummer's sawmill on Black River; everything in King County outside the Seattle settlement except the buildings at Alki, which were out of his path. The gay crowds of today at Leschi bathing beach have little knowledge of what dread the word "Leschi" meant to the pioneers.

The attack on Seattle, which was to have been the Indians' decisive and triumphant act, had failed. Although the war continued in other parts of the Territory all that year. it was this battle that decided the struggle in Washington Territory between the Indian and the white man.

The Indian chiefs miscalculated in many ways. For one thing, the fierce tribes that were leading the uprising defeated their own plan of uniting the Indians, for they had terrified the weaker tribes for so many years that it was now hard to gain their cooperation. Grant makes much of the fact that the suspicions and jealousies existing between the tribes tended to weaken them, when otherwise they might easily have overpowered the whites and succeeded by their greater numbers.

Furthermore, the morale of the natives was destroyed by the shells from the cannon on the *Decatur*. They were well used to guns, for they had been using them ever since the Hudson's Bay Company had come into their territory, but these shells that lay still and then "mox-poohed" or shot twice, filled them with superstitious fear. It was something they had not counted on and proved too much for them. Then, too, the noise of those old cannon was terrific.

So when Leschi sent back word to the captain that he would return, his threat was more boastful than confident. He had heard the cannon and seen the shells that "mox-poohed."

But for the presence of the *Decatur* Seattle might have been wiped off the map. But the ship alone could not have saved the village. The friendship of the settlers with the Sound Indians, and the fact that there was not one of these pioneers but did active service in the protection of the settlement helped immeasurably. At every step in its history, whatever the need, those enthusiastic young men swung an axe or shouldered a gun to make their vision real.

CHAPTER XV

AFTER THE BATTLE

AN INVALUABLE first-hand picture of the battle is preserved for us in a letter written two days after it occurred.

Hon. A. A. Denny   Seattle, Jan. 28, 1856
Dear Sir:
    Sebastopol is not taken yet. We had an engagement with the Indians, Saturday, Jan. 26th. It commenced at 8:30 o'clock A. M. and continued until dark incessantly and resulted in the death of two Bostons—Milton Holgate and Robert Wilson. Fortunately none were wounded. I have no idea how many Indians were killed but there were a number.
    My house was burned on my claim during the action but the outhouses are still standing but your house in town was robbed of flour and perhaps other things on the night of the attack.
    The Indians we suppose are back near the lake where they must be from 500 to 1000 strong and say they will give us two or three months siege.
    Our company is disbanded and another has been formed this morning for the protection of Seattle; and from the best information I can obtain the majority of Indians on the Sound will join them.
    Shirley [Sarah] is true grit. Please find out and inform me what course I must pursue to obtain remuneration for the loss of my house. Only a part of my cattle came in last night. Should this state of things continue there will not be six families left here in the spring. The *Decatur* is afloat and most of our women and children are on board of her.
                                    Yours respectfully,
                                    W. N. BELL

The pioneers began immediate preparations to defend themselves more securely against what they expected to be a long siege. Citizens and soldiers quickly built a stockade about the town and a second blockhouse near Plummer's house at Occidental and Jackson Streets, about two hundred feet east of the Felker House. This fort stood on top of the ridge overlooking the swamp to the east. As far as we know this fort was not lived in, but was used by marines and sailors.

The stockade, built of sawed lumber contributed by Yesler, consisted of two parallel fences, five feet high, and a foot and a half apart, with the intervening space packed solid with sawdust to make it bullet-proof. The inclosure ran from the shore on "the Point" east beyond Plummer's house; north past the first blockhouse at First and Cherry; and then west over the bluff to the water's edge. Almost all of the village was included. So quickly had the builders worked that both structures were finished by February 15th in a little over two weeks.

A new volunteer company, called Company A, was organized on the 28th for six months' enlistment with Judge Edward Lander, captain; Arthur Denny, first lieutenant; and D. H. Neely, second lieutenant.

The fear and tenseness of those days immediately after the battle have been caught and preserved for us in Mr. Blaine's diary. He wrote:

Tuesday. This morning the Indians are said to be within 5 miles of us but did not disturb us through the night. The Steamer *Active* came up from below us with Governor Stevens and other dignitaries on board. A new company was organized in town, volunteers for present defense, officers elected, and stockades are commenced in different places to protect the soldiers. The Governor and others say Seattle must not be given up, else 10,000 men could not subdue the Indians. It is the key to the Sound and the most vigorous efforts must be made to save it. The Governor asked me for the church to be used as a blockhouse. I told him to take it and fortify it. . . . . Last night ten men quartered in the house, tonight it is left to run its chances.

Wednesday. No Indians last night but scouts report them in the woods within three miles of town. The defenses are progressing. Steamer *Active* went to Olympia yesterday, came back to-day. . . . . I had most of our things moved from the house down to the wharf, within the barricade. We stay in the *Decatur*. Kate has not been ashore since the fight on Saturday. It is reported that some 15 or 16 Indians were killed Saturday. Every precautionary step is being taken to resist them if they come again.

Thursday. Last night two Indians were fired upon while attempting to creep into town, as supposed to set fire to buildings. The Indians are at Collins' place.

The speed with which the news of the attack traveled is shown by the return of Governor Stevens from Whatcom on Tuesday, the 29th. Mr. Blaine recorded the changed—

and chastened—attitude of the governor who only the preceding Friday had been so sure that there would be no Indian attack.

When returning from San Francisco where he had gone to buy supplies for his store, Dexter Horton heard cannon fire at Port Townsend on the day of the battle. When the ship stopped at Port Madison, he learned that the cannonading had been at Seattle. In his own words:

> I couldn't sleep that night for my wife was over at Seattle. The next morning with difficulty I hired an Indian and his squaw to paddle me over to Seattle. They crept along and every little while the Indian would pause, look around and listen for enemies. When opposite Seattle, seeing no canoes, they paddled with haste toward Seattle. As we came alongside the *Decatur* I was hailed and informed that my wife was safe on board that ship.

After hearing of the attack Arthur Denny, as Speaker of the House, was obliged to put in the longest days of his life while the closing business of the legislative session was carried on. After adjournment on Thursday following the battle, he hurried home. As he neared Seattle he could see fires against the dark, evening sky. Mother remembered his telling of the sick, terrified feeling it gave him; how he fully expected to find the village in ashes.

The fires he saw were along the Duwamish, for he returned on Friday or Saturday and Mr. Blaine reported the Indians at Collins' place on Thursday. The natives burned houses, barns, and fences all along the Duwamish and White Rivers as they moved on.

When the stockade was finished, families whose cabins near the fort had not been burned returned to their homes during the daytime and attended to their household duties and at sundown went back to the blockhouse to sleep. Those who lived at a distance remained in the fort all winter.

Within the walls of the fort in the midst of all the sadness and discomfort, Mrs. Bell lay ill in her bed. Her little girls did all they could to make her comfortable where there was no comfort. She would say to them, "Your little hands have brought me everything I have needed today." As soon as he could, Mr. Bell took his wife to California in search of the health that she was never to regain. She died the following June. In 1870 Mr. Bell returned to Seattle.

It was dark and crowded in the blockhouse. One of the mothers told afterward that when it was too dark to sew, and her eyes had grown tired, she would rest them by folding a hem and sewing for a while with her eyes closed.

One of the notable accomplishments of the women during those days in the fort was the making of an American flag. To this day the red flannel of its stripes, although moth-eaten, is still red. The white cotton stars are yellowed, and the blue field is faded. The flag is fastened to the staff with some figured dress material. The stitches taken in the dark fort are not so fine as they might be, but no Betsy Ross flag could be more precious. This flag is now in the possession of a granddaughter of David and Louisa.

The families crowded in the blockhouse took turns doing their cooking. Water was carried from Yesler's mill.

The pioneer children had little milk to drink, for most of the cows had been either stolen or killed by the Indians. One of Louisa's memories was of the children crying for milk. Seventy-five years later, Susan Mercer told how she and her sister mourned the loss of their cow. They had had her only one day and were anticipating the milk and butter they were to have.

In March, in the blockhouse, a second daughter was born to David and Louisa Denny. She was named Madge Decatur for her birthplace, which was now called Fort Decatur.

Living in the blockhouse was not a happy experience for any of the pioneers, but the children found diversion in trips to the *Decatur*, where they became warm friends with both officers and marines.

Mrs. Blaine's baby boy on board the ship was thriving.

For the first week or two, Mrs. Horton was taken aboard each day to bathe and dress him. No matter how busy they were, some marine was delegated each day to row Mrs. Horton out to care for the baby.

On February 20th Mrs. Blaine wrote:

The baby is a month old today and I guess has been tossed about as much as a child of his age ever was. The ship is some distance from shore so that we have to go back and forth in a small boat. He has been taken ashore some half dozen times or more. I have been off to wash and iron and do some other work. He stands it pretty well though he cries considerably from wind on his stomach, is as fat as a pig and dreadfully homely.

In the same letter Mrs. Blaine refers to a matter which was troubling the settlers at this time. She said:

A report which is believed by many has been brought recently that a formidable tribe from the British possessions have leagued with other hostile Indians and that 1200 of them are on their way here now. A steamer started yesterday to look for them (as they will have to come by water) but I do not think she will find them as it is so easy to hide their canoes.

So they lived in constant terror of an Indian attack, from the woods back of them, and from the water in front of them. It was a heartbreaking winter. Food was now giving out, and the children continued to cry for milk. Of those days Arthur Denny wrote afterward, "Those were times of pinching want and great privation such as we had never experienced except in the winter of '52-'53."

Many of the settlers were leaving for Oregon and California as fast as they could get passage. It was hard for those who were left to see the others go. It took courage to remain. A few months after the battle there were but seventy-five or eighty men left, and less than a dozen families. It was Seattle's darkest hour.

The Blaines accepted an offer from a church in Portland. They delayed their departure only long enough to see Charles Terry on his return from the Atlantic Coast with messages from their relatives whom he had visited in New

York State. Years later the pioneer minister and his wife returned to Seattle to spend the leisure years of their lives.

"The White Church" was closed. In these discouraging days the pioneers had nothing left to sustain them but their own integrity and faith.

The hostile Indians did not return to the village as Leschi had threatened, but the settlers kept close watch through the remainder of the winter. Protection by water was strengthened. For part of the time, the *Decatur* was joined by two other ships of the United States Navy—the *Massachusetts* and the *Active*.

This left the volunteers of Company A free to do scout duty. They were stationed at the blockhouse fort on the Duwamish, named Fort Lander. Hanford says the volunteers were "patiently and thoroughly watching by day and night in drenching rains, the trails used by the Indians and especially the portage between Lake Union and Lake Washington." The command of the company fell to Lieutenant Denny in the spring, when Captain Lander resigned because his judicial duties prevented his active service.

Yesler was not a member of Company A, but his friendship with the Indians continued to be of great value. He was sent to persuade some of the unfriendly natives to give themselves up and be placed on the reservations. At one time he crossed Lake Washington and went to the hiding place of the Sammumpsh Indians, who trusted him, and persuaded them to come out of hiding and go across the Sound.

An incident, ghastly, but still a part of the history of the war, is told of Pat-ka-nim. He had been promised by the military authorities twenty dollars a head for every hostile Indian that he could kill—a promise made in the heat of war and carried out to the letter by the chief, who arrived at the *Decatur* in February with several of these ghastly trophies. They were sent to Olympia, and the chief followed to receive his hostage money.

Later the settlers saw a canoe approaching. When it arrived at Yesler's wharf out stepped Pat-ka-nim elaborately dressed in "Boston" clothes. As described by one who saw him:

> He was arrayed in citizen's garb including Congress gaiters, white kid gloves, and a white shirt with standing collar reaching half way up to his ears and the whole was finished off with a flaming red tie.

Dr. and Mrs. Maynard resigned from their work on the reservations. They had done a very valuable service in keeping the friendly Indians from joining the enemy. Governor Stevens wrote of Mrs. Maynard:

> I take this occasion to express my sense of the courage and devotion of Mrs. Maynard and to acknowledge her services in soothing the troubled and distempered minds of the Indians. In sunshine and in storm, on the water and on the shore, in a mat lodge and under a roof, her presence, her acts and her words of kindly charity, exerted a potent influence for good.

An account of how Mrs. Maynard "saved Seattle" by bringing the news of the coming attack from Port Madison to the *Decatur* in a canoe is discredited by many old-timers who were in a position to know the facts. Prosch, however, who came to know Mrs. Maynard very well, gives the story as authentic.

One version of it, and a very probable one, is that Mrs. Maynard did make such a night ride, but that her warning was only one of many reports brought in during those days previous to the attack. Most authorities give Indian Jim credit for passing word of the coming attack to Yesler, and to Yesler for taking the news to the *Decatur*. In his official report Captain Gansevoort credits Yesler with having warned him.

As romance gradually colored accounts of the battle, there were several who "saved" Seattle. A wild night ride by Princess Angeline was one of the favorite stories —a story which, according to the old settlers, had no foundation.

As Prosch told the story of Mrs. Maynard's heroism.

Chief Seattle, who was kept informed of the movements of
the enemy, reported to Dr. Maynard on the 25th that a
large number of hostile Indians were hovering in the woods
back of the town ready to make an attack. Mr. Prosch said
further:

The agent and his wife discussed the situation and concluded that
warning from them to the people on the east side of the Bay was due.
Indians upon whom they could rely were called in and as a result
a canoe was got ready in the darkness of the night for the fourteen-
mile trip across the stormy waters. Sally, the daughter of old Kitsap,
said also to have been a cousin of Angeline, was captain, and under
her were five other women and one man. Mrs. Maynard was the
one passenger, she going as a courier or messenger to convey word of
the threatened attack upon the town.

The wind blew fiercely that night. The waves rolled high. With
all their strength and skill the Indians could hardly keep their frail
vessel afloat and moving. At one time they were blown upon West
Point. Hostile Indians were there and they examined the party. Finding that they were women and only one man they let them go. Before
doing so however they inquired what was under the mats in the bottom of the canoe. Sally told them clams. In truth it was Mrs. Maynard secreted there by Sally when she found that they were in danger.

After a hard struggle the canoe was placed alongside the *Decatur*.
Mrs. Maynard told the men on guard that she must see Captain
Gansevoort. He was awakened and acquainted with her and the
object of her visit. She gave him a letter from Agent Maynard. The
Captain had hot coffee and food provided for the Indians and he
urged Mrs. Maynard to stay at least until daylight. She said no that
she must be back by six in the morning, before daylight, so that her
trip would not be known among the reservation Indians. On the
return the wind blew harder than before, but it was a stern wind
and although dangerous did not prevent the arrival of the party
before dawn.

Not only Prosch but others who doubtless got their information from the Maynards describe Chief Seattle as having been in great mental distress when he heard the booming of the guns of the *Decatur*, and as having made "pitiful
demonstrations of the anguish he was in." No figure of
either race is more compelling than the old chief, who loved
his own race, who loved the white man, and yearned for

both, always praying that they might be reconciled to each other.

The only houses outside the village that were not burned belonged to Thomas Mercer and David Denny. These were spared, according to the word of the Indians, because Mercer and Denny had been especially kind to them.

When stock was taken of the losses which the pioneers had sustained in the war in the destruction of their belongings, a list was sent to the government for recovery of damages. No compensation was ever received. They were entitled to compensation because their property had been attacked by the Indians, who were wards of the government.

The following list includes part of the names of those who sent in claims:

```
D. S. Maynard, cow .................. $  75.00
Eli Maple, grain and lumber ...........    387.37
Francis McNatt, dwelling and barn ......   1749.50
Thomas Mercer, crops destroyed .........    267.00
Henry Adams, house ..................    370.00
William N. Bell, dwelling ..............   1568.00
George Frye, an ox stolen ..............    100.00
L. M. Collins, house destroyed ..........   2873.00
Plummer & Chase, sawmill destroyed.....   8200.00
Henry A. Smith, dwelling and stock......   1728.00
Samuel Maple, house and goods ..........   1673.50
```

AFTERMATH

Spring came and still there was fear and danger of an Indian attack. Farmers on the Duwamish returned to their claims for the spring planting under the protection of the armed volunteers. It is a picture reminiscent of Revolutionary days, when men took turns at the plow and with the gun. Walter Graham of Company A told afterward of doing a goodly share of the spring plowing.

This planting was most vital to the life of the little group. Trade on the Sound was paralyzed, thus cutting off their supply of provisions outside their immediate settlement. Arthur Denny said, "There was sufficient ground cultivated in the lower valley to supply the few families that remained with vegetables for next winter."

Returning to the Duwamish claims was like beginning all over again, for houses, barns, and fences had to be rebuilt. Most of the settlers spent their nights in the blockhouse.

What the conditions were early in June are told in a letter which Lieutenant Arthur Denny wrote to Adjutant General Tilton after receiving orders to leave one officer and eight men to garrison the Duwamish blockhouse and proceed with the remainder of the company to assist in cutting a military road to Snoqualmie Pass. Mr. Denny said in part:

> The future well-being of the citizens, if not their very existence, demands the presence of a greater force than your order designates or than I could possibly leave here. There are now a few farmers endeavoring to raise produce for the future subsistence of the families in King County and who are relying upon the presence of my command while so doing as a safeguard. But if they are deprived of this they must eventually abandon all hope of success as they will deem it unsafe to continue the work of their farms if I abandon the occupation of the lakes by the scouts, not even mentioning their fears of hostilities from the Indians on the opposite side of the Sound.
>
> I earnestly desire to execute all orders promptly and efficiently and I am sorry to be compelled to say that by so doing in this instance I shall prostrate the interest and put in jeopardy the lives of the citizens of this section of the country.

This letter started a controversy that became one of the major events of the post-war period. Tilton's answer countermanded his original order, but gave a new one wholly impossible of execution, in which he showed a lamentable lack of knowledge of the geography and conditions of the Territory.

Again Lieutenant Denny replied, respectfully pointing out why it would be impossible for him to follow the course outlined, and raising the point that the company had been formed expressly for the protection of Seattle.

As a result of this second letter, Denny was discharged from the command of Company A, which then fell to Second Lieutenant Neely.

Immediately Company A adopted resolutions which they sent to the governor informing him that they "did fully endorse and approve the course pursued by Lieut. Denny." They expressed themselves as considering the action of the commander in chief as "an act of injustice and an insult to the company wholly unjustifiable and uncalled for."

These sharp resolutions, signed by the entire membership, Company A was asked to rescind by an officer sent from Fort Steilacoom. In his report the officer stated:

After a great deal of talking with a great number of them privately I requested Mr. Neely to muster his company before Mr. Yesler's door, made a full and lengthy explanation to them in a body, told them that they had placed themselves in a false position, that they were the only company in the service that had disobeyed orders &c. &c. I said all that a man could say . . . . . but when the command was given "All who wish to rescind those motions, stand forward," no one stepped from the ranks.

For this obdurate stand Company A was refused an honorable discharge, which meant that they were also refused pay for their services. The matter was then taken up in the next session of the legislature. The hearing of the case covers many pages of the records. A joint resolution was finally passed demanding that the company be restored to full military standing and receive their pay.

Hanford attributes this unfortunate affair to "jealousy and spite" on the part of Tilton. He draws attention to the fact that when a few years later Tilton and Denny were opponents in the race for Congress, the people of the Territory gave Denny, strongly Whig, a large majority over Tilton, a Democrat in a Democratic Territory, which victory Hanford considers a complete vindication of Denny. After years have passed we can see that much of the injustice to Denny and Company A was due to the confusion and suspicions engendered by war.

There were other cases of misunderstanding. Judge Lander and Governor Stevens very seriously disagreed, the judge being arrested at one time. Relations between the legislature and the governor were decidedly unfriendly; the governor was condemned by one legislature and the condemnation rescinded by the next.

All through the Territory misery abounded. Nerves were on edge. When the time for the annual election came, little interest was shown. In all of King County only thirty-five votes were cast. Arthur Denny was elected to the Territorial Council, and Dr. Smith, T. D. Hinckley, and David Phillips to the House.

In this trying time the King County commissioners were again called upon to arrange for the pauper who had been sent to Steilacoom in '54 to be cared for by a doctor. The legislature had failed to appropriate funds for his care, and now he was returned to Seattle.

The decision of the commissioners is found in the brief records for '56:

Ordered that Edward Moore, the pauper, now in Seattle, be sold at public auction to the lowest bidder for his maintenance to be paid out of the county treasury, said bid to be left discretionary with the commissioners to accept or reject.

Harassed as they were, they did not realize that their attempt to board the fellow out sounded much like trafficking in slavery. But happily the man's family was found in the East. The settlers cleaned him up and sent him off in charge of the master of a ship.

This incident of the country's first pauper is of more than passing interest, illustrating as it does the embarrassment in the new Territory before provision was made for caring for public wards. An itemized bill of $621 for Moore's support had been presented by King County to the legislature the previous winter, but the lawmakers, admitting that it was "a case that should touch all the finer feelings of our nature," still felt that they could not establish a precedent by paying the bill

In the latter part of August, when danger from an Indian attack seemed reasonably removed, the *Decatur* set sail.

Sadly the pioneers watched the friendly vessel depart. It
was like seeing an old friend sail away. Now they felt quite
alone. The excitement was over. They turned wearily to
the wreckage of their once flourishing town—and to their
persistent fear of the Indians. It was not so much fear of an
attack as a lurking fear that was always with them. Inez
Denny wrote that for years afterward it was easy to imagine Indians everywhere.

The village now entered upon a period of depression that
lasted for ten years. Of that period Arthur Denny wrote:

> Those who remained until the close of the war were so discouraged
> and so much in dread of another outbreak that they were unwilling
> to return to their homes in the country and undertake the task of
> rebuilding them. As a consequence it was years before we recovered
> lost ground to any extent.
> Business was generally stagnant. Little in the way of building or
> improvement was attempted. Roads that had been opened before the
> war had mostly become well nigh impassable and some of them en-
> tirely so. Active efforts were not resumed to improve the roads and
> open communication until 1866, a period of ten years.

During the depressing aftermath of war even the opti-
mistic Dr. Maynard lost faith in the town he had helped so
glowingly to start and moved away, but not far. As Bagley
tells it:

> At the close of the Indian War the people of Washington were
> left in an almost hopeless condition. Many of them abandoned their
> homes and moved away. There was little money afloat and little
> business. In this Maynard was no exception. He saw no promise of
> success in returning to a business life so he decided to become a
> farmer. He still had 260 acres unplatted of his donation claim and
> Charles Terry had about 320 at Alki. On the 11th of July, 1857,
> they exchanged properties. Terry moved over to Seattle and the May-
> nards moved to Alki.

Henry Van Asselt had been so impoverished by the war
that in order to get money to rebuild on his claim he was
obliged to go down into the Willamette Valley and work
for a period as a farm laborer.

Not only the white men but the Indians suffered. Their

condition in the years following the war was deplorable. They were poor, diseased, and disorganized, and lived in squalor along the beaches. The government at Washington. vexed by the beginnings of the Civil War, gave little attention to them, and was not fulfilling the promises made in the treaties.

Leschi, the rebel leader, was tried and after months of controversy was hanged. This tragedy was deeply regretted by many of the settlers who contended that Leschi had surrendered and should have been treated like any other defeated leader. The story is told most feelingly by Ezra Meeker in his "Tragedy of Leschi."

Chief Seattle, old and nearing his end, pleaded for the rights of his people and tried to save Leschi. His great heart was broken by the confusion of his race and by the failure of the government to fulfill its promises so solemnly made.

An attempt was made by Joseph Brannan to avenge the massacre of his brother and family at White River. It is said that he killed eight of the twelve Indians who were in that attacking party. The first one was killed when Mr. Brannan was returning from east of the mountains and met an Indian wearing clothes which he recognized as his brother's. Realizing that his brother had been murdered he dispatched the Indian at once.

He vowed then never to rest until he had killed them all. especially Nelson who had led the attack. For three years Nelson was in hiding. The news of Joe Brannan's intended revenge spread throughout the Territory.

In the meantime, Mr. Brannan became engaged to marry; but the romance was darkened by his morbid pursuit. The young woman of his choice refused to be married until he gave up his quest for the remaining fugitive Indians.

Love won the day. Nelson was allowed to come out of hiding. He was deeply repentant for his part in the killing and vowed never to touch a gun again. Bagley tells that he even refused to shoot a hawk for a woman he was working for.

Nelson lived for many years a quiet, peaceful life in Auburn, not far from the scene of the massacre. Mr. Arthur Ballard, of Auburn, who has gained much information from native sources, tells us that all of Nelson's children died of tuberculosis in after years, and that the old Indian always considered this as a punishment for his part in the tragedy.

Gradually and inevitably the grim memories of the siege became less acute. There came a time when the pioneers could even smile at some of the incidents. Dexter Horton told with a relish how the gunner of the *Decatur*, aiming in the direction of the woods, shot through the little lean-to back of his store, and shot a dress of Mrs. Horton's out into the woods. Months afterward the gunner insisted on presenting Mrs. Horton with a new dress.

David Denny told how during the battle he tore a great rent in his trousers; how he tried to get in some corner of the fort away from the eyes of the women in order to repair the damage temporarily; and what big stitches he took in the process.

Trouble with the fierce northern Indians, which engaged the attention of the officers of the *Massachusetts*, forms an interesting chapter in the history of Washington Territory, but it is not a part of the Seattle story. However, the murder of Colonel Isaac Ebey on Whidby Island by these dreaded warriors in the summer of '57 caused a wave of renewed horror and dread in Seattle, and filled the settlers with sorrow for the loss of one of the greatest of Washington pioneers. Because he was a "hyas tyee" Colonel Ebey was killed in revenge for the killing of an Indian chief by one of the whites.

In '58 and '59 the famous Fraser River gold strike in British Columbia occurred. Thirty thousand men came up from California. Victoria changed from a fort to a town. Whatcom became a tent city of ten thousand. While Seattle did not share in the boom, there was excitement aplenty. A number of single men went to the mines.

None of the original founders of Seattle went; none budged from their task of holding together the little community they had founded. Wretched as the outlook was in this hour when the quest for gold might have tempted them, they proved themselves to be essentially founders and builders. Yesler, Terry, Plummer, the two Dennys, Horton, Mercer, Frye, Smith, Boren—not one left his post. It is as if they were holding all through those doubtful years a frail thread that connected the prosperous beginnings of Seattle with all that came after, even up to the modern city of today.

CHAPTER XVI

THE OUTLOOK in Seattle from '56 to '60 was dark. But happily adversity knit together the village life in intimate friendliness. The pioneers were young. The same spirit of youth that had brought them west survived the gloom. Any opportunity for merriment was seized upon avidly.

The settlement was agog with excitement in the summer of '56 when it learned that Edmund Carr and Olivia Holgate, who had taught together in the Sunday school, were to be married. The townsfolk proposed a wedding. A wedding meant a feast and a cake. Hanford says:

> The market was nearly destitute of delicacies usually supplied for such an affair but it is wonderful how pioneer women with scant provisions can delight appetites of the hungry when they try; they did try and made the feast a great success.

He tells further how three cakes were made with the milk from the one cow that had been saved from the Indian slaughter, and with the eggs from their few chickens. One cake was for the feast; one for Captain Samuel Swartwout of the *Massachusetts*, then in the harbor; and the third for the officers of the ship. These compliments were acknowledged by a salute to the bride and bridegroom from the ship's guns. In the absence of a minister the marriage ceremony was performed by E. A. Clark, then justice of the peace.

When the holidays approached, in the spirit of creating their own cheer, Ira Woodin and George Frye initiated secret preparations for Christmas. They bought up all of the town's stock of candy—the hard kind that came in wooden buckets—a few oranges and apples, and all the trinkets that could be found in the settlement stores.

Their plans leaked out; so the parents prepared the children by telling them again the old, old story of Santa Claus. By Christmas morning they were gleefully excited. To their amazement, when Santa Claus appeared he was twins, and had gone native in his Indian blankets; but the children were not critical, so happy were they that he had remembered them.

Another occasion for celebration was the completion of Plummer's new store building with a hall in the second story, called Snoqualmie Hall. Someone said, "Let's have a ball!" and someone else said, "Let's ask everybody around the Sound!" And so they did. As Hanford describes the occasion.

Delegations came from Port Townsend, Port Madison, Steilacoom and Olympia; and in Plummer's hall with old-fashioned violin music, cotillions, polkas, the Virginia reel and the lancers were danced by feet, the lightness of which surprised their owners. Some who had been for many months without expectation of ever being happy again were jollied and encouraged to carry on the struggle against adversities and tribulation.

A number of other notable weddings took place, none more important in town history than the union of Charles Terry and Mary Jane Russell at Port Madison, on July 13, 1856, which consummated the romance begun in the cabin home of Samuel Russell at Alki. The only account we have of this wedding is Grant's masculinely terse description—"a pleasant social event of the time." Mr. Terry bought Bettman Brothers general store and became active in the life of Seattle.

In '57, the fourteen-year-old homemaker of '53, Mary Jane Mercer, was married to Henry G. Parsons of Olympia; and, later in the year, Eliza Mercer to Walter Graham. Mrs. Ursula McConaha, the plucky, hard-working widow of George McConaha, was married to Lewis Wyckoff. S. B. Hinds, Charles Plummer's partner, married Nellie Andrews, the daughter of Peter Andrews, a newcomer from Maine. Another daughter, Addie, was married to a well known sea captain, John S. Hill.

A double wedding ceremony united Thomas Russell and Susan Crow, the step-daughter of Dr. Josiah Settle—who with his wife was a recent newcomer—and a young bachelor, Harry Hitchcock, and Maria McMillan, the daughter of the Rev. J. R. McMillan from Illinois, who had taken a claim on White River. Another daughter of Mr. McMillan was married to John Ross.

In Pierce County "one of the beautiful Bonney girls" —Mary—became Mrs. Oliver C. Shorey, in 1860, and she and her husband moved to Seattle a year later. On the Duwamish, Henry Van Asselt and Jane Maple were married in '62.

Tragedy followed romance in the beautiful home that Mr. Plummer had built for his bride when the young mother died in giving birth to twin sons. Later, Mr. Plummer married Mrs. Sarah Harris, a widow from Massachusetts.

Women did not remain single long after their arrival in the Territory, nor did the little pioneer girls as they grew up. The men still far outnumbered the women. The bachelor problem was acute. In 1858, editorials by Charles Prosch on the need of wives in the Territory began to appear in his paper in Steilacoom, the *Puget Sound Herald*.

Thomas Mercer often spoke half jokingly, half earnestly of getting territorial or government aid in bringing a party of young women from the New England states. This idea led to an interesting chapter in Seattle history. But Judge Mercer—as Mr. Mercer was called after being appointed judge of probate—was fortunate in finding a bride for himself in Oregon. In the fall of '59, he and Miss Hester Ward were married by Mercer's old friend, the Rev. Daniel Bagley, with whom he had crossed the plains.

On the Mercer's return to Seattle they lived in the little home near First and Washington where Mr. Mercer and his children had lived after the battle. With them came Mrs. Mercer's brother, Dillis B. Ward. It is interesting to know that Mr. Ward's most lasting memories of his arrival in Seattle were of the bullet holes in "the White Church" and of the dinner of baked salmon at the home of David and Louisa Denny.

Each arrival of newcomers was a huge event in the quiet life of the village. Two young girls, Susie Mercer and my mother, Kate Denny, took great pleasure in calling on each new family.

One of their social calls was made when Captain S. D. Libby and his wife Sarah moved to town. Captain Libby built a pleasant house with a piazza at James and Second, opposite Hillory Butler's and back of Yesler's. Here, soon after, Mrs. Libby opened Seattle's first millinery, which perked up the spirits of the women without question. The men may have had misgivings.

Another of Mother's memories that crowds in here is of sometimes helping Mrs. Libby by ripping apart the braid in straw hats that they might be fashioned into more modish bonnets. No matter how depressed Seattle women became, they never lost interest in their hats.

The number of immigrants during the period following the war was not large, but there were men who had come to the Northwest at the time of the Fraser River gold rush and had remained to settle at different places, some coming to Seattle. Besides there was a slow filtering of men toward the West, especially unmarried men.

Several who came to Seattle were: Henry A. Atkins and William H. Shoudy, who later became partners in a general mercantile business; Edwin Richardson, a surveyor; Hugh McAleer, who set up a tin and plumbing shop; D. K. Baxter, who opened a saloon; Manuel Lopez; John Webster; Samuel Coombs; L. C. Harmon and family, who ran a small hotel at first and later established the well known New England Hotel; William W. White, a blacksmith, and his family; and John A. Suffern, who opened a small foundry.

Three other members of the party of the four wagons

joined the Seattle group when John Denny—Arthur and David's father—and his wife, Sarah Boren Denny—Mary and Louisa's mother—and their eight-year-old daughter. Loretta, came to the village to live.

John Denny captivated the village at once and continued to be immensely popular to the end of his days. Tall and white-haired, with a broad-brimmed hat and a Kentucky accent, and with both wit and wisdom, he was soon "Uncle John" to all.

Mr. Denny had lived on frontiers all his life—Kentucky, Indiana, Illinois, Oregon, and now Washington. He had moved west with American history. His father had served under General Washington in the Revolutionary War. He himself had served in the War of 1812. He was a strong Whig; a warm friend of Abraham Lincoln with whom he had served in the Illinois legislature. Now on the Northwest frontier at the age of sixty-six, he took hold with the zest of a young man and entered into every civic enterprise from that time on. He possessed the quality of eternal youth. In addition he brought the wisdom gleaned from a rich background of experience. Coming as he did just before the Civil War, he became an emblematic figure sponsoring the Lincoln principles.

A charming picture of Seattle in the summer of 1859 is furnished us by Thomas Prosch, son of Charles Prosch:

On the 22nd of July, 1859, John H. Scranton gave to the Olympia and Steilacoom people the opportunity of coming to Seattle on the new steamer *Julia* for the low price (at the time) of three dollars a person. Two hundred people availed themselves of the privilege. Scranton advertised up the Sound one of the attractions as follows:

"In order to give zest to the entertainment, Dr. Maynard hyas tyee of the Seattle tribe of Indians will superintend the grand clam bake."

Seattle made every effort to properly receive and care for her guests. A salute was fired from the wharf. Mrs. Terry threw open her house to the upper Sound ladies. The attractions of the town then consisted of three wharfs—Yesler's, Horton's and Plummer's; the Woodin tannery; the Methodist church; the Yesler's sawmill and cookhouse and the old blockhouse fort, in addition to stores, hotels and saloons. . . . . A free ball and supper was given in the Plummer Hall at night. All went on successfully and happily except the grand event—the clam bake. To the great disappointment of the citizens 1 to Maynard's utter humiliation the tides served badly and for several days they refused to go out and so uncover the beds.

Mr. Prosch—one of the visitors from Steilacoom—also wrote that after he and his brother had looked over the town, they decided that it was far inferior to their home town.

It was not so large, so well built, so clean, so handsome. Many of the houses were unpainted; not one was plastered. By comparison we were proud of our home place. Seattle was not and never could be the equal of Steilacoom.

This attitude the two boys did not altogether conceal. and the town boys were well aware of it. Years later Judge Hanford told Prosch how the Seattle boys felt. Prosch writes:

They were very anxious to tone us down, believing we were far too cocky, and that ride on a rail, ducking in the slough, Sunday clothes and all, and other performance of like character, were due as a part of our just entertainment, the lack of opportunity only pre-venting our receiving the full measure of our desserts at their hands.

"YET IN THOSE DULL AND QUIET TIMES"

Of the period following the Indian War Grant writes. "Yet in those dull and quiet times were begun many of the things that now make Seattle illustrious." The spirit of youth still prevailed and during the first session of the legislature following the battle, the young lawmakers were found organizing nothing less than a Northern Pacific Railroad Company. Even an Indian War did not make them lose sight of their railroad. We find the same men who had differed seriously on matters pertaining to the war at the head of the new company—Isaac Stevens, Edward Lander. and Arthur Denny.

This railroad was to extend from Puget Sound to the Rocky Mountains, then the eastern boundary of Washington Territory. Several meetings were held but nothing came of the plan. As Prosch says, the enterprise was "too large an undertaking for so small a community and possessed too few attractions for capitalists abroad."

Likewise was a wagon road through the Cascades never lost sight of by the pioneers. Its need was emphasized anew in '58, when repeated rumors of gold in eastern Washington tantalized the people in Seattle with the realization that they were still cut off from the rich land east of the mountains.

Consequently on August 29, 1859, the settlers held a "mass meeting" to promote the idea of building a wagon road. Prominent speakers at this rally were Maynard, Yesler, and Arthur Denny, who were also appointed a committee to solicit funds. Always the association of these three names, which formed a tripod upon which rested many of the great enterprises of pioneer Seattle. How they did it we cannot conjecture, but at this meeting the sum of $1050 was subscribed to begin building a road through Snoqualmie Pass.

Signatures were also obtained to a petition to the legislature asking for assistance in building such a road. T. D. Hinckley was made superintendent, and without waiting for legislative aid work was begun at once.

A part of the road between Snoqualmie Falls and what is now North Bend was surveyed, logs and trees removed, and some grading done before the winter snows came.

That winter, through the good offices of Arthur Denny in the Council and his colleagues in the House, Dr. Henry Smith and David Phillips, the legislature memorialized Congress on the need of connecting eastern Washington with the seaports of the Sound, and on the advisability of a military road to Walla Walla through the Snoqualmie Pass. The logical reasons in favor of this pass rather than Naches and other passes were set forth.

This memorial was favorably received in Congress. A bill appropriating $75,000 was introduced, but was lost because of the dominating interest in the Civil War. For this reason this road remained but little more than a trail.

The trend of legislative activity during this period is indicated by the measures in which Mr. Denny was interested. The records show him as introducing a resolution relative to the settlement of the San Juan Islands dispute, as working for a road to Whatcom, for a geologic survey in the interest of coal production, for a lighthouse for the Straits of Juan de Fuca, and for a bill against legislative divorces.

The lawmakers were often on as many as eight committees at a time and Mr. Denny in '56 served on the committees on education, claims, military, enrolled bills, Indian affairs, commerce, memorials, and rules and orders. Grant writes of him, "There were many measures, memorials and acts introduced by him and he did much toward moulding the early policy of the territory."

In the village of Seattle through those slackened years the pioneers managed somehow to support a school in the same building where Mrs. Blaine had opened the first session. Miss Dorcas Phillips succeeded Mrs. Blaine. Other teachers named by Grant were: E. A. Clark, Edmund Carr, David Graham, Miss Addie Andrews, and Edwin Richardson. About all we know of those school sessions is that Eugenia McConaha, who must have been like her illustrious father, was "the smartest scholar in school." School was also held in the Duwamish blockhouse, but it is not known who taught there.

Occasional church services were held in "the White Church" when the presiding elders of the Methodist Episcopal Church, the Rev. John F. Devore and the Rev. Nehemiah Doane held quarterly meetings.

During these "dull and quiet times" Yesler's sawmill kept going, but that is about all. The San Francisco building boom was almost over. Besides there were many other larger mills on the Sound by this time. Only occasionally was there a shipment of lumber from Seattle.

Arthur Denny and Frye were now associated with Yesler in the sawmill. The three were also associated in a grist mill and in a hall known as the "Yesler-Denny Hall." No one had money. All had to help each other. Frye, who was still sawyer in the mill, had to take a good part of his wages in lumber and in this way started building.

The Woodin tannery was rebuilt on the same site at the present Prefontaine Place. Hides were plentiful and Woodin & Son did a good business for a number of years, shipping their leather not only to points on the Sound, but to San Francisco.

Charles Plummer, one of the most energetic business men in town, built a wharf in connection with his new store building, constructed a water system so that he was able to supply ships with water, and had a financial interest in other business activities. He and Charles Terry were filled with unlimited energy and enterprise. The town owed much to them in these doubtful years.

These two men took advantage of the gold boom east of the mountains and supplied pack trains going over the road, which Seattle had built for the purpose in the fall of '59. with necessary provisions from their stores. This was the beginning of Seattle's great outfitting business of today.

In 1860, when the gold excitement was at its height, so many men went to the mines from Seattle that for a time the mill had to close. Luther Collins was one who left for the mines. As was the case in the Fraser River excitement, placer mining made every creek a potential source of gold. Rock Creek near Wenatchee, and Lewiston, Idaho, then eastern Washington, became centers of mining activity. While this gold rush never materialized into a permanent mining industry it did open up eastern Washington to settlement.

Charles Terry's interests at this time included his farm on the Duwamish and his mercantile business in the village. The Terry home in town was a small frame one at Second and James, later replaced by a pretentious Victorian mansion. At this time the Terrys had three children—Nellie May, Betsy Jane, and Edward Lander, the son named after his father's best friend.

The land deal by which Terry had traded his three hundred and twenty acres at Alki for Maynard's unplatted town property had not turned out so well for the Maynards. At their Alki home they were noted for their hospitality. It is said that the Indians camped in such numbers about the home of their "tillicum" that they made him poor with their demands on his generosity. The doctor soon tired of farming and moved back to Seattle. His property at Alki Point, which is today a part of the city and worth thousands, was worth so little that he could hardly give it away. He reduced the price until in '68, according to Prosch, "He found a man who was willing, able and sufficiently courageous to pay him $450 for the 314 acres of land then remaining. This venturesome individual was Knud Olson, known to all the old settlers for his long residence on the Alki place."

A bulwark during these years was Dexter Horton, who. with David Phillips was still conducting a general store at First and Washington. In this store continued a business that led to the biggest banking system in the Northwest. When the mill and farm hands and the trappers and loggers from the surrounding country were paid, they would ask Mr. Horton to keep their money for them. They gave it to him tied in little bags with their names attached. He tucked these moneybags away behind boxes, or more often. in the coffee barrel. Weeks after, perhaps, when someone came back for his money, Mr. Horton would dig around in the coffee barrel until he finally found a little cloth bag, smelling of coffee.

As time went on Mr. Horton found himself more and more frequently the custodian of other people's wealth without the proper facilities for guarding it. Finally he bought a safe. As before, men brought their money in sacks, which Mr. Horton marked and tossed into the safe. If some one wanted to take money out or add to it, a little slip of paper with the amount taken or added was put into the sack.

The greatest drawback to business advancement in Seattle was its continued isolation. "A mania for roads" persisted. The fond hope that the village would have a railroad and a wagon through the Cascades by this time was unrealized. Communication by water had been interrupted by the war. The *Traveller* had continued to do some business afterwards, but had not been dependable. Then in the spring of '58 she followed the other early steamboats to Davy Jones' locker in Puget Sound.

She was succeeded by the *Eliza Anderson*, one of the historic boats on the Sound; but the regular once-a-week service of this vessel was not enough to promote much town growth.

"Yet in those dull and quiet times" there continued to be humble beginnings of business. Henry Van Asselt, who was by trade a skillful cabinetmaker, opened a shop, and found his work in curly maple in great demand. E. A. Clark, who seems to have been a versatile man, opened Seattle's first photograph gallery, his specialty being "ambrotypes."

Each settler found something to do. Dutch Ned continued to pack sawdust in his wheelbarrow filling in the low land about the mill. Lewis Wyckoff ran the village livery stable. Captain John S. Hill with his little stern-wheeler, *Ranger*, did the jobbing on the Sound. Dr. Settle turned to nursing when his professional services were not in demand. Later he went into the clothing business.

All of the pioneers were rich in spirit but poor in pocketbook. Henry Yesler lived in the small house by the mill, and Arthur Denny still occupied his house at First and Marion. How little they realized the turn in fortune that awaited them when the town started to grow subsequently.

David Denny was farming and logging on his claim, but he and his family lived most of the time in their home at Second and Seneca. Around this little whitewashed cottage of three or four rooms they had cultivated quite an orchard and vegetable garden and, of course, a flower garden. In the front yard, fenced in from the cows by a white picket fence, Louisa grew old-fashioned perennials.

Their farm, where the Civic Auditorium stands today, was a tract of open, boggy land, overgrown with swamp shrubs. Inez Denny writes of this rich meadow-land where hundreds of birds gathered, and describes the trips of the children out to the farm with their father.

We went with father in the wagon over the "bumpy" road when he went to haul wood, or perhaps a long way on the county road to the meadow, begging to get off to gather flowers whenever we saw them peeping from their green bowers.

Driving along through the great forest which stood an almost solid green wall on either side we called "Oh, father, stop! Stop! Here is the lady-slipper place!"

These precious memories of a pioneer girl have become the rich heritage of the city of today and transform the thoroughfare out to the Civic Auditorium into a green-walled forest road and a sanctuary for lady's slippers. It is good to know that, sixty years later, when the city dedicated the auditorium, Clarence Bagley placed in the cornerstone a little sprig of sweetbriar, in memory of the sweetbriar bride and her family.

THE BAGLEY'S ARRIVE

When, after ten days of driving, the Rev. Daniel Bagley, his wife, Susannah, and their son, Clarence, came riding into Seattle from Salem, Oregon, in October, 1860, they came like true aristocrats in a buggy drawn by horses. A chariot could have created no greater stir in the village, for this was the first time anyone had arrived on wheels.

It was as if Mr. Bagley, like John Denny, had been destined to become one of the Seattle group. The Bethel party with which Bagley, Mercer, and Horton had crossed the plains, had left Illinois in April, 1852, just a year after the four wagons group had left. After his arrival in Oregon Mr. Bagley had engaged in ministerial and missionary work of the Methodist Protestant Church. In '59 he came to Seattle as an agent of the American Tract Society. Influenced by his old friends, Mercer and Horton, and by the fact that the change of climate might benefit Mrs. Bagley, who was an invalid, he decided at that time to make Seattle his home.

The Bethel party was largely reunited. John Pike, another member, had moved to Seattle a short time previously, and two others, Aaron Mercer and William Shoudy, came soon after. Bagley, Horton, Mercer, Pike — names which were to be inscribed large in the history of the city.

Coming not only from the same state of Illinois as the Denny party, but from the same cultural, religious, and political background, together they formed a group whose characteristics were identical. Whig in politics, anti-slavery in conviction, teetotalers, intellectual, and deeply religious.

Clarence Bagley at that time was a youth of seventeen. In his *History of Seattle* he has described the village as he saw it the day of his arrival. All of the business section was on Commercial Street, four blocks long. "Its northerly end butted up against the sawmill and at the south it jumped off into the Bay at King Street." First Avenue, then Front Street, was water front. All of Seattle was encompassed between Third Avenue, which was the edge of the forest, and the Bay, and between Seneca and Jackson Streets. There were about twenty families and a much larger number of unmarried men, making a total population of one hundred and eighty-two white people.

This youth was to see in his lifetime Seattle grow into a city of over 400,000 population. In the crowd that gathered about the buggy of the Bagleys was another boy who has seen the city's growth to the present time—a red-haired lad of nine, Rolland Denny. These two boys were to see the primitive forest replaced by another forest of tall, towering buildings; the beach, which was then occupied by Indians and their canoes, lined with the docks of a great world port.

The Bagleys rented a house from Henry Adams near the southwest corner of Third and Columbia Streets, the site now occupied by the Chamber of Commerce. A big tree standing in Columbia Street furnished firewood, and when that was gone there was plenty more on the lot now covered by the Seattle National Bank.

Even at that time the settlers were afraid of the Indians. Clarence Bagley remembers how the women would call out to him to be careful of Indians when he set out to hunt in the woods back of the village.

Ever since the departure of the Blaines, the pioneers had been a great part of the time a flock without a shepherd; consequently, Daniel Bagley entered at once upon his duties and held services in "the White Church." He also taught the village school that winter.

He was called upon to perform a marriage ceremony shortly after his arrival. How time had flown! The oldest of the little covered wagon girls, Louisa Catherine Denny, was sixteen on October 20th and five days later was married to George Frye, who was then twenty-five.

This young couple married that day in the little home at First and Marion became my parents. The stories of pioneer days which the girl-bride told in later years became the inspiration for this narrative.

Not only as a minister but as a citizen Daniel Bagley entered at once into town activities. He was just the ally the ambitious young settlement needed. In August before he came, Hillory Butler and seven other pioneers had petitioned the Grand Lodge of Free Masons of Washington Territory for a dispensation to organize a lodge. A charter was granted the petitioners and they became a lodge on September 15, 1860. Bagley at once transferred his membership from Oregon and became active in the work.

But the most ambitious enterprise that the town had ever attempted was one that Bagley and Arthur Denny planned soon after the former's arrival just before Mr. Denny went to the legislature for the seventh time. Let us remind ourselves that these two men were not venerable, as we commonly think of them, but men in the very peak of manhood, Bagley being forty-two and Denny only thirty-eight. The plan they discussed had to do with the location of the territorial university in Seattle.

According to the Act of Congress that had made it a territory, Washington was entitled to a territorial university and had authority to sell two townships of land to pay for such an institution. In each session of the legislature this mythical university was "located" in some town. The location was considered a choice political plum; hence there was rivalry among the little towns of the Territory to secure it, not because they thought that they could handle such an undertaking, or even wanted to try, but because it was a handy thing to trade for political favors.

After its site had been bandied about several times, and none of the settlements had the strength or inclination to proceed with its organization and building, "locating the university" became a joke. It remained for Daniel Bagley to take the joke out of the matter. He conceived the idea that it would be a good thing for Seattle to have it. He talked the matter over with Arthur Denny and said to him. "If you get the university located here at Seattle and have me appointed commissioner with full powers to sell university lands, I will get the buildings so well started before the next legislature that it will be hard to change the site again."

Joseph Foster of Mox La Push, who was also a member of the legislature that year, and Arthur Denny thought it would be an excellent plan to get the university "located" at Seattle and then in a few years trade it for the capital. To quote Joe Foster's own words, "I told Daniel Bagley our nice little plan and he knocked it into a cocked hat in two minutes. He says to me, 'Nonsense, Joe, we'll get the university, and keep it, and I will show you and Denny that a university is better than a capital'." Time has proved that he was right.

When Denny and Foster left for Olympia, they went primed to work for the university. Later in the winter Bagley went down to help them.

While he was away his son, Clarence Bagley, taught the school. For discipline the youthful teacher put the pupils on their honor; but there is no record as to how they behaved. At recess and at noon he went out and played a lusty game with his pupils.

Those attending were: Maria McMillan, Susie Mercer. who was married the following spring to David Graham; Alice Mercer, who became the bride of the youthful schoolmaster five years later; Emma Russell; Lenora Denny; Loretta Denny; Rebecca Horton; Martha Crow; Eugenia McConaha; Gertrude Boren, who continued to live in Seattle with the John Dennys after the Carson Boren home was broken up; Robert Hays, who lived with Hillory Butler and was the son of Gilmore Hays who had crossed the plains with Butler and Frye; John Libby; Rolland and Orion

Denny; Inez Denny; and Clarence himself, when he was not acting as teacher.

Young Clarence became the envy of the village beaux by taking the girls of the village buggy riding in the only buggy in town. There were only two roads to take, one north out to Uncle Tommy Mercer's place and the other south over the ridge of Beacon Hill from which he drove down to Lake Washington where Walter Graham had taken a claim.

Looking back over the history of the United States, one wonders at such interest in establishing a university on the frontier when civil war was imminent. There was lively debate and considerable bitter feeling between the Secessionists and Abolitionists in Seattle in the winter of '60 and '61 when national excitement ran high; but the town was so completely isolated from news of the Civil War with only occasional letters and papers from the East, and the weekly visit of the *Eliza Anderson* its only touch with the outside world, that the excitement could not parallel that of other sections of the country. Their big interest that winter was to win the university for Seattle.

CHAPTER XVII

THE UNIVERSITY

IT WAS NOT difficult to get a bill locating the territorial university at Seattle through the legislature. The legislators did not take the matter seriously. Who would take a university seriously in such a small village?

Journals of the House of Representatives and of the Council for 1860-61 record that on December 12th B. R. Stone of Kitsap County introduced house bill number 17, an act to re-locate the territorial university. The bill passed. On January 10th Arthur Denny introduced council bill number 27, an act to provide for the selection of the lands to be sold for university purposes; to appoint a board of commissioners; and to provide for the selection of a university site.

On the following day this bill was referred to a legislative committee of which Joseph Foster, faithful and eloquent friend of the bill, was a member. This measure was also passed. Three university commissioners were appointed —Daniel Bagley, John Webster, and Edmund Carr. The University of Washington was legally on its way. Nothing had been said about buildings, however, and the commissioners were prohibited from incurring indebtedness.

Bagley and Denny wasted no time. They realized that they must have the lands located and sold, a university site chosen, buildings constructed, and school commenced before the legislators again convened and again changed their minds.

Mr. Denny had offered to contribute the site. Early in February he and Mr. Bagley went out to the northern boundary of Denny's land in the neighborhood of his first cabin at Western and Battery to make the selection. The tract was an almost impenetrable tangle of trees and underbrush. After the two had worked for hours and had made no progress in making a suitable choice, Denny suddenly threw down

his surveying instruments and exclaimed, "Bagley, I'll give
the knoll!" "The knoll" was that part of his claim now occupied by the Metropolitan Buildings in the city blocks lying between Seneca and Union, Fourth and Sixth.

It was no sudden impulse. Denny had thought of the
knoll before as a university site, but had hesitated to give
away what he realized to be the choicest acres of his donation claim. It was not a light gift to be measured by its
value in money at that time. It had cost Mr. Denny more
than money. It had been dearly bought. It had cost him
years of toil, of danger, and of want. He had risked all
that was dear to him for those acres.

Mr. Denny's part of the knoll comprised eight and a
third acres. Charles Terry then came forward and gave the
remaining one and two-thirds acres for himself and Judge
Edward Lander. At that time this tract, covered with gi-
gantic firs, seemed very far out from the straggly little settlement that had been cleared only as far north as Seneca
Street and as far east as Third Avenue.

With the land donated and the site selected, the next
steps were the raising of funds and clearing the land preparatory to erecting the buildings. The commissioners held
their first meeting on Washington's Birthday, and the clearing of the land began on March 1st, although the deeds
were not executed until April.

One is awed by the stupendous nerve of starting out on
the venture with no funds of any kind. The legislature had
made no appropriation and made none for fifteen years. Although there was no money and Mr. Bagley had to borrow
twenty dollars on his own credit for incidental expenses.
the work of clearing the land was pushed with vigor. It was
done by men who afterward became prominent in the town's
history. Nothing was too menial or too big for any of them
to do. John Pike, for whom Pike Street was named, grubbed stumps, drew plans for the buildings, and later helped

in the building. Clarence Bagley little thought that he was helping clear the forest for a university that he would live to see become one of the largest in the United States.

The pioneers made short work of clearing the site. In early May it was accomplished. Dynamite was then unknown for use in land clearing; the stumps were grubbed and pulled, then piled and burned. Thousands of feet of valuable timber were burned to get it out of the way. According to Prosch, the site was cleared at a cost of $3345.

Meanwhile the big task of the commissioners was to select and sell the two townships of land which Congress had granted the territorial university. The legislators had authorized the selection and sale of these lands when the university was located in Seattle, but they had not expected to be taken at their word. According to Grant's interpretation of their action, they put the price of $1.50 an acre on these lands to make sure that they could not be sold, for land could be bought from the government for $1.25 an acre, or could be had for nothing by homesteading it.

But Daniel Bagley chose the choicest pieces of land from the public domain in the vicinity of Seattle that were still unclaimed and put them on the market. What are some of the most valuable sections of the city today, including commercial sites on Lake Union and view properties on Lake Washington, were opened up at that time and sold for $1.50 an acre.

People bought even at the higher price. It was easier to buy direct from the university commissioners than to go to the land office in Olympia, which was then far away. It was not uncommon for a settler to select some good site and then go to the commissioners and buy it. Lumber companies bought land for its valuable timber. Meig's mill bought a tract valued at $25,000.

At first, the men who cleared the university site were paid their wages in school land, as were the carpenters and

workmen. The workman was given a receipt for the value
of work done, and he in turn selected his own land.

The value of this opening up of the land about Seattle
has never been duly emphasized. While the object was entirely to get funds to build the university, it proved to be a
wise civic move in attracting homebuilders and extending
the population to the outskirts of the settlement. Arthur
Denny wrote of it whimsically in after years, "We needed
neighbors at that time more than we needed a university."

Afterwards when the storm of criticism broke on Seattle
for actually having had the temerity to sell the lands, it
was claimed that they should have been saved for an en-
dowment fund. But those young pioneers knew whereof
they acted. If they had not selected the lands quickly and
sold them at once there would have been no university in
Seattle to endow.

Again destiny seemed to play directly into the hands of
the Seattle founders. After his inauguration in March, Abraham Lincoln replaced many Democrats, in federal offices
throughout the land, with Republicans, as the Whigs had
now become. It was natural that he should give an office
to the son of his old friend, John Denny; consequently.
Arthur Denny was appointed to the land office in Olympia
where he became a staunch ally of Daniel Bagley in his
selling of the university lands. It couldn't have happened
more fortunately.

The school lands had sold so well, that by the time the
site was cleared in early May the commissioners began
building. A road for hauling building material was built
from Front Street and Columbia diagonally up the hill
through the forest. Hillory Butler, Thomas Mercer, Josiah Settle, and Lewis Wyckoff did the hauling. On May
21, 1861, the pioneers were ready to lay the corner stone
of the first building.

The laying of the corner stone is a bright, brave picture.

From the little whitewashed town, white against the ever-greens with the blue waters of the Bay sparkling out beyond the people climbed the trail that led up to the knoll. There was some complaining because it was so far out. When they reached the place it was very much in the rough with the smell of soil and burning stumps, and with the deep forest all about that hid the glorious panoramic hilltop view of mountains and water; but they enjoyed the ceremony.

The corner stone was laid near what is today the entrance of the Olympic Hotel. The pioneers were reluctant to spare one of their precious Bibles; but they had to have a Bible in the corner stone; so they put in one that had both Genesis and Revelation missing. Copies of the Declaration of Independence, the Constitution — down to the Twelfth amendment—and the laws of Washington Territory were also deposited. They were too poor to give even a single coin for the customary deposit in the tin box to be sealed in the stone, but they conducted the ceremonies as if they were endowing the institution with millions.

Thirty years later, when the university had outgrown its location and the city crowded too close about it so that it had to be moved, both Daniel Bagley and Arthur Denny were present when the corner stone that was laid on that May day in '61 was uncovered.

While the workers dug out the stone the two founders then white-haired men, amused the bystanders with reminiscences of the early days. Mr. Denny assured them that he remembered the date because it was the day of the birth of his son Charles, and his attention had been divided between the ceremonies on the hill and those at home.

The workers strove hard to dislodge the corner stone. which difficulty gave the two pioneers much satisfaction. "You see," said one, "we did our work well then." At last. imbedded in the mortar, they found a small copper box so tightly sealed that they had to have a blacksmith open it.

Inside was another box just as tightly sealed, and inside that a tin box bright as new.

The contents of this box were examined carefully. When some one asked who owned the Bible with Genesis and Revelation missing. Mr. Bagley confessed that he had furnished it. "Bibles were scarce in those days and that was all we could spare," he said.

"Where are the coins?" said someone, looking for the customary deposit.

"There weren't any," replied Mr. Denny. "They didn't put in any of my money in the box because I had none. Who was flush then? I don't believe that a man in town had money to put under corner stones in those days."

Work on the main building, a president's house, and a dormitory, went on rapidly. Yesler's mill could supply only the rough lumber. The better building material came from Meig's mill at Port Madison, with the exception of the white pine for finishing lumber, which came from the mill at Seabeck.

Stone for the foundations was quarried near Port Orchard; sand was dug from a bank near Third Avenue and Marion Street; lime and brick were brought down from Whatcom by Captain Henry Roeder; and the cement, oils. glass, and hardware had to be imported from Victoria.

Most of the townsmen who were not otherwise employed worked on the buildings. Whatever each knew of carpentry. masonry, plastering, or any of the building trades was made use of. As the work progressed, the sale of school land made it possible to pay the men in money instead of in land.

It was a lively summer. From the knoll up in the woods came the sound of saws and clattering hammers; and from the road that went ambling its crooked way around the big trees on its way to the university site came "Gee!" "Haw!" as the oxen hauled the lumber from Yesler's mill and from the wharf. New people were being attracted to town because of the land sale and the building of the university. It was not a great growth, for national business and immigration were at a standstill because of the Civil War, but it centered much of the business of Washington Territory in Seattle.

The builders made amazing progress. By August the three buildings were well on their way. The main building was 50 by 80 feet, two stories high, and surmounted by an observatory and belfry. To give it a classical touch befitting a great university, the porch was supported by four Ionic pillars. The capitals were designed and carved by A. P. DeLin and Oliver Shorey. Mr. DeLin had worked in the Chickering piano works and was a most skillful craftsman in wood. The fluted columns were wrought by Ossian Carr and D. C. Beatty.

The president's house was 40 by 50 feet, a pleasant home-like building with green blinds and a porch. The boarding house or dormitory, 24 by 48 feet, was a plain, frame building. All of the buildings were painted white.

As if to make sure of the university lest it be taken away, a picket fence was built entirely around the ten-acre "campus." A bell from Troy, New York, was brought around the Horn. The belfry was covered with tin by Hugh McAleer to make it shine. Good water from a spring to the east was brought through hand-bored logs. In his report to the legislature later Daniel Bagley said, "A full supply of the purest of spring water is constantly running, brought a distance of 1400 feet in charred pump logs."

By late fall the buildings were fairly well completed. Where, eight months before, there had been an untouched forest, there gleamed white through the green trees—a university. A miracle had been performed and a handful of men had wrought it.

News traveled slowly in those days, but still word came to the founders of the criticism and disapproval caused by their going ahead and actually selling land and building a university. These were but hints of the storm that was to break soon, mainly about the head of Daniel Bagley.

Having completed the buildings, the founders had to fill them. They had no students and no faculty. However, they decided to use the buildings and open an elementary school for the time being. There was controversy among the townspeople over using the buildings in this way. At a public meeting Henry Yesler objected very vigorously but as he had no better solution, there seemed nothing to do but to begin school with what pupils were available. The point was actually to open school in the buildings which had been constructed. There was derision from many quarters and the university was called "the Seattle High School" for many years after.

After looking about for a teacher, the commissioners decided upon Thomas Mercer's youngest brother, Asa, who had been graduated from Franklin College the year previous, and had come west to join his brother. He was "employed for $200 over a period of five months to teach arithmetic, spelling, grammar, and other essentials." This elementary school received no support from university funds and is not to be confused with the actual opening of the university in '63. Funds were raised by a tuition fee.

This school opened on November 4, 1861, with thirty pupils, and with Mr. Mercer—then twenty-two years old —janitor, principal, and faculty. On that day the children of the village took their dinner pails and school books and went up the hill over the winding road to "the university."

Clarence Bagley was the only pupil advanced enough for a university course. All the others were below high school grade. Again we see familiar names enrolled among the students—Eugenia McConaha; Inez and Madge Denny; Rebecca Horton; Alice and Susan Mercer; Rolland Denny and his brother, Orion; Lenora Denny; Gertrude Boren; Loretta Denny—some of them names that we saw in the list of pupils attending Mrs. Blaine's little kitchen school.

As soon as the legislature convened, Daniel Bagley reported on the building of the university. His report hidden away in old legislative records, is still a document of dignity and simple Biblical beauty. Dated "Washington Territory, Dec. 4, A. D. 1861" and addressed to "Your Honorable Bodies," it enumerates and describes briefly what had been accomplished: how the president's house was on a "good foundation, a brick and cement cellar"; that Franklin Matthias had supplied fifty-four window frames at $5.50 a frame; that they had "cleared (grubbed) and fenced the ten-acre site with a good picket fence with cedar posts and the same is substantially painted"; and that the grounds were sown with wheat and blue grass.

The report that "We have sold 20,524.7 acres at $1.50 per acre, making $30,787.05" must have startled "the honorable bodies" most.

In closing, Mr. Bagley said:

We began in April without one dollar. We have done the work specified above. We have never dishonored an order. We have kept clear of debt as required by law, and have not had any serious accident or misunderstanding. Have endeavored to do our duty and no more. That we have not erred in judgment is too much to hope.

This splendid report did not stay the storm of criticism. In fact it was too good a report. That the land should never have been sold and that Seattle was no place for a university were the complaints.

Opposition to the university was led by Mr. B. C. Lippincott, superintendent of instruction in the Territory. Mr. Lippincott said that the whole procedure had been hasty and ill-advised and demanded that an investigation be made.

But there was a peacemaker in the legislature, John Denny. Like Henry Clay, his contemporary Kentuckian, Mr. Denny did much to stem hostility. He had been elected to the legislature that year, and was now chairman of the committee on education. He agreed that the best way was to send a committee from the legislature to Seattle to investigate. Accordingly a committee of five, including Mr. Lippincott, was chosen.

Taking its cue from Uncle John Denny, Seattle prepared for a cordial reception of the committee and decided to make the date of their visit the day of the dedication of the university.

With grim determination to investigate, the committee approached Seattle, but as their boat sidled up to Yesler's wharf they were greeted with stirring strains from the newly organized Seattle Brass Band. It was disconcerting. The music was in honor of their coming. The leading citizens were there to greet them. They were escorted importantly up the hill to the university where it was explained to them that they were to have a part in its dedication.

What could the committee do but respond graciously? Even the weather combined with the band to win them over. Prosch says, "It was the last day of the year; the sun shone unclouded. It was warm and pleasant and all felt cheered and good." A bountiful lunch prepared by the ladies also had its cheering effect.

At the dedication ceremonies young Asa Mercer made an eloquent address and Mr. Lippincott was asked in the name of the honorable members of the legislature to respond. He complied with an eloquence to match Mercer's. Mrs. Suffern played the melodeon.

A somewhat irrelevant memory of my mother's was of a long prayer offered by Mr. Bagley. The welcome sound of "Amen" at the close was followed so soon by the firing of a cannon that it always seemed to her that Mr. Bagley said in one breath, "Amen, fire the gun."

The committee investigated Mr. Bagley's books and reported to the legislature that the affairs of the new university were being conducted "with commendable economy.

prudence and energy." What was perhaps the most crucial moment in the beginning of the university had passed.

But the storm broke again. Prosch says that there were "several investigations." Due to confusion in the discrepancy between coin value and the greenbacks of the Civil War period it was difficult to keep money accounts untangled, and one committee investigating Mr. Bagley's books found a shortage in his accounts. But another committee made an exhaustive audit shortly after and found instead that Mr. Bagley had cheated himself by about eight dollars.

The legality of Mr. Bagley's selling the land was next called in question. It hinged on the technicality as to whether the lands were "granted" or "reserved." Mr. Bagley was obliged to make several trips to Washington City to have the land sales confirmed in order to make good the warranty of the university. It was years before the matter was settled. During this time he was supported by Mr. Denny in the land office at Olympia, and later—again as if the hand of destiny had directed it—in Congress.

Clarence Bagley says, "During Mr. Denny's term in the land office at Olympia and as delegate in Congress his counsel and aid were of infinite importance to the commissioners and the university."

Of his father, Clarence Bagley writes, "He had for twenty years to suffer an unlimited storm of calumny and reproach because of his connection with the university."

Daniel Bagley's name has come down to us as "The Father of the University," and no title was ever more bravely won. The energy of this splendid man and the business sagacity he displayed in obtaining funds and in starting and then maintaining a university against terrible odds in a town of less than two hundred inhabitants can never be quite appreciated.

After the dismissal of Asa Mercer's five-month session

of the elementary school, Mrs. Ossian Carr was employed
by the town for $60 a month to conduct a primary school
in one of the rooms of the main building during May, June.
and July.

Mr. Mercer set out to drum up trade for the university.
Without any means of advertising other than his own voice
and personality, he paddled all around Puget Sound, from
Whatcom to Olympia, visiting the towns and logging
camps trying to persuade the young people to come to college. As an extra inducement he offered young men the opportunity of earning their tuition by cutting cordwood.

This tour was good advertising for the university. When
it opened in October of '62, again as a private school, there
were sixty pupils, including five young men from Olympia.
three from Victoria, and two from Portland. Mr. Mercer
had arranged with Arthur Denny for the young men to cut
their tuition wood from the land in front of the university
grounds. They averaged two cords on a Saturday for which
they were paid $1.50 a cord.

This wood was sold to Captain D. B. Finch at $2.50 a
cord for fuel on the wood-burning *Eliza Anderson.* Yesler
allowed the university the usual wharfage charge of twenty-
five cents a cord, thus increasing the profit considerably.

Besides helping the students, this woodcutting helped
clear the forest in front of the university buildings so that
they were visible not only to the village but to ships coming
into harbor. Other land was cleared and soon the reproach
that the university was "too far out in the woods" was removed.

Although the school had started out briskly in '62, it did
not continue to prosper. Just why is not quite clear. Victor
Farrar says, in his history of the university printed in the
Washington Alumnus, that it "rapidly declined." He also
speaks of Mercer as being ill and of some insubordination
among the pupils.

Whatever the reason, the school closed its second session on March 12th and Mr. Mercer declined the position of president. The commissioners began at once to look for a new president and to plan to open the university on a higher basis.

On September 7, 1863, it was opened formally "by authority of law and under the direction of the Regents," with William E. Barnard, a graduate of Dartmouth, who had recently come west from Massachusetts, as president. Lizzie Boise was preceptress. Tuition charges a quarter were: primary, $6; academic, $8; and collegiate, $10. It can at least be said that the curriculum was far-reaching though in the wrong direction.

In '66 President Barnard was succeeded by the Rev. George Whitworth, who had moved to Seattle from Olympia because of his interest in the development of the coal mines near by.

The new seat of learning was well started, but in the succeeding years its light flickered alarmingly at times. It never went entirely out, however; although the university was actually closed at different times. Just how hopeless and discouraged the people were about the situation is shown by an advertisement to lease the institution that appeared in Washington, Oregon, and California papers in April, 1868:

This institution embraces ten acres of ground, well cleared and fenced; the University building proper, president's house, boarding house and out buildings, with a good supply of running water. It is pleasantly and healthfully situated in Seattle, W. T. Proposition to lease it as a sectarian institution will not be entertained.

Fortunately no one responded. In '69 the university was opened again under the presidency of John H. Hall, a graduate of Yale.

Perhaps no chapter in the history of Seattle is better illustrative of the staying courage of the far-seeing pioneers than the building of this university and the carrying on through those lean, hard, Civil War years when business was slow and the Territory was poor—carrying on for fifteen years before receiving any legislative aid. Yet from the first this struggling school identified Seattle and gave it its first definite gain over rival towns. Seabeck, Port Madison. and Utsalady were all more important than Seattle until the university was built. A quotation from the San Francisco *Bulletin* of that period illustrates how the university identified our early city. It will be noticed that it was necessary to locate Seattle in its relation to larger towns.

Seattle is situated about equidistant between Steilacoom and Port Townsend on the east side of Puget Sound. It has three or four stores, one sawmill and about 200 inhabitants. The only attraction of the place and the object of general comment is the University which has just been completed. It is a fine building located on a beautiful eminence and commands a grand view of the Sound.

The efforts of the pioneers were ably supplemented by a self-sacrificing university faculty. Salaries had to be paid from the tuition fees and these were not sufficient to support the teachers properly. For many years the number of the faculty was limited. Its status throughout the struggling years is aptly illustrated by a story told of Professor O. B. Johnson, who was connected with the university from '82 to '94. President Eliot of Harvard once asked Professor Johnson what chair he occupied. The latter replied, "I don't know what chair you would call it, Mr. President. I teach zoology, botany, physiology, psychology, physics, astronomy, and—"

"Oh, yes, I see," interrupted President Eliot. "You don't occupy a chair; you occupy a settee."

So faithful men, and women too, gave of their services unstintingly, keeping alive the feeble school by their untiring efforts.

For thirty years the university stood on the site known today as "Metropolitan Center." For thirty years its bell pealed forth not only to summon the young to school, but to summon the town to important meetings, and during dense fogs to enable ships to get their bearings. It became a beacon, literally and spiritually—a beacon of education on the Northwest frontier. Many still remember it with love and smiles.

When the university outgrew its ten-acre campus it was moved to its present commanding site on Lakes Union and Washington. There four fluted pillars stand arrestingly. classic and white, in the green beauty of the sylvan theater. These columns of the first building, placed by the class of 1911 on the campus of the new university on the fiftieth anniversary of its founding, stand out as a reminder of those other days, and of those other men who brought the institution into being. And those men, how far their candles have thrown their light! Ere the flames flickered and died other candles were lighted and other candles—on down through the years.

I wish that a March of Tribute might be a feature of commencement week; that each member of the Senior class would lay a flower at the foot of each stately white pillar. as a tribute to the men who gave us the university and to that first little class of thirty. A step out of the beaten track; a moment of time, a single flower; it is not much to give in acknowledgement of the wealth received. One flower in honor of Daniel Bagley, that man of wisdom, who dreamed a dream and first conceived the idea of the university for Seattle; one for Arthur Denny, whose efforts and generosity helped make the dream come true, and for Charles Terry and Edward Lander, who completed the land donation for the site; one for Asa Mercer, first instructor, who, to the dip of his paddle, sounded the call to the young people; and a fourth in honor of that first little class who heeded the boatman's call, and led the way through the corridors of the university out into the world where thousands now follow. A step—a thought—a rose—it is not much to ask.

CHAPTER XVIII

NEWS OF THE CIVIL WAR came slowly to the people of Seattle. When the eagerly awaited news did arrive on the *Eliza Anderson,* it was months old. Still the pioneers' interest in the war was intense, and was whetted by the very scarcity of news. In his *History of Washington* Snowden says:

> While the people were too depleted by the Indian War and too far away to participate actively in the Civil War, the feelings and sympathies were very keen and often partisan. It was so strong at one time in Seattle that the opposing factions would hardly trade with one another, the Unionists being on one side and Copperheads on the other.

This account of their partisanship is borne out by Clarence Bagley who remembers that Mercer, Bagley, the Dennys. and Dexter Horton, Republicans, were decidedly opposed politically to Yesler, Maynard, Terry, and Plummer, who were Copperheads, as Southern sympathizers were called.

During the Civil War the women of Seattle made another flag—this time not in the blockhouse but in Yesler's Pavilion. Asa Mercer, who was the moving spirit, bought the bunting and cut out the stars. The belles of Seattle— many of them "Mercer Girls"—rallied around the colors and basted the stripes and sewed on the stars by hand. Mrs. O. C. Shorey and Mrs. Dexter Horton loaned their sewing machines and did the stitching. Mrs. Shorey remembers that the flag was "forty feet long and the stripes so wide that the bunting had to be pieced and every stripe had to be stitched twice." As the workers sewed they sang "The Star Spangled Banner" and "Rally Around the Flag, Boys," but, according to Mrs. Shorey, there "wasn't a boy in sight. they were all out getting a tall, straight tree for a flagstaff." They found just the right tree for the pole. It was 120 feet high and was erected near Yesler's mill about where the Totem Pole now stands.

When the flag was finished and raised some of the Secessionists cut the rope and let the flag down, but a nimble-footed sailor climbed the pole and soon had the colors flying again. Later when a prominent Democrat died, his admirers raised the flag at half-mast. This time the Unionists cut the halyards. The Democrats thereupon hired Billie Fife to climb to the top and rig a new rope—a fine sailor feat for which he was well paid—and the flag was flown at half-staff. This flag was burned in the Seattle fire of 1889.

The King County Rifles, a military company of the young Whigs of the county, was formed in the early days of the war ostensibly for protection against the Indians but actually for defense of the Union, if needed, in the Northwest. Hugh McAleer was captain and Clarence Bagley one of the officers.

This partisanship, however, was a party feeling rather than any fundamental difference of belief concerning slavery. It was not bitter. The Northwest settlers were too far from the national struggle for that. Their common danger and common problems served to draw them together. It was through the years of the Civil War that they accomplished some of the biggest community projects.

The attitude of the people of Washington Territory is best interpreted by Professor Meany, who says:

*While the majority of them adhered to the Democratic party, their democracy was fundamentally different from that in the East, and especially in the South. Every time the question of slavery arose the people of the Northwest spoke and acted in favor of free soil and against slavery. They would continue as Democrats but not pro-slavery Democrats.

The Republicans of the Territory gained some ascendency with the election of President Lincoln. Another local appointment besides the appointment of Arthur Denny to the land office was that of Christopher Hewitt, who had led the volunteer forces in the Indian War. Mr. Hewitt had prac-

---

*From *History of the State of Washington* by Edmond S. Meany. By permission of Macmillan Company, publishers.

tically given up the practice of law and was engaged in mechanics, including the making of oxbows; but, as it is told, a brief of his on a case in admirality reached the Supreme Court of the United States and attracted so much favorable comment that Lincoln, finding this young Washington mechanic legally and politically qualified, gave him the post of Chief Justice of Washington Territory.

The appointment of John J. McGilvra, of Illinois, as United States Attorney of the Territory was also of much local interest. Mr. McGilvra did not come to Seattle to live until three years after his appointment, but from that time on he was one of the most active townsmen.

President Lincoln did not make an immediate change politically in the Seattle post office. In '61 Plummer, who had been postmaster for over seven years, was succeeded by Timothy Hinckley, another Democrat. But Mr. Hinckley had no store in which to have a post office, and soon resigned in favor of Samuel Coombs of the same political faith. At that time the postmaster received only twelve dollars a year for his services; consequently, the post office had to be a casual adjunct of some more paying business. Mr. Coombs had a small notion store in which he acted as notary public as well as postmaster. In '63 the President appointed a Republican for the position. Gardner Kellogg, who had come up from San Francisco in the spring of that year, took office in December, and conducted the post office in his drug store.

President Lincoln's approval of the Northern Pacific Railroad was cause for rejoicing in 1864, when the road was chartered and given a land grant by the government. The railroad for which Governor Stevens had surveyed was actually to be built from some point in Wisconsin to Puget Sound. They had no way of knowing that building would not begin until 1870.

Throughout this Civil War period a new organization—the Seattle Brass Band—literally played a vital part. Al-

though this band played its first tune in the early spring of
'61, its actual origin was much earlier than this, for it had
been the dream of George Frye for years.

When Mr. Frye returned to his cabin from work, and
silence and darkness closed down on the little village, his
thoughts turned back to his home in far-off Germany, where
there had been a wealth of music. Under the spell of the
great primitive forest, there awoke in him the urge for
musical expression. He had broached the subject in the old
cookhouse, but the Indian War had interrupted any plans
he may have had. But in 1860 the idea developed into a
definite organization. Twelve young men without much
knowledge of music sent to San Francisco for music and instruments, hired a teacher somewhere, somehow, and began.

After the day's work, when the sawmill was hushed for
the night, the pioneers heard weird sounds while the enthusiastic musicians practiced. Their zeal was great and in
a remarkably short time they were playing Yankee Doodle.

The Seattle Brass Band performed a real service to the
community. It tooted on every possible occasion. As we
know, it doubtless did much to put the university investigating committee in an amiable mood.

Years ago the pioneer band played its last tune. The
leader's cornet has long been silent, and still lies where he
laid it, so modest, small, and mute. Who can say that a note
once breathed ever dies? Perhaps even now the notes of
that first backwoods band, too faint for earthly ears to hear.
are still in the air, mingling with the music with which Seattle now abounds—with the strains of its Symphony as
they radiate north, south, east, and west.

When the news of the firing on Fort Sumter reached Seattle, weeks late, a meeting was held in the unfinished university building to show territorial sympathy with the Union. The band was there with Yankee Doodle. There was

singing and prayer and Daniel Bagley read the fifty-eighth chapter of Isaiah with the stirring call "to loose the bands of wickedness, to undo the heavy burdens, and to let the oppressed go free, and that ye break every yoke."

That evening there was a mass meeting, *probably* in Plummer's hall, and the pioneers organized themselves on the Union side. The band, which did much to give their patriotism proper expression, again played Yankee Doodle. and later a new acquisition to their repertoire—Nellie Gray. Then there were speeches by the orators of the day.

This was the decade of noble oratory, of debate, of spelling matches, and singing schools, and Seattle was not lacking in these endeavors. Hanford writes of this period:

John Denny, Judge Hewitt, Jasper W. Johnson, and Ira W. Utter were strong in debate. Denny had been a member of the Illinois Legislature contemporaneously with Lincoln. Johnson was an ambitious young lawyer and Ira Utter was a college man, living as a hermit, except when he came to the village for necessities, news, and opportunities to be heard in debate. In his cabin in the forest he had a collection of classical books and he kept his voice trained by reading good literature to his cows, who were very patient listeners.

Although Ira Utter practiced on his cows, John Denny was the orator who never came off vanquished, his ready wit succeeding when other means failed. A story is told of a debate between Mr. Denny and a young lawyer from the East, who was on the opposite side of the political fence. The young man made a brilliant speech; then Mr. Denny took the stump. He opened with a few well-chosen words espousing his side and then suddenly raising his voice and pointing his long, lean forefinger at his opponent exclaimed: "And no little huckleberry lawyer can blind us to the facts!" The "huckleberry lawyer" turned scarlet, the audience roared, and the debate was won.

In the university the teachers were all Unionists. The pupils sang "Rally Round the Flag," stamping their feet vigorously at the word "down," when they came to the phrase, "Down with the traitor and up with the stars." Some of the pioneer children used one of the available sour apple trees in the village to hang in effigy "Jeff Davis on a sour apple tree."

As the war progressed, the Democrats of the Territory, under the leadership of Terry, Plummer, Joe Foster, and Thomas Russell, formed a branch of the Union Democrats and held a convention in which they strongly denounced slavery. They were so strong in their stand that the Republicans, not to be outdone by the Democrats, had to make a still stronger statement of their opposition to slavery.

There was considerable fear in the Northwest lest the English to the north might join the Southern cause. In 1859 this danger seemed very acute and as the war progressed, it did not lessen. The dispute over the San Juan Islands was more bitter than it had ever been.

One of Seattle's closest contacts with the arena of war was John Denny's trip to Washington City. Someone was needed to help Daniel Bagley in the interest of the university, and who could be more persuasive than John Denny?

His meeting again with Lincoln was characteristic of both Thinking to test Lincoln's memory, Mr. Denny joined the line that was greeting the President. When it came his turn. he simply shook hands and was passing on when his old friend called out, "No you don't, John Denny. You come around here and we'll have a talk after a while."

The two friends sat and talked and laughed over old times. Doubtless they recalled the time back in Illinois when they had broken a quorum and defeated an anti-Whig measure by jumping out of the window of the committee room when the Democrats had locked the door.

When Mr. Denny returned from "the States" he made a strong impression on his granddaughters with the silk hat he wore when he walked up from the dock. As far as I know this was the first silk hat in Seattle. Worn by this tall, sil-

ver-haired old gentleman, it brought Washington City quite
a bit nearer.

One of the saddest events of the war to the people of
Washington Territory was the death of their first governor.
After being governor, Mr. Stevens had been elected delegate to Congress from the Territory. Until he enlisted in
the war, he brought all of his tireless energy to bear upon
getting the Northern Pacific Railroad through the Snoqualmie Pass. While his death was sad, it was of such a nature
that it made the Territory rejoice in his bravery.

It was at the Battle of Chantilly where, as Major General, he was riding at the head of his troops bearing the
colors which he had taken from the color bearer who had
been killed, that the former governor met his death—in the
same gallant manner that he had lived his life.

"He was a Democrat and I was a Whig," said Arthur
Denny, "but he paid the supreme sacrifice and I have only
praise for his memory." That was the way all felt who disagreed with him politically. His death caused the most pro-
found sorrow throughout the Northwest. It was said that
President Lincoln had intended to place Major Stevens at
the head of the nation's army.

The Territory had a personal interest in several others
of the leaders of the war: General George B. McClellan;
Generals U. S. Grant and "Phil" Sheridan, each of whom
had been stationed at Fort Vancouver; and General George
E. Pickett, who had been stationed at San Juan Islands when
he heard that his beloved Virginia had seceded from the
Union.

By the fall of '64, telegraphic communications had been
established between San Francisco and Seattle, and some
news of the war came that way. News of Sherman's march
to the sea was one of the first items received. The following
spring came the sorrowful news of the President's assassination.

The university bell was tolled; flags were hung at half-staff; and an appropriate memorial service was held. No one was so shocked and saddened as John Denny. He was in the habit of going each day to visit Lyman Andrews in his little coal office, and Mr. Andrews wrote afterward that on this occasion the door opened with none of Mr. Denny's usual alacrity. Slowly he entered and sat down, the picture of sorrow. The two sat silent until Mr. Andrews spoke of the tragedy. Then, unable to restrain his grief any longer, the old gentleman buried his head in his hands and cried as if his heart had been broken.

Early in '65, when his term as registrar of the land office was about completed, Arthur Denny was elected delegate to Congress from Washington Territory. His opponent, oddly enough, was James Tilton, who nine years before had removed Mr. Denny from the command of Company A.

Feeling, caused by the assassination of President Lincoln. ran high at the time of the election on June 5th, resulting in the first big victory for the Republicans in the Territory. However, it had not been an easily won victory. One has only to read the territorial papers of the period to learn that there existed echoes of the strong war talk of the East.

All through the campaign the Seattle *Gazette*, Seattle's first newspaper, waged warfare on the Copperheads. Until the election, "ARTHUR A. DENNY, UNION CANDIDATE," headed their editorial column in bold type like a challenge.

Nor was the *Gazette* lacking in the forensic eloquence characteristic of the period. "Come out from among the Copperhead gang and touch not the slimy reptile," was the editor's appeal to Union Democrats. They were assured that if they voted for Denny, they would vote for an honest man and a true Union sympathizer, but that Tilton was "the most consummate blockhead in the country."

In the thick of the campaign, the *Gazette* reported, "The Copperheads are industriously circulating that Mr. Denny is in favor of negro suffrage and equality, which is one of the numerous falsehoods invented by the Copperhead organ in Olympia."

According to the papers, Mr. Denny was kept busy making speeches throughout the Territory denying immoderate sympathy for the negroes. The rival Olympia papers, the *Pacific Tribune* and the *Washington Democrat*, kept up a steady firing back and forth on the same issue.

It was also reported in the non-Union papers that Asa Mercer, who was at that time East on the second expedition of "the Mercer Girls," was intending to bring back a shipload of negroes, and that *that* had been his *real* reason for going to New York.

Selucius Garfielde, of Olympia, used his silver-tongued oratory in favor of Denny's candidacy and made forty speeches throughout the Territory. This was a remarkable record in those days of long distances and slow going.

When the Union ticket finally won with a large majority, the *Gazette* came out with the headline, "LUCIFER FALLEN"; that in the *Pacific Tribune* read, "THE TERRITORY REDEEMED. GLORIOUS ELECTION RETURNS."

The *Gazette* declared it to be as great a victory to the Territory as the fall of Richmond was to the nation and continued, "Washington Territory is redeemed. King County is all right and the world progresses."

And then the *Gazette* ends with a grand flourish:

Mr. Denny is elected by nearly two-thirds of all the votes cast for delegate to Congress and the Legislature is strong for the Union in all its integrity and for the constitution as it was, is, and as it may be constitutionally amended by the voice of the people. Vox Populi! Vox Dei!

A NEWSPAPER AND A WAGON ROAD

Before the close of the Civil War, Seattle had a newspaper. It was not much either of news or of paper, but it chronicled the war for the pioneers and it boosted their civic ambitions and enterprises. The newspaper followed the establishment of the university; a town energetic enough for a university was unquestionably ripe for a newspaper.

From Bagley, Grant, and Prosch, all newspaper men, we get delightfully humorous descriptions of this first newspaper and its editor, J. R. Watson, or "Our Ollapod," as he was called and as he referred to himself. Bagley described him as a typical newspaper man of those days who was editorial writer, reporter, business manager, and mailing clerk all in one, besides being a capable printer who could set type, run a press, make up forms, and make a roller.

After conceiving the idea of a newspaper for Seattle, Mr. Watson cannily printed sample copies in Olympia on the historic old printing press, the Ramage. Olympia, being at that time a vastly more important place than the little sawmill town, Seattle, had had a newspaper for some time.

The samples took. Much encouraged, Mr. Watson immediately went about establishing a plant here. In August of '63 he began printing the Seattle *Gazette* in Olympia, and on December 10th first published an edition in Seattle. Mr. Yesler furnished the office for the little paper free of charge, and helped in other ways to get it started. The *Gazette*, which was supposed to be a weekly but really came out only when there was sufficient news to warrant an issue. consisted of four pages, each having nine and a half by fourteen and a half inches of printed matter .

Its first copy was not too ambitious nor did it claim to be. It stated editorially that although it was "not as big as a barn door or the London *Times*," it was the best that could be offered. But the little newspaper had a mission; later when the first telegraphic message came into Seattle, there was a newspaper in which to print it.

At one o'clock on the afternoon of October 26, 1864, a cannon was fired to celebrate the completion of the Western Union Telegraph line to Seattle. Up to this time the "news" had consisted of sections of a New York paper, which came irregularly by way of the Isthmus of Panama and thence by steamer to San Francisco and Portland. From Portland it was taken by pack train or wagon to Olympia, and then by boat to Seattle.

The day before the completion of the telegraph line to Seattle, the news was flashed from New York to Kansas City, then from Kansas City to Portland on the 25th, and from Portland to Seattle on the 26th that "A courier from the front reports Price in full retreat, closely pursued by our forces," and that "Sherman was pushing Hood and was rather trying to coop him up in the valley and starve him to death."

When this first dispatch, bearing its Civil War news. reached Seattle, this little paper on the very outpost of civilization was thrown into feverish activity, and lost no time in issuing its "extra" under the title of the *Citizen's Despatch*. As each war dispatch came, Editor Watson, who had no bank account and little credit, was at his wit's end to get money to pay for the telegram. At last he worked out a plan, which, though rather uncertain and sketchy, worked fairly well. It was this: when some important news came over the wire, the telegraph operator would hunt up Mr. Watson and tell him that there was "important news." The editor would then bestir himself and go around to various liberal citizens and collect "two bits" apiece until he had enough to pay for the telegram. Then he would rush to his office, set up the type and run off a copy of "an extra" for each subscriber. Later the same news would appear in the *Gazette*. So with the aid of a young Indian as roller boy, the *Gazette* came out from time to time, and also an occasional extra, and both were received with great admiration and affection by the little town.

Interesting and temperamental as the *Gazette* and "Our Ollapod" were, even more interesting and romantic was the historical old printing press, "Ramage," on which the paper was printed. Not only was the first newspaper in San Francisco printed on the old "Ramage," but the first in Portland, in Olympia, in Seattle, and in the State of Washington. Now venerable with age, it rests as one of the most cherished relics in the museum of the University of Washington.

In the first issue printed in Seattle, the *Gazette* exclaimed: "We want roads, bridges, wharves, school-houses, churches, printing presses and population!" And then it went on to emphasize the need of roads, saying that the people of Puget Sound might "secure a share of the travel which now passes around us on every side."

Judged by our standards of today the *Gazette* was a funny little sheet and "Our Ollapod" spent far too much space on facetious personalities. Grant describes the editor as witty and full of humor, as one who soon became

the central figure of a coterie of jovial spirits which congregated on "the sawdust" or gathered nightly in the editor's sanctum or at the "Gem" or some other place with a bar, a large red-hot stove, a score or more of chairs with rawhide bottoms, and sawdust covered floors.

But "Our Ollapod" and his paper still had an important part in helping the village with its ambitious program of "roads, bridges, wharves, school-houses, churches, printing presses, and population." Quickly sensing that the big desire of the townsfolk was for roads, especially one through the Cascades, the *Gazette* seized upon that topic as something to live for, and began a campaign to that effect. It was encouraging to the pioneers to see their need for a road through the mountains in eloquent print; consequently in the summer of 1865 they held another of their famous "mass meetings." Congress was too busy with the Civil War to help them—very well; they would help themselves. They must have a road!

While "Uncle John" Denny with his eloquence, and Henry Yesler with his popularity went about soliciting funds, Lewis Wyckoff, Arthur Denny, John Ross and William Perkins set out on a very determined exploration of the passes through the Cascades "for the purpose of finding a more favorable line for a wagon road than that by the Cedar River pack trail."

The mountain pass followed by their first pack trail. which they had built the year before the Indian War, had been called the Snoqualmie Pass, but was not the real Snoqualmie Pass. The explorers went out to Jeremiah Borst's place in the Snoqualmie valley and proceeded from there.

Mr. Denny writes, "We could find only one Indian. Chief Saniwa, who had ever been through." The old chief. a Klikitat described as "a very dignified Indian, small but very erect with an exalted idea of his own importance," would not make the trip, but gave directions to two young braves who accompanied the party. The chief encouraged the explorers by telling them that this pass was lower than the pack trail.

With their Indian guides, Denny and Perkins, accompanied by Borst, set out on foot and for three days went through a trackless wilderness where no white man had ever been before. When they joined Ross and Wyckoff who had come by the old trail with the horses, they announced the discovery of a better pass, the Snoqualmie Pass that we know today.

The solicitors for funds raised $2500. After the exploring committee returned with its report, a contract for building the new road was given to William Perkins, who left Seattle with a force of twenty men. When he returned in November they had opened twenty-five miles and intended to finish in the spring. It was a road of terrific grades but still a road. In October a train of six wagons came over it.

That fall Arthur Denny set out for Washington City. From the most primitive wilderness, surveying for roads, he was within a few months presenting a bill in Congress to provide for the construction and improvement of roads in Washington Territory. In the record of his work as reported in the Congressional Globe, roads were his chief interest and formed the bulk of the memorials presented by him from the legislature.

After the winter storms and spring freshets had done their worst, the people of Seattle realized what a tremendous undertaking the maintenance of the road was, for trees were blown across the road, bridges destroyed, and grades washed out. Not only was the condition of the road itself discouraging but it ended at Lake Keechelus, a beautiful lake with mountains towering near the water's edge on all sides. Here the traveler had to face the problem of loading wagons and horses on a log raft and poling across the lake. If the day was sunny, and the waters smooth, it did not seem such a formidable task; but reaching this lake on a stormy day was anything but cheerful and made even the stoutest heart fearful.

Nothing was done to the road the next summer. The mighty Cascades did indeed loom up as an impregnable barrier between Seattle and the rest of the world. The pioneers had made a determined onslaught and seemed to be defeated. But they did not know defeat. This time they attacked not the mountains but the legislature, and in 1867 a bill was passed appropriating $2,000 on condition that King County raise a like amount. Again the citizens called a mass meeting and again they sent John Denny and Henry Yesler with the young lawyer, John McGilvra, to solicit funds. This time the road actually went through. Arthur Denny says, "We took up the work where Perkins left off and opened the road to a connection with the Cedar River pack trail at the foot of Lake Keechelus." In the fall two men came over from Umatilla. Grant says:

Even at that late date the Kittitas Valley was an almost unknown region and the Umatilla men described its scenic beauty and natural fertility and salubrity with all the enthusiasm of fresh discoverers and the Seattle people listened in the same spirit.

The road had broken down the barrier between the region east of the mountains and the Puget Sound country. For the first time they were really aware of each other. J. E. Wyche, district judge, came over the road that fall on his way from Walla Walla to Port Townsend, thus making the tie even stronger. Not only that, but when he passed through Seattle he told of having met surveyors in the mountains who were surveying for the Northern Pacific Railroad. The spell of the ten dark years that had followed the Indian War was now broken. The little town was again up on its toes with excitement over a railroad through their famous Snoqualmie Pass.

The road became a subject of general public attention everywhere. The governor, Marshall F. Moore, gave it serious attention in his annual message and urgently recommended a mail route between the Sound and the Yakima and Walla Walla Valleys. Arthur Denny writes:

Thus at last after years of effort, was accomplished a work which had been a favorite enterprise with the people of the middle Sound from its first settlement. The road was far from good, but it was, at the time, a great work, considering the means available to accomplish it, and though poor, it served to open up direct communication with the country east of the mountains.

These quiet, conservative sentences—characteristic of Mr. Denny, who was not an orator like his father, but reserved in his expression—written years later, convey something of the importance of this accomplishment. It marked one of the important milestones in Seattle history. More important than the actual road itself was the fact that they had at last conquered the Cascades. Today when we motor so easily through Snoqualmie Pass over the broad Sunset Highway. or speed by the electrified trains of the Chicago, Milwaukie. St. Paul & Pacific Railroad, we may know that our privilege to cross was won by the infinite faith and courage and hard work of Seattle's founders.

There was to be more labor, more surveying, more legislating, for the building and maintaining of the Snoqualmie wagon road was a problem that came up all through the early years. The pioneers not only built the road but struggled to make it permanent. In 1875 we find Mr. Yesler sponsoring the "First Grand Lottery of Washington Territory," the proceeds of which were to go for the improving of this road. The old handbills show the startling item of "First Prize, The Steam sawmill and mill property, valued at $100,000.00." Tickets to this unique lottery were sold. but before the "grand distribution" the whole thing was declared illegal and consequently ended.

This lottery seems a strange way for a town to raise money. Although it failed, it shows how hard pressed the settlers were for money and how keenly they felt the need of a road. It is all a part of what makes one of the most determining chapters in Northwest history.

CHAPTER XIX

THE MERCER GIRLS

As a child, I remember my mother's speaking of "the Mercer girls." This one was a "Mercer girl," or that one was a "Mercer girl." So many of her friends were Mercer girls that I remember thinking what a large family of girls Mr. Mercer must have had. It was years later before I really understood that the story of "the Mercer girls" was like a chapter from *To Have and To Hold*, only in the case of "the Mercer girls," the ladies came of their own volition after hearing Asa Mercer discourse eloquently on the wonders of the West; for it was the first instructor of our university who was responsible for this interesting and romantic chapter in the history of Seattle and Puget Sound.

In following the history of Seattle we have seen that one of the pioneers' most serious problems was the lack of white women in the settlement. Snowden speaks very gravely of the Territory's need for "more ladies." Both Mr. and Mrs. Blaine mentioned this need of marriageable women repeatedly, and deplored the conditions that caused the existence of the squaw man.

It will be remembered that as early as '58 Charles Prosch wrote stirring editorials in the Puget Sound *Herald* of Steilacoom on the virtues and values of good wives. That year he wrote:

There is probably no community in the Union with a like number of inhabitants in which so large a proportion are bachelors.

And again in '59:

Here is the market to bring your charms to, girls. Don't be backward but come right along, all who want good homes in the most beautiful country and the finest climate in the world.

These editorials encouraged ninety-six bachelors to call a meeting to form some plan to encourage the emigration of marriageable women to Puget Sound.

We smile when we think of those ninety-six earnest young

men trying to find a way to bring girls and women to the Sound that they might have homes. Most of the men kept bachelor quarters in their cheerless little cabins; many of them prepared their own meals—hurried affairs of salt pork and potatoes—and awkwardly sewed on their own buttons. They sorely needed good cooking and women's care. They knew it. They admitted it.

After several meetings and much talking nothing definite was done. It remained for young Asa Mercer, full of ideas and ambition, to actually accomplish something. His elder brother, Judge Thomas Mercer, who had realized the need for a number of years, doubtless influenced young Asa; but it was the imagination and venturesomeness of youth that carried out one of the amazing expeditions of western history.

The plan for importing women sounded simple. Mr. Mercer was to go to New England to persuade young women, many made fatherless by the Civil War, to come to Puget Sound as school-teachers and seamstresses. However, money was needed to carry out the plan. He went to Governor William Pickering and to the legislators but received no financial help, for the treasury was empty. All approved of the idea however.

Undaunted, Mr. Mercer went from place to place collecting money to pay his expenses to Boston, with the same resourcefulness and energy that he had evinced in his work for the university. The unmarried men hailed him as a public benefactor and gladly contributed until in the fall of '63 he was able to be on his way.

"Our Ollapod" of the Seattle *Gazette* treated the matter a bit humorously at first and exclaimed, "Bachelors bring out your boiled shirts!" At that time the editor, campaigning for the promotion of coal mining, said he had "coal on the brain," but when the matter of importing women came up, he wrote that he had "calico on the brain." It is very noticeable though that the jokes ceased as the project matured, and by the time the girls arrived, the *Gazette* published the news in a serious and dignified vein in a prominent position.

On reaching Boston, Mr. Mercer went to Lowell where he delivered an address in which he pictured in glowing words the attractions of Puget Sound—the climate; the abundance of fish, game, and berries; the fertile land to be had for the taking. He told of the financial advantages. especially for women, because of the scarcity of music teachers, school-teachers, and dressmakers. He said nothing about marrying the bachelors.

Mr. Mercer's pleasing personality, his oratory, his wonderful description of the land of plenty, and the opportunity to make their fortunes in a new country appealed to some of the women. The cotton mills in Lowell had been silenced by war, affecting general prosperity, and the prospect of economic advantages carried weight. Eleven well educated and accomplished young women came west with Mr. Mercer by steamer to San Francisco by way of the Isthmus and then by sail to Seattle.

Arrangements had been made in the village to care for the newcomers at the hotel the first night, and a reception at the university was planned for them the following day. But keenly as "the Mercer girls' " arrival was looked forward to, it finally came as an anticlimax in the night when the pioneers were sound asleep. They had no wireless to inform them when the casual sailing vessels might arrive.

The girls had been obliged to come from San Francisco to Puget Sound on the lumber bark *Torrent*, bound for Port Gamble. There they boarded the sloop *Kidder*, which arrived at Seattle at eleven at night on May 16, 1864. Did any wakeful, young bachelor hear the sound of the ship's chains and know by the beating of his heart that "the Mercer girls" had arrived? We do not know.

The arrival lacked something of the glamour that the girls had pictured for themselves, as, led by a smoky lantern, they stumbled through the dark on their way to the DeLin House at the corner of Commercial and Main Streets. But the next morning left them with no doubt of the cordiality of their welcome.

The village was early astir. "Asa Mercer and the girls are here!" the word went quickly round. Immediate preparations were made for the public reception to be held that afternoon at the university.

Most of the girls were from eighteen to twenty years of age. A few were younger, the youngest being sixteen. The girls could not have fallen into safer hands. They were from good New England homes, many of them prepared to teach school.

Modern versions of their reception which picture bachelors clamoring boisterously to meet them are not true to the historic fact. The very scarcity of women increased respect for them, and bachelors, long denied the company of women, were bashful and came into their presence with twirling thumbs and much embarrassment.

The meeting at the university on that happy, spring day in May was called to order by no more appropriate host than the gallant Dr. Maynard. A prayer for their health and prosperity was offered by the Rev. N. Doane, who followed it with a speech in which he hoped, in the good Victorian manner, "that blessings may attend thee and prosperity crown thy every effort." Asa Mercer was extended a vote of thanks and given a rousing cheer to which he responded in the elegant phrases of the day.

The newcomers were soon made welcome in the different homes until they could find positions in the fall. Everything possible was done to make them happy. That summer was Seattle's first gay, social season.

To the accompaniment of melodeons and parlor organs

the summer evenings were made sweet with singing as the lusty bass of young bachelors mingled with the girls' soprano. Sewing bees and quilting parties, picnics, and old-time balls were given in honor of "the Mercer girls" that summer of '64.

The Misses Josie and Georgia Pearson were accompanied on the trip by their father, Daniel Pearson. Mr. Pearson sold shoes which he had brought with him from Massachusetts in King and Pierce Counties for a time, and then procured a position as light keeper at Admiralty Head on Whidby Island, a position he filled for thirteen years.

Before the summer was over a number of the girls had found positions as teachers.

Josie Pearson began teaching in what is now Coupeville on Whidby Island, but died suddenly soon after. Her sister also taught on the island and then became assistant light keeper at Admiralty Head. Three years later she was married to Charley T. Terry, a prominent Whidby Island pioneer.

Mrs. Pearson came on the second Mercer expedition with her fifteen-year-old daughter, Flora, who later wrote an account of the expeditions. This account has furnished us with many valuable details of these trips.

Although Mr. Mercer did not stress the loneliness of many bachelors when he was enumerating the charms of the Northwest to his listeners in Massachusetts, the real motive of his experiments was fulfilled. Few of those girls who began teaching continued long as teachers. It is interesting to read the names of the fortunate men and the brides they won: Sarah Cheney, who taught at Port Townsend, was married to Charles Willoughby; Antoinette Baker, who taught in Pierce County, to Mr. Huntington of Monticello; Aurelia Coffin to Mr. Hinckley of Port Ludlow, where she had taught for some time; Kate Stevens to Mr. Henry Smith, a customs inspector of Port Townsend; Kate Stickney to Walter Graham, whose first wife, Eliza Mercer, had died the year before; Sarah Gallagher, who had remained in Seattle where she taught music and also taught school in the university building, to Thomas Russell, whose first wife, Susan Crow, had died; and Annie Adams to Mr. Robert G. Head, a printer of Olympia.

Ann Murphy was the only one who did not remain in the Territory. Lizzie Ordway never married. She succeeded Josie Pearson in the Whidby Island school for a time and in 1870 became Seattle's first public school teacher. She also taught at Port Madison and later became superintendent of schools in Kitsap County.

So successfully did "the Mercer girls" fill the need of the Territory that Asa Mercer was quite the hero of the day. He was nominated by the Union Republican party as their candidate for joint councilman for King and Kitsap Counties and was elected by a large majority. According to his own account he was elected without being obliged to spend a nickle, make a speech, or buy a cigar or a drink of whiskey for anybody. This smart filip in the local paper may have helped in his cause:

Mr. Mercer is Union candidate for joint councilman for King and Kitsap counties and all bachelors, old and young, may on election day, have an opportunity of expressing through the ballot box their appreciation of his devotedness to the cause of Union, matrimonial, as well as national.

On all sides the young crusader heard praise of his undertaking, which created in him a desire to go on another expedition bigger and better than the first. Early in '65 Asa Mercer was again on his way East.

THE SECOND "MERCER GIRLS" EXPEDITION

When Asa Mercer started out on his second expedition it was with the express purpose of laying his plan before Abraham Lincoln. He wrote afterwards, "Having sat upon Lincoln's lap as a five-year-old lad listening to his funny stories and knowing the goodness of his heart, not a shadow of a doubt existed in my mind as to its outcome."

So with this memory of Lincoln's kind eyes smiling down at him, the young man stepped off the boat in New York on April 15, 1865. He describes his arrival in a letter which he wrote to Clarence Bagley thirty-six years later:

The steamer arrived in New York about noon and I arranged matters so as to leave for Washington on the morning train. Reaching the hotel office at 6 o'clock crepe greeted me from all sides and a bulletin announced the assassination of the President at Ford's theater the night before. I was at sea without a compass.

If the great Emancipator had lived, who knows but that he would have understood and helped Mercer in his plan to take widows and orphans from the near-impoverished East and give them a better opportunity in the West! The government had ships and seamen left idle by the ending of the war, and Mercer's plan was to ask the President to use these in the transportation of the women to Seattle.

Although left "without a compass," Mercer soon found his direction and went to "the most talked-about and seemingly most popular man and politician in the country"— Governor John A. Andrews of Massachusetts. The governor was taken with the idea and introduced Mercer to Edward Everett Hale, who was also enthusiastic over the plan, and helped by putting Mercer in touch with other influential people.

Armed with letters of introduction, Mercer went on to Washington where he saw "everyone from President Johnson down the line." While all agreed that it was an excellent plan, no one would take the responsibility of authorizing a ship for such an expedition.

But when Mercer went to General Grant he received not only sympathy but help. Grant knew the situation. He had been stationed at Vancouver Barracks and knew not only the loneliness of "single men in barracks" but the beauty and possibilities of Washington Territory.

Telling Mercer to wait until he returned, this man of action went immediately to interview the President and the members of his Cabinet. When he came back he wasted no words of felicitation but turned brusquely to his aide and commanded, "Captain Crosby, make out an order for a steamship, coaled and manned, with capacity to carry 500 women from New York to Seattle for A. S. Mercer and I will sign the same."

Instead of going to the quartermaster and having a vessel definitely assigned and the order made secure, Mercer did very much what impetuous youth of today would do; he rushed off to New York to get the girls to go on the ship which General Grant had ordered.

Bagley writes of this choice of young women:

Letters had been received in the eastern homes of the members of the first expedition, telling of their warm welcome and good treatment and of their success in obtaining positions. No doubt they also made mention of the delightful Sound climate and the beautiful scenery of the Pacific coast. Their contentment and the fact that every promise made them had been fulfilled, gave more confidence to the second expedition. No trouble was encountered in enrolling hundreds of names but the selection was made with such great care that upon investigation many applicants were refused. Western territory had known of the shipment of young women from the slums of London to the colonies and they and their authorized agent, Mr. Mercer, showed great tact and prescience in being firmly determined that the future generations of Washington should have the best parentage possible to obtain. None but women of high moral character were considered, many were cultured and well versed in the good New England methods of home making and housekeeping.

In three months' time a sailing date was set. On July 23rd, Mercer wrote to the *Gazette* in Seattle the following letter, which arrived in the middle of September:

On the 19th of Aug. I sail from New York with upward of 300 war orphans, daughters of those brave, heroic sons of liberty whose lives were given as offerings to appease the angry god of battle on many a plain and field to perpetuate freedom and her institutions. I appeal to every true, warm-hearted family to open wide the door and share your home comforts with those whose lot is about to be cast in your midst.

At the prospect of feeding and lodging three hundred young women, the village was appalled. Where would they put them? To be sure, beds could be made on the floor, but where could they get enough quilts to go around, for they had hardly enough for themselves?

The tone of the *Gazette* is anxious but it rises nobly to the occasion. While it questions the propriety of Mercer's bringing so many women, it adds:

> Be this as it may they will soon be here and depending upon our citizens for homes. They have strong claims upon our sympathies and . . . . . come to us unprotected orphans of the heroes whose lives were freely given for our country's salvation. The graves of their natural protectors now roughen the battlefields of freedom. We, on this distant shore, enjoy the fruits of their valor and sacrifices but we did not share their sufferings, toils and dangers. We are called upon by every emotion of gratitude and sense of duty to protect and provide for their children.

A meeting was called for September 16th and the Rev. Daniel Bagley, who served the community in so many offices, was made corresponding secretary of a committee to make arrangements, and C. C. Terry, treasurer. Copies of the editorial in the *Gazette* were sent to all communities in the Territory; also a circular letter, which said in part:

> We cannot now stop to question the propriety of Mr. Mercer's action. Humanity and patriotism alike call upon us to make their condition as comfortable as possible. They may be expected here in a few days hence something must be done without delay. Please report at once how many we may send to your care upon their arrival here.

The towns responded nobly, sending back answers as to how many each one could take. In Seattle a fund for "the girls'" entertainment was raised to which the bachelors contributed generously. Mrs. Yesler was made chairman of a special women's committee. All was made ready—*and then the girls did not arrive for many months.*

While the letter written July 23rd had been taking its slow circuitous way to Seattle, Mercer had run into difficulties. Having secured girls enough to fill the ship, he returned to Washington to have the vessel made ready and turned over to him.

While he waited in line to see the quartermaster general. the man ahead of him so angered the general that the latter was "still black in the face" when Mercer's turn came. He promptly refused to honor the order from Grant. He said brusquely, "There is no law justifying the order and I will not honor it."

The general would not relent and it looked like the end. Weeks passed and just as Mercer was about to give up and return home he received word that he might have the government steamship *Continental* for the sum of $80,000.

Mercer was in no position to raise money, having spent all his funds and borrowed from every available source. In this perplexing hour a man named Ben Holladay came to him and agreed to fit the *Continental* for the trip and carry the passengers to Seattle for a nominal figure if Mercer would turn the boat over to him. He seemed like a friend and Mercer gladly accepted the offer. Mercer was getting transportation for his party and the stranger was getting the boat at the very reasonable price offered Mercer.

Again things were going well until a few days before the time fixed for the departure, when an article appeared in the New York *Herald*, attacking Mr. Mercer and questioning his motives in taking the girls West. It described the men of the Northwest as immoral and profligate and prophesied that the girls would be used for evil purposes.

The article was widely copied and before Mr. Mercer could counteract the story and show his references, it had done incalculable harm. Letters began to pour in from women declining to go on the trip. Mercer went to his erstwhile friend, who was to take charge of the ship, and then discovered that there was what he described as a joker in the deal. The contract called for five hundred girls and now that that number was not forthcoming the contract was void and the usual fare would have to be paid.

Just what Mercer's financial arrangements with the girls were, we do not know. Some of the girls he had agreed to bring for nothing and was largely responsible for most of them. After all his months of complications, the finances of the young man were, to say the least, in a tangled condition. There is one picture of him, hiding below—just before the ship started, when some distraught creditor came on board calling for him.

Mr. Bagley likens him to Dickens' Micawber. One writer compares him to a Don Quixote beating at windmills which he didn't know what to do with after he had conquered them. But with our perspective, we can be thankful that he was not too sensible, else Seattle would have missed the colorful, romantic, and beneficial episode of "the Mercer girls."

One wonders that the ship ever sailed, but on January 6. 1866, at ten minutes past three, according to the diary kept by one of the young women, the *Continental* set sail from New York.

On board were exactly one hundred passengers, including men, women, and children. The size of the second Mercer expedition has been greatly exaggerated and the number of five hundred has persisted. As a matter of fact there were only thirty-six unmarried women, ten widows, thirteen men with their wives and some with children, and fourteen single men. Two babies were born on the trip.

The expedition created considerable interest. *Harper's Weekly* for January 6th carried pictures of ladies in voluminous skirts grouped gracefully about the ship's salon. The accompanying article had apparently been prepared before the attack in the New York *Herald* appeared. One news reporter known as "Tod of the New York *Times*" accompanied the expedition. Apparently he was quite lacking in personal charm, for although he tried to impress the girls, none of them responded.

The party sailed down the coast of South America and then on around the Horn. They were three weeks in passing through the Straits of Magellan. They stopped at the Galapagos Islands and finally reached San Francisco on April 24th, ninety-eight days from New York. Several accounts of this trip on which these one hundred people were crowded for three months in the close quarters of an old-time steamer have been furnished.

One written by Mrs. Flora Pearson Engle—then Flora Pearson—describes the poor fare on the ill-provisioned boat, as consisting of fried salt pork as the staple food accompanied by tea steeped in salt water. She tells how for seventeen days in succession the principal dish at dinner was beans only slightly parboiled.

The most complete account was furnished by Harriet Stevens, who wrote cleverly a day-by-day journal of the voyage, which was printed in serial form in the Puget Sound *Daily*, the successor of the *Gazette*, after her arrival.

After the first storms and seasickness she writes:

As we began to recover our normal condition we began to look about us. With great satisfaction we found that we had a party of intelligent, amiable, sprightly people. The unmarried ladies were mostly from New England and can boast a fair share of the beauty, grace and culture that characterize the best society of that region.

Miss Stevens described the trip through the Straits of Magellan, across the equator and up the west coast of the Americas and speaks of the keen sight-seeing interest of these New Englanders. For amusement she speaks of the games they played: proverbs, and another guessing game, invented by Mr. Mercer, in which subjects printed on cards required the players to talk for five minutes on a subject which was guessed by the others.

Mr. Mercer's responsibilities were also that of chaperon.

When the ship stopped off the coast of South America and Spanish officers came on board and paid court to the young ladies, Mercer had to assert his authority with unmistakable firmness in order to prevent some of the girls from taking up their abode in South America.

Mrs. Engle writes of three married engineers who flirted outrageously. Both she and Miss Stevens tell about the handsome California miner, about whom a group of girls hovered until they were called "the constellation." Miss Stevens explains that this miner was by birth a Virginian but was bred in Kentucky, which facts, together with his handsome appearance, made him quite irresistible. On reaching California, he was the first to point out the Golden Gate, but somehow gave his admirers the slip and was lost to them after arriving in San Francisco.

While "the Mercer girls" had been traveling around the Horn, the story from the New York paper had reached San Francisco, and the girls were greeted by a well intentioned group of people who were there to save them from their fate. Miss Stevens reports one woman as saying, "Of course no respectable women came on the *Continental*." San Francisco women offered homes and protection but the girls continued on to Seattle, for those who sailed were women who believed in Asa Mercer in spite of the attacks upon him. The long, trying trip had only proved to them his honesty of purpose.

Mr. Mercer's description of their arrival in San Francisco, which we also quote from the Bagley letter, furnishes another amusing angle of the difficulties of managing such a trip:

There were many trying and some amusing incidents in connection with the enterprise, one of which, no doubt, even the nervous, active reader of today will appreciate. One of the most enthusiastic supporters of my contemplated "raid on the widows and orphans of the East," as he was wont to call it, was Governor William Pickering. The day before I started to New York the Governor met me, shook my hand warmly and said: "God bless you, Mercer, and make your undertaking a great success. If you get into financial trouble and need money, do not hesitate to wire me and I will give you help.

When I arrived in San Francisco I was broke—three lonesome dollars being my all. With hotel bills of the party to pay and transportation to Seattle to secure the situation was somewhat embarrassing to say the least. Remembering the Governor's promise, I spent $2.50 sending him this telegram: "Arrived here broke. Send $2,000 quick to get party to Seattle." The next day I received a notice from the telegraph office to call, pay $7.50 and receive a dispatch awaiting me. Having but 50 cents, I could not buy the message. However, I called at the office and asked to see the superintendent. Explaining my impecunious state, I told him of the message to the governor, and suggested that he, the superintendent, open the dispatch and see if it contained an order for money. If so, I could pay, otherwise it was the company's loss. He opened the envelope and read, then burst into a hearty laugh, and passed the envelope to me. It was made up of over one hundred words of congratulation, but never a word about money.

Some months before leaving New York I purchased $2,000 worth of agricultural machinery, mostly wagons, shipping them by sail around the Horn to Seattle via San Francisco, where they had to be reshipped. Arriving in San Francisco without any money and having these women on my hands to feed and care for, I rushed to the shipping office, Coleman & Co., and fortunately learned that the wagons and machinery were still in the warehouse in the city. I sold them and got money necessary to pay the transportation of the girls to Seattle.

In justice to Governor Pickering it should be explained that he was not possessed of ample means and had no such sum available as Mercer required. But he was sufficiently interested to call a special session of the territorial legislature and ask for an appropriation of $4,000 for the enterprise. The bill was hotly debated, for the *Herald* story had crossed the continent and the bill was killed.

Getting the girls to Seattle from San Francisco was a problem, for the small vessels that plied between San Francisco and the Puget Sound ports were ill-equipped to carry many passengers. The party had to be divided and the several groups took passage on different barques bound for ports on the Sound—the *Gold Hunter* for Port Madison, the *Scotland* for Port Orchard, the *Vendetta* for Freeport, the

Sheet Anchor for Port Gamble, and the *George Washington* for Seattle.

The first group to reach Seattle arrived on May 11th on the *Anderson,* as the steamer *Eliza Anderson* was usually called. Which vessel brought them to the Sound where they transferred to the *Anderson* we do not know. The next group arrived on the *George Washington* after a sixteen-day trip from San Francisco, with splendid weather. The *Sheet Anchor* was driven south of San Francisco by contrary winds and arrived in Puget Sound the last of all.

In the Seattle *Gazette,* right under a notice of the arrival of one of the contingents, a notice appears of a "social party" which read, "The young gentlemen of Seattle will give a social party at Yesler's Hall this evening. A general invitation is extended."

In the next issue of the Puget Sound *Daily* the party is described with a few stanzas of most romantic poetry in among the prose. It speaks of the collation that was served at the Occidental Hotel after the dance, which closed at twelve. Miss Stevens made the naive comment soon after her arrival that there was much more of comfort and refinement than she had expected.

The stir and gayety caused by the arrival of the young ladies was welcomed by the pioneer women. It was a great treat for them to hear news from the States and to see the latest styles in the pretty clothes—it was a breath of the old life "back East."

Criticism of Asa Mercer had reached Seattle from "the public prints," as the Puget Sound *Daily* had it, and the young man was given a chance to defend himself at a meeting in Yesler's Hall. "Turn out, everybody, and hear the other side of the question," the friendly local paper urged.

Daniel Bagley presided, and "the Mercer girls" turned out to show their faith in the man who had sponsored their trip. Mercer explained how every paper from "leading pictorials to penny-a-liners" had assailed him. His speech entirely convinced his audience of his sincerity, "the presence of the fair sex" doing much to aid his cause.

Under date of July 15th, there appeared in the *Daily* the notice of a marriage performed by Daniel Bagley— that of Asa Shinn Mercer and Miss Annie E. Stephens of Baltimore. Cupid had done effective work on the ocean voyage, for four marriages resulted.

The newcomers soon found their places in the community and some of them became the territory's school-teachers as the first group had. Most of them married and all of them entered upon the privations and hardships of pioneer life without complaining.

The uplifting and stabilizing effect of this emigration of New England women to Puget Sound cannot be overestimated. Their influence was felt throughout the state. From these two groups of women, known as "the Mercer girls," sprang many of Washington's most substantial families. In more recent times when President Hoover picked a man from the West in choosing men from the nation to form the famous Wickersham Committee he chose a son of one of "the Mercer girls."

Of them Clarence Bagley remarked simply, years after, "Not one of the Mercer girls ever went wrong." And Asa Mercer wrote in his letter about them:

> The young ladies comprising the party were selected with great care, and never in the history of the world was an equal number of women thrown together with a higher average of intelligence, modesty and virtue. They are now going into the sere and yellow leaf of life with, as a rule, sons and daughters risen up to call them blessed. I have drifted away from them, but I know that their influence upon the State has been, as a whole, for good. God bless them and theirs.

CHAPTER XX

ROADS, bridges, wharves, schoolhouses, churches, printing presses, and population"—those things which the *Gazette* made a plea for—along with other advancements—began to take definite shape in the Sixties. The discouraging years following the Indian War were being succeeded not by any sudden growth, but by a strong, steady progress.

The settlement of Seattle had never had agricultural possibilities nor were her citizens farmers; but she adjoined a rich agricultural district. In June of '63, the King County Agricultural Society was formed with Christian Clymer, a farmer at Black River—now Renton—president, and Dr. Maynard, secretary.

In the fall a first modest agricultural fair was held, which was succeeded by a still more ambitions one the following year. At this time horses, cattle, and pigs; fruit and vegetables; and the women's handiwork were exhibited in the Yesler-Denny Hall. Mrs. Maynard won prizes for her cookery; Mrs. E. W. Smithers and Mrs. F. M. McNatt for their fine pats of butter. The pioneers continued to marvel at the size of the vegetables grown in this lush Northwest. Jacob Maple's apples, which measured seventeen inches around and weighed about two pounds each, elicited much comment.

In January of '65 Seattle became, by act of legislature. "the town of Seattle." We must never again speak of her as a village. The first trustees were Charles Terry, Henry Yesler, Hiram Burnett, David Denny, and Charles Plummer. The first ordinances levied a municipal tax, provided for wooden sidewalks on Front Street, forbade "reckless and fast driving through the streets," and prohibited swine from running at large within the town limits. Any offending swine was put into a hog pound and released only after his owner's payment of one dollar for the marshal's fee, four dollars fine for each animal, and fifty cents a day for the offender's lodging and board.

The town grew so fast that in '69 the legislature granted it a more expansive form of government with a mayor. Seattle's first mayor was H. A. (Dick) Atkins.

The first water system was inaugurated in 1865 when by legislative enactment Charles Terry and Henry Yesler were given the exclusive privilege of furnishing water in the town. As most of the people at that time had their own wells in their back yards, it was largely vessels and places of business that needed to be supplied.

This water supply came from the springs in the hill back of the town and was distributed through V-shaped flumes elevated above the streets high enough for vehicles to drive under. Old pictures of the Yesler home show these flumes. Later Yesler supplied water through hand-bored logs, which system operated until 1886.

No better record of the growth of the town at this time can be found than in the news items and advertisements appearing in the Seattle *Gazette*. They are: "D. Horton Staple and Fancy Dry Goods"; "Cheap Cash Store, Charles Plummer"; and "Yesler, Denny & Co. Seattle Lumber and Flour Mills." Gardner Kellogg's advertisement for his drug store occupies a prominent column with its "golden balsam" and "sarsaparilla" and the "best brand of coal oil." Coal oil, a great luxury in the 60s, appears very prominently. It could be had for "50 cents a quart in bottles or $1.50 a gallon." Mr. Kellogg also carried coal-oil lamps, some with reflectors and other elaborations. Charles Terry's Eureka Bakery is advertised; L. V. Wyckoff's Livery Stable; the Woodin Tannery; Shorey & Libby's tiny millinery, which also did dressmaking and carried ladies' furnishings; and a new venture that announces that "The new photographic establishment of E. M. Sammis is in full blast."

Fortunately photography came early. We can almost trace

the history of Seattle and her citizens by these quaint pictures. They form a record that cannot be exaggerated, nor disputed. Precious old daguerreotypes by E. A. Clark and photographs by E. M. Sammis are among the cherished possessions of this generation. Seattle in her metropolitanism dare not grow haughty or we will turn the pages of the family album and show her humble beginnings.

One advertisement reads, "John Welch, tailor, Commercial Street, Seattle, W. T. The old soldier once more in the field." (He had been in the Mexican War.) "The old soldier" advertises cashmeres and vestings and the latest styles with full satisfaction assured, and urges the pioneers to "Give him a call." Bagley remarks that he would have fared poorly had it not been for the patching that the unmarried men in the town needed.

"The Eureka Bakery," selling as "Cheap as the cheapest," announces a cracker machine that is warranted to turn out all types of hard breads and crackers. This bakery became quite an institution. It was taken over later by George Frye, and still later in '71 by William Meydenbauer, who ran it famously for years.

The university runs a large advertisement in each issue outlining its courses in primary, academic, and collegiate. The strict standards of conduct which President Barnard tried to enforce on the frontier are clearly set forth. The students must read the Bible, observe the Sabbath, attend church, and not attend "balls, saloons and theaters."

One of the most significant advertisements is that of Dr. Maynard's hospital—Seattle's first hospital—opened in 1863 in the Maynard home with Dr. Maynard as superintendent, surgeon, and physician, and Mrs. Maynard as nurse, and also in charge of a lying-in department. This hospital performed a much needed service in ministering to injured loggers and men from the sawmills and ships. The Maynards at this time occupied the old Felker house which became the first hospital as well as having been the first hotel.

There was much gossip in the *Gazette* about the comings and goings of the ships, especially the *Eliza Anderson*. No history of Seattle would be complete that did not mention that little, old steamboat, which now arrived twice a week. In March of '64 the editor tells us that "The propeller. *George S. Wright* called in at this port Monday evening last. The *Wright*, *Libby*, and *Anderson* were all at the wharf at the same moment giving quite a business air to the harbor."

The *Libby* and the *Wright* subsequently became rivals of the famous *Anderson* and also household names at every port; but the *Eliza Anderson* retained first place for some time, charging high prices when she could and lowering them when competition compelled her. The fare to Olympia was usually about $6.50, to Port Townsend $12.50, and to Victoria $20.

Just as the sailing vessels had been the pioneers' only means of contact with the outside world, so were these first little steamboats. In '65 a mail route was established with Whatcom. The boat stopped at such important points as Mukilteo, Tulalip, Coupeville, and Utsalady.

Freeport came into prominence during the early sixties when a large, new sawmill was built by J. R. Williamson across the bay near Duwamish Head, and with wharves. shipyards, a store and dwellings made the beginning of what is now West Seattle. It became a busy port and sometimes there would be four or five ships at one time loading lumber for foreign countries.

As the town grew it gradually adopted the social customs of the Sixties with church socials and patriotic celebrations. As early as '64 it had grown to the dignity of a regular Christmas celebration held in Yesler's Hall, with a tree and a Santa Claus that looked like a Santa Claus. I think Mr.

Yesler was the good saint on that occasion. Trinkets such as Seattle stores could not furnish were procured in Victoria and in Olympia. When at last the curtain was drawn aside there was the tree shining in the light of homemade tallow candles and festooned with strings of popcorn and local cranberries. The town loved its children. A few years later it held a more elaborate Christmas entertainment in the university with speaking, a tree, and a program.

In '67 Seattle even had a circus, the Great Western. I record with pride in the pioneers that no one stayed home on the day of its performance.

Yesler's Pavilion became the meeting place for town "doings." Yesler had put the pavilion up as a temporary place for a Fourth of July celebration in the lower end of his orchard at the corner of Cherry and Front Streets, but decided to finish it, since there was frequent need of a large meeting place. For years this pavilion was the scene of every type of gathering just as the old cookhouse had been in its day.

At all functions there was the Brass Band, still the pride and joy of the town. It was one of the few bands in the Territory for a number of years and played its gay tunes at celebrations from Olympia to Victoria.

A distinctive work in the reclamation of tidelands at the mouth of the Snohomish River was being done at this time by Dr. Smith. Dr. Smith was a student, as well as a poet and physician. He was much interested in the way Holland had reclaimed tidelands and followed the same method here. His articles telling of the seventy-five acres he had reclaimed appeared in the territorial press. It was largely through his influence that the people of Seattle later did much in reclaiming acres of land which form the present industrial sites of the city.

While at the mouth of the Snohomish, Dr. Smith conducted an infirmary. He was the only physician for five counties, traveling about in an Indian canoe to remote logging camps. Later he was appointed physician for the Tulalip Indian reservation. He also owned and managed many logging camps himself. His widely useful work was not so closely identified with Seattle as Dr. Maynard's but he likewise did invaluable service as a pioneer doctor.

AN OPPORTUNE INDUSTRY

But with all these things—"roads, bridges, wharves. schoolhouses, churches, printing presses, and population"— there was still one thing lacking in Seattle—an industry. Furthermore, all this time while the pioneers were trying to find out what to do next to keep things going, they always had the all-abiding faith that some day the railroad would come to Seattle. This prospect only added to their need of some substantial industrial development. Meanwhile what could they do?

The university had given dignity and distinction to the town but it had not assured its economic stability. The sawmill, its first means of support, had long since been supplanted by mills nearer to accessible timber. Farming could not be depended upon, for, though the land was rich in the surrounding region, most of it was covered with timber. and the clearing of it so difficult and tedious that Seattle could not hope to make shipments of farm produce and become an agricultural center for a long time, as Portland, encircled by her wonderful valleys, had done from the beginning.

It was a critical time. If steps had not been taken when they were, again Seattle might have continued as an obscure sawmill town "at the mouth of the Duwamish."

In looking about, coal seemed to be the solution. Coal had long been known to exist in the Puget Sound country. It will be remembered that in '53 Dr. Bigelow had discovered coal on his donation claim on the Black River, a mile or so

from the present Renton mines, and that there had been
some development which was destroyed by the Indian War.
No further attempt had been made during the ten years of
desolation following the war.

In '63 the second coal excitement occurred when Lyman
Andrews discovered coal on his donation claim on Squak
Lake, the lake that is known to this generation as beautiful
Lake Sammamish. One day Andrews came trudging into
town with a sackful of coal on his back—a significant incident, for it was not by luck that Seattle's coal industry was
developed, but by back-aching effort. Andrews took his coal
to the blacksmith shop of W. W. Perkins, who tried it in
his forge. Finding it good, Mr. Perkins gladly went into
partnership to mine it.

The *Gazette* became highly excited over the venture and
from that time until it ceased to be was enthusiastic about
the local development of coal. As we know, "Our Ollapod"
admitted that he had "coal on the brain." If publicity could
have mined coal, the *Gazette* would have accomplished it.
It even published a diagram showing exactly where the new
Northern Pacific Railroad would run in relation to Squak
Lake and the mines.

But the pioneers needed more than publicity; they needed
capital, for the unsolved question of transportation handicapped the miners just as it had handicapped Seattle from
the very first. So nothing came at that time of this project
which years later became the profitable coal industry at
Issaquah.

The next discovery of coal was made in '63 by Edwin
Richardson, who was surveying on the eastern side of Lake
Washington, and accidentally uncovered a bed of coal on the
bank of Coal Creek, now known as Newcastle. A minister
in Olympia, the Rev. George Whitworth, became interested
in this coal and moved to Seattle. Mr. Whitworth had lived
in a coal district before coming west and was also somewhat

of a geologist. When asked to look at specimens of coal from Coal Creek he recognized its good quality. Daniel Bagley was also convinced of its good quality and became enthusiastic over the value of coal in the development of Seattle; so these two ministers of the gospel became leaders in the economic as well as the spiritual welfare of the town. They became prime movers in the Lake Washington Coal Company organized in '66, to develop this coal.

The other incorporators of the company were Josiah Settle, John Ross, P. H. Lewis, and Selucius Garfielde— the last named being closely identified with the life of Seattle, though his home was in Olympia. Garfielde's eloquent oratory did much to stir the plucky little group of pioneers to some of their big endeavors. Furthermore, he was surveyor-general at that time and it was considered fortunate to have his name among the incorporators because of his influence and prestige.

In far-away Washington City, coal in the Northwest was being championed by Arthur Denny. In that spring of '66 Mr. Denny rose from his seat in Congress and said:

Mr. Chairman. I have noticed in listening to the discussion upon this bill [trade with British America] so far as it relates to coal and lumber particularly, that it seems to be regarded as applying especially to those interests in the Atlantic region of the country. I wish to say that it applies with equal force to the interests of the far-off Pacific coast. In the territory which I represent here, the Territory of Washington, we have an extensive coal field and we are endeavoring to develop that interest. But as the original bill stands we will be wholly without that protection which enables us to do so. . . . . I simply rise for the purpose of stating the naked fact that this bill does interest the extreme Northwest, perhaps equally as much as it does the East and the Northeast.

Work in developing the mine at Coal Creek began. Again coal was transported in sacks on the backs of men, for there was no wagon road. I cannot but linger over that picture of men loaded down with heavy sacks, toiling along the trail for miles through the forest.

The first thing on reaching town was to have the coal tested, so a quantity was given for experiment to the United States Revenue Cutter *Lincoln*, then on the Sound. The coal created such heat that the iron of the smokestack was nearly melted. The captain reported that it was too inflammable to be safe. The two preachers and their associates smiled; and, realizing that coal is valuable in proportion to its burning properties, doubled their efforts and carried an extra load on their backs.

Their troubles were many. First they had to build an expensive wagon road through the forest from the mines to Lake Washington. When that was done the coal was brought by wagon to the lake, then taken across on a barge, and landed on the western shore, near the eastern end of Jackson Street—at a section of the forest known at that time as "Fleaburg"—and then hauled by wagon over the steep hills to Elliott Bay.

This method of transportation was not very satisfactory; so they tried another plan. They constructed a barge, which they named *Good Templar*, and bought a tug, named *Fannie*, and tried bringing the coal into Seattle by the Black and Duwamish Rivers. But the barge grounded in the Black River; then, when they finally got it down to the dock, it was seized by the customs officers for operating in salt water without a license. Clarence Bagley describes the affair humorously as a "little detail which the coal barons had overlooked." He says further, "There was lots of money in coal, they had the coal, but they did not have the capital with which to build the roads, barges, cars, and tugs necessary to transport that coal to the anxiously awaiting market."

"The coal barons" tried to sell their product and arranged with a certain steamship skipper for its sale in San Francisco. He was not reliable and neglected to bring a reply. On hearing that he was on the Sound again and that he would pass Seattle sometime in the night on his way from Olympia back to San Francisco, Mr. Whitworth, Clarence Bagley, and P. H. Lewis rowed over to Alki Point, built a bonfire to attract his attention, and waited there to signal him. All night they watched. Toward morning the ship came in sight and on seeing the signal anchored out from shore, when the watchers went aboard and had their interview. As Bagley remarks, "The steamer was held while the party discussed the coal question, which goes to show that schedules were somewhat elastic in those days."

The interview was disappointing, for the master brought no help or encouragement from outside; consequently, the pioneers had to depend upon themselves again. In 1870 they reorganized the company with Bagley and Whitworth again at the head. A separate company was organized to handle the transportation and to build a tram road and bunkers. Of this project Grant says:

> The usual, old Seattle plan of every man going at it with his own hands was pursued. Everyone who was willing and able to work— and that meant almost all in the village—went out with pick and axe and shovel and crowbar and drove the work. At the end of the season the tramways were constructed, ready for cars.

The new process of transportation seemed even more laborious than the old, for the coal was handled more times from the mine to the bunkers. The cars were loaded at the mines, run down along the tramway to Lake Washington. and taken across the lake on a barge. Then on a portage tramway which ran from Lake Washington to Lake Union, where the Montlake Bridge canal is today. After taking the cars across Lake Union on a barge, they were loaded on the tram rails which led from the south end of the lake to the bunkers at the foot of Pike Street.

But the whole undertaking was more than the promoters could manage financially. Fortunately, now that they had made the effort and Seattle coal had become known, some San Francisco men with capital bought the company out and continued its development. But the Seattle people led by two preachers had first demonstrated their own faith by actual back-breaking endeavor.

The new company put on a small locomotive, called "The Bodie," to operate between Lake Union and the bunkers. "The Bodie" was Seattle's first locomotive engine. The advent of this tiny engine was a big event. The *Intelligencer* of March 25, 1872, speaks of it as "the first locomotive that ever whistled and snorted and dashed through the dense forest surrounding the waters of Puget Sound." When it arrived, the company offered everyone a free ride. As far as I know everybody in town took a ride some time during the first day. "The Bodie" and eight coal cars were kept moving from eleven in the morning until five in the afternoon. the round trip being made in half an hour.

By the end of May in 1872, long trestles had been thrown out into Elliott Bay from the foot of Pike Street and many men were employed in mining and transportation. Large ships were stopping for coal for San Francisco. That year 14,830 tons were shipped. The whole industrial life and atmosphere of the town had been changed, and made vital and enduring. The men who had started the coal project. not for their own gain, but for Seattle's, had accomplished their purpose. They had seen the town through another crucial point.

Now that their coal mines were being developed, the town was all the better equipped to become the terminus for the railroad. News of the definite building of the Northern Pacific Railroad came even as they worked on the coal problem and gave them an added incentive for its development.

Afterwards, when the tram route from Lake Union to Pike Street had been abandoned by the coal company for a more practical one, the rails were still left, making a path through the forest. The opening through the woods let the sun in, and wild flowers seeking warmth and light bloomed along the sides of the track. Here the university students gathered flowers for their specimens in botany. It was their favorite walk, an ideal "Lover's Lane," which it was called. Gathering specimens was a wonderful excuse for a stroll and often, while looking for trilliums, lady's-slippers, and bleeding hearts, a sweetheart was found. Many a pioneer man and maid plighted their troth by the wild roses that bordered the track. There are gray-haired men and women today who remember the old railroad track with tender smiles.

FROM BLACK COAL TO WHITE CHENILLE

One must not picture the town of Seattle as having only "coal on the brain" during the years between 66 and '72. Coal is one picture of the panorama. Let us unroll the other pictures of those years of marked development and try to catch the whir of progress that led all the way from the black coal of the mines to the white chenille of a wedding gown in a real church wedding.

Prominent in one picture of the town was a big, modern hotel—the famous Occidental Hotel, which stood in the triangle formed by James and Yesler Streets, and Second Avenue. Seattle has no hotel today more grand and important than "The Occidental" was to the pioneers. The space in front, now Pioneer Place, became the gathering place for all town doings from political rallies to strawberry festivals. The hotel advertised as furnishing a good livery stable, as today we advertise a garage, and tomorrow a hangar. It had a billiard table. Board was "fifty cents a meal; one dollar per day; six dollars per week."

The hotel was built in 1865 by M. R. Maddocks, Amos Brown and John Condon. Two years later the hotel was bought by John Collins, and the Seattle Hotel which stands on the same site today is owned by the Collins family.

Seattle's first brick building was put up in '68 by Dexter

Horton at First and Washington Streets. True it was only
28 by 72 feet, one story high, and only the front was brick.
but it was called proudly "the brick building" for many
years.

The new firm of Atkins & Shoudy first occupied the building. Two years previous these men had bought the mercantile business of Dexter Horton and David Phillips.

Shortly after selling his store Mr. Horton went to San
Francisco and engaged in the brokerage business in that city
for a short time. In January, 1870, he returned to Seattle
prepared to enter the business life of the town in a much
larger capacity; he brought with him a new, steel safe and
books and papers for a banking business.

In the institutions which the Seattle *Gazette* had listed
that "We want," the editor had not mentioned a bank; but,
of course, the tiny village of '63 had no need of one. The
safe in "D. Horton's" store did very well. But, just as the
safe had taken the place of the coffee barrel to hold the depositors' sacks of money, so the safe grew into a bank. The
story is best told in a booklet which The Dexter Horton
National Bank got out on its golden anniversary:

From this practice [of tossing their sacks into the safe] grew the
habit of depositors taking money from their sacks as needed and
leaving a receipt within for the amount extracted. The evolution was
natural. The business of handling the money grew beyond the bounds
of the facilities of the little store. Horton found himself overrun
with money entrusted to his care.

So in April of the year of Mr. Horton's return from San
Francisco, the bank was opened in a little one-story frame
building at First and Washington with a capital of $50,000.
and with Dexter Horton and Mr. Phillips again as partners.
This was the first bank in Seattle and for ten years the only
bank in town. In 1872 Mr. Phillips died and Arthur Denny
bought his interest in the bank, which then became Dexter
Horton & Co. Quoting further from the booklet:

"Horton and Denny's bank is good enough for me" became the

universal expression among men from Victoria to Olympia. From all parts of the Puget Sound country in the 70's came men to deposit their money with the confidence of Englishmen in the Bank of England.

The story of Seattle's first bank is one of the most fascinating in pioneer annals, not only because of its evolution from coffee barrel to armored vault, but because of the evolution of Dexter Horton himself from a penniless arrival, glad to get work cooking in a lumber camp, working in Yesler's mill on a twelve-hour shift, and teaming for Thomas Mercer part of the day, to the head of the famous Dexter Horton Bank.

The pictures disclosed in the panorama of pioneer Seattle are not wholly those of a model town. It was a frontier town, and as it grew, the distillery, the saloon, and gambling places also arrived. Although it was never a "wild west" town still its "Main Street" south of the mill or "south o' Yesler," was not unlike the business sections of the typical western town of that period. But, fortunately, the town was dominated, not by the saloons "down on the sawdust," but by the steeples and belfries on the hill.

One of the organizations formed to combat the influences "down on the sawdust" was a "Ladies Mite Society," organized in '65, which had for its object the securing of lectures on temperance and other reform subjects. Great was the members' pleasure when they were able to hold their meetings in the "finest home in W. T.," the hospitable home of Mrs. Charles Terry.

The following year a lodge of the Independent Order of Good Templars was formed. The temperance movement was very much in thought at that time. In the first town plat filed by David Denny, still to be seen in the county records, are streets named "Victory," "Light," "Banner," and "Temperance." David Denny, with others, felt very keenly the white man's responsibility in preventing the Indians from getting whiskey. Drinking did more to ruin the Indians than any other thing.

The Good Templars started off with a big temperance rally in Plummer's Hall with an outside speaker, after which they organized with the Rev. Mr. Whitworth as Chief Templar; Rebecca Horton, Vice-Templar; David Denny, Chaplain; and Louisa Denny, Secretary. A hall over "The Brown Church" was prepared for a meeting place.

The record of the lineup of a Fourth of July parade in '68 shows two prominent organizations in the town. The "procession" was led, of course, by the Brass Band, which was followed by the Good Templars and the Free Masons. The chaplain of the day was Daniel Bagley; the marshal. riding proudly on horseback, Samuel Russell; the president of the day's program, John Denny; the orator, James Mc-Naught, a young lawyer just arrived in town; and the reader of the Declaration of Independence, Mr. Whitworth. A salute was fired. In the afternoon there was horse racing along Front Street in clouds of dust; in the evening, fireworks and dancing.

Women were highly respected in this young community. One of the first speakers of national note to lecture was Susan B. Anthony, who spoke in "the Brown Church" in '71. A Female Suffrage Society was formed at that time in which Mrs. Henry Yesler and Lizzie Ordway were very prominent. John Denny and Daniel Bagley were both active supporters of the cause.

In '67, the very year in which the university was necessarily closed for a time, the pioneers expressed their love of learning by forming a library association. Mr. James Mc-Naught was elected president and Mrs. Yesler, librarian. Both Mr. and Mrs. Yesler were active for years in the support of this work.

While this association was primarily to organize a library. and may be said to have been the forerunner of the present library system, it was also of the nature of a lyceum, so popular in those days. The best talent in the Territory was employed the following year to give a series of lectures: Selucius Garfielde; Elisha P. Ferry; Elwood Evans; John McGilvra, who spoke on "Republican Liberty and Government"; and John Denny, whose lecture traced the "Progress of Art and Science."

Seattle had been forearmed in the matter of a university, and although they had supported private elementary schools, had been a bit slow in the matter of public schools. Realizing that they must have a free common school in the town, the pioneers held a public meeting in the spring of '67 to discuss the matter. They voted a tax, and later bought a school site at Third and Marion for $500. By the autumn of '70 the forest had been driven back, and "The Central School"—a two-storied building crowned with a belfry— had been added to the Seattle picture. On an exciting morning the bell rang its gay summons and the town's children trooped up the hill through the stumps to Seattle's first public school. There to greet them was Miss Lizzie Ordway, Seattle's first public-school teacher. So many children came that Miss Lizzie had to turn the younger ones away. Back they trudged with their dinner pails to wait until the second room in the building was ready.

One by one the churches appear in these growing-up years of our city's history. Each denomination made its humble beginning, realizing that "where two or three are gathered together in my name, there am I in the midst of them." In '66 the Rev. Mr. Whitworth who, as we know, had come to Seattle in the interest of the development of coal and then had been persuaded to take over the presidency of the university, organized a small group of the Presbyterian faith. As they had no church building they used "the Brown Church." For a number of years Mr. Whitworth and Mr. Bagley carried out the happy arrangement of preaching on alternative Sundays in this church and of holding Union Sabbath school and prayer meeting. The first Presbyterian church was built in 1876.

In 1865 the Rev. Peter E. Hyland of Olympia established Trinity Episcopal Church with Henry Yesler and Charles Terry as two of the charter members. The members held services alternately with the Methodists in "the White Church" until they could build their own—the little Gothic church at Third and Jefferson Streets, which is seen in all of the old pictures. This church had the first pipe organ in King County.

Two years later a young Catholic priest, Father Prefontaine, came to live in Seattle. He fitted up one room of a tiny two-room cottage—opposite where the County-City Building is today—for a chapel and lived in the other. In order to raise money for a church, this kindly, democratic priest, who, too, becomes one of the pioneer traditions, held fairs all about the Sound, traveling in a canoe, the way of all Seattle pioneers. There were very few Catholics in the town at that time, but every one of the citizens set to work to help the young priest raise money.

The lots on which the first Catholic church was built in 1868, The Church of Our Lady of Good Help, were on the edge of a steep ravine with a creek flowing through where Prefontaine Place is today. The land was covered with monster firs, one being eight feet through. No wonder that it took three months to clear the site for the church.

Plymouth Congregational Church was organized in '69 with the Rev. John F. Damon as its first pastor. Meetings were first held in Yesler's Pavilion and then on alternate Sundays in "the White Church." Arthur Denny, who withdrew from "the White Church," became one of the first members and gave the land for the first church building, which was built in 1873. Traveling about in an Indian canoe. Mr. Damon preached in most of the towns on Puget Sound.

He made many friends among the young people. So many of them came from all around for him to marry them that he became known as "the marrying parson."

In that same year of '69 "two or three are gathered together" in the home of Edward Hanford for the purpose of establishing the First Baptist Church. Both meetings and socials were held in the Hanford home until 1872, when the church steeple went up at Fourth and James.

Although many of our modern churches were organized between '65 and '70, "the White Church" and "the Brown Church" continued to be *the* meetinghouses with alternate Presbyterian and Methodist Protestant services in one and alternate Episcopal and Congregational and Methodist Episcopal sermons in the other; and no one the worse for it.

With so many churches in the little town, there was no staying the next step—a church wedding. The first one was in "the White Church" in '65. The romance dated back to the winter when young Clarence Bagley kept school in his father's absence, and little Alice Mercer, the youngest of the four Mercer sisters, was one of the pupils. The ceremony was performed by the Rev. C. G. Belknap. The bridegroom confessed, over a half century later, that he was afraid the young fellows would laugh at him if he were married by his own father, thus having his marriage ceremony performed free of cost.

When he was eighty-six years of age, Mr. Bagley wrote:

In it [the White Church] all the young folks went to church and Sunday School. Among the children was a little girl who became my wife on Christmas Eve, 1865. She and I trudged through two feet of snow that led around stumps standing in Second Avenue to the little building that was already filled by friends, young and old.

What a pretty picture is unfolded! The lighted church on the edge of the dark wood; the frosty night; the moon on the snow; and the happy voices of young and old. There was no music at the wedding, for, at that time, even a melodeon in the church was considered an instrument of the devil; but there was music as the pioneers returned to their warm, little homes from Seattle's first church wedding— the music of laughter.

Seven years later, the same spring that the little engine "Bodie" snorted and whistled into Seattle with its load of coal, buoying up the men of the town with a feeling of confidence in the future, the women were all aflutter over another church wedding.

Virginia Bell, one of the children that had landed at Alki from the wind-tossed schooner *Exact*, was the bride; George Hall, the bridegroom. From the two-story Boren home. which the Bells had occupied after their return from California, the bride went to be married in the new Trinity Episcopal Church.

The story of this wedding has come down to me as a bit of daintiness in the frontier town. Fortunately, I do not have to depend on memory or hearsay for this fragment of early history, for I have before me a letter written as late as 1928 by that selfsame bride. She tells in this letter that she sent to Victoria for the white silk for the wedding gown. and that a dressmaker just out from New York made it. It was made pannier style, trimmed with white chenille fringe and crystal beads. Of course, the bride had a long train orange blossoms, and a veil and beneath the veil a rose tucked in her hair. Everything else, including the announcements and white silk slippers, came from Held Bros., San Francisco. Truly, if all the world loves a lover, it loves a bride too, for when she opened the box from San Francisco she found a dozen beautiful handkerchiefs and a note of congratulation. One can imagine the flourishes and curlicues and the Victorian phrasing of that note.

The wedding cake was a work of art. Mr. Meydenbauer made it himself. He would not let anyone touch it, but carefully carried it to the house with his own hands. With what pride he presented it, all decorated with cupids and clasped hands.

The town did not have a suitable conveyance for the bridal party; consequently the bride and bridegroom rode to the church in a bright, new express wagon, sitting in state in the back of the wagon on two kitchen chairs. I do not know who was in the driver's seat but I like to think that perhaps it was Thomas Mercer with the faithful Tib drawing them. I can picture the dainty bride in all her wedding finery being carefully and tenderly lifted from her high seat in the wagon. When they arrived at the church they found that everything with four wheels had been commandeered and the church was so crowded that they had difficulty in getting in for their own wedding.

It may have been this very wedding that stirred in the town the desire for a hack, for it was not many years afterward that Seattle had its own carriage, if you please, which is delightfully described by Charles T. Conover in his *Mirrors of Seattle.*

Since my story of pioneer Seattle is concerned with *first* things, perhaps I may be forgiven for transcending the chronological bounds of my story and including the first hack. How grand that first hack seemed as it threaded its way among the stumps and through the mud! How everybody stared at it! And how the small boys gathered around it!

After the advent of this hack, no two couples arrived at a party at the same time, or left at the same time, for each couple had to wait their turn and grandly arrive in state. Poor hostess! Her party was a long time beginning and a long time ending. If perchance it was a dinner, her guests who were first on the driver's list might arrive before she was ready to receive them; or, on the other hand, she might have to wait dinner for those who were on the end of the list.

And oh, the thrill of hearing the carriage roll up to the

door, and hearing the door slam! There was no other sound in all Seattle like it. And the luxury of the upholstered seats! It was like a story book; one could sit back and imagine one's self a princess, and pinch one's self to make sure it wouldn't all vanish at the stroke of twelve. And the young swains! Didn't they think they were doing it right and proper? And didn't the town itself begin to feel its oats? A library—a bank—church weddings—orange blossoms—coal —chenille—and a hack!

CHAPTER XXI

SOME OF THE MOST intrepid pioneers that had served Seattle all through her wilderness years were not permitted to enter the promised land of achievement. Luther Collins, who had gone to a mining camp in eastern Washington Territory— now northern Idaho—was drowned in the Snake River. Soldier of fortune, rough but brave, he had been the Daniel Boone of the Seattle group.

John Holgate, another adventurous soul, who had been the first to explore the Duwamish and the first to discover its value, was led by the same seeking spirit to leave Seattle and follow the lure of mining to Nevada, where in 1868 he was shot in a dispute over a claim.

In August of '66, Charles Plummer died. Bagley says of him, "He ranked with Yesler, Terry, Maynard, and the Dennys in the earliest development of Seattle and its resources." He had been a most active town-builder, a postmaster, and a leader in every event. It was with a feeling of deep bereavement that the members of St. John's Lodge of Masons and his other fellow-townsmen followed his body over the little woods trail that led to the cemetery on the hill north of town.

This was Seattle's first cemetery; David Denny had given the tract. After the cemetery was moved it became Denny Park, since razed to make way for the march of the city. Most of the bodies were moved to what was called the Masonic Cemetery, now Lakeview Cemetery near Volunteer Park. This is the resting place for many of the pioneers.

In February of '67, Charles Terry died. Young he came into the Seattle story and young he went from it at the age of thirty-seven. While he lived he lived abundantly; no one ever crowded more into so few years. Fifteen years before he had landed at Alki and started to build a New York of the Pacific. His vision is being realized today in the city which men are beginning to call "The New York of the Pacific." However, he was much more than a dreamer. His little old notebook in which he recorded the days the pioneers worked loading the *Leonesa* and the list of groceries ordered from Captain Howard is typical of the practical service he rendered.

In among the list of groceries and the record of the sitting hen is a scrap from a poem, which reveals the romantic side of this young Charlie Terry. What was in his heart. one wonders, when he wrote these words of Burns':

"Had we never loved so kindly,
Had we never loved so blindly,
Never met or never parted,
We had ne'er been broken-hearted."

Old Chief Seattle died at Oleman House on the Port Madison Reservation in '66, in the same place where about eighty years before it is thought that he had been born. It will be remembered that Chief Seattle had been baptized by a Catholic priest and had been a faithful Catholic for many years. His funeral, attended by hundreds of white men from all over the Sound, was conducted by a native priest according to the rites of the Church, with Indian customs added. One of his sons delivered an oration at the close of which he drew a photograph of his father from his breast and said these prophetic words:

The white man will not forget him, for here is his picture, made by the lights of the heavens, the older it grows the more it will be prized. When the Seattles are no more, their chief will be remembered and revered by generations to come.

Seattle today can be proud that it was named, not merely for an Indian chief, but for him that was one of the greatest of his race. In his day he had been a great and aggressive warrior, but in age, under the influence of the Church, he had grown benign, and charitable, yet very sad, for he had lived long enough to see the breaking down of his race.

When the town had grown to a city, a group of the chief's old friends, headed by Hillory Butler, Samuel Crawford. and Arthur Denny, erected a monument over his grave at Suquamish on the Port Madison Reservation on which was inscribed.

SEATTLE
CHIEF OF THE SUQUAMPS AND ALLIED TRIBES
DIED JUNE 7, 1866.
THE FIRM FRIEND OF THE WHITES, AND FOR HIM THE
CITY OF SEATTLE WAS NAMED BY
ITS FOUNDERS

On the other side of the monument were these words:

BAPTISMAL NAME, NOAH SEALTH
AGE PROBABLY 80 YEARS

Chief Seattle's death ended a chapter not only in local history, but in the history of the white man's westward-moving conquest.

The old chief left behind him his daughter, Princess Angeline, whose fame was the reflected glory of her father. She became a notable figure. For many years after Seattle became a city, the princess was seen on the downtown streets sitting on the curb, scanning the many palefaces that passed her as she looked for some of her old friends. Though the city crowded around, Angeline lived for many years in her little shanty near the water front—an ugly, untidy, old woman—but she was not forgotten by her pioneer friends who remembered her with presents of food and clothing. She grew to love them very tenderly.

It was Mrs. Maynard who named Angeline. When she first met the young Indian woman, known as the widow of Kick-is-om-lo Cud, or familiarly "Cud," Mrs. Maynard laughed and said, "You are far too handsome a woman to carry that name and I hereby christen you 'Angeline'."

All unsought fame came to the poor old Indian woman. Souvenir spoons and photographs of her have been eagerly

bought by the tourist. In her last sickness she said her prayers to the Socalee Tyee (the white man's God). She was
buried according to her wish in the burying ground of her
friends, where one may see her monument, inscribed "Princess Angeline," beside those of her "hias tillicums," the
pioneers of Seattle.

The old cookhouse was torn down in '66, and this was
like the passing of another old friend. But the town had
outgrown it. It was the last log building in the commercial
part of town and its smoke-blackened walls looked shabby
among the smarter board buildings. It had to go. A fine
two-story building took its place.

But the hearty jokes that were told in the cookhouse lived
on. They are almost as historic as the achievements of the
pioneers. Possibly the most famous of these historic jokes is
one told on a group of territorial legislators who had come
from Olympia to see the town of Seattle. They were to return by steamer early in the morning. When they heard a
shrill whistle, they hurried into their clothes and hastened
in the direction of a light on Yesler's wharf. Carpetbags in
hand, they stumbled through the dark until they were safe
in the engine room. The engineer seemed busy, but the boat
did not start. After waiting a while, one of the lawmakers
asked when the boat left for Olympia. "This sawmill doesn't
run to Olympia, sir," answered the engineer gravely.

The local paper had an indignant editorial on the blowing
of the mill whistle for such a long time at five o'clock in
the morning. Apparently the whistle served as an alarm
clock to waken the mill hands; but blowing intermittently
until it had wakened them, it also aroused the entire population.

In his *Reminiscences of Puget Sound* the elder Prosch
tells a number of these famous jokes and also gives a happy
picture of the sociability of the times in describing his visits

to Seattle. At the approach of the steamer all of the men of the village hurried to the wharf. Mr. Prosch says:

Invariably as the steamer neared Seattle the same familiar faces were seen coming to meet her, Henry Yesler, Hillory Butler, Frank Matthias, Charlie Terry, John Collins and others at the head of the procession. When within hailing distance the salutations commenced with "How are you, Smithers?" and "How are you, Denny?" etc. and continued until all were duly recognized.

This rush of the entire male population to Yesler's wharf was one of my mother's distinct memories. No doubt she chafed at viewing the steamer's arrival from the cabin windows because "nice girls don't go down to the wharf."

Another famous pioneer story was on Dexter Horton. One Sunday Mr. Horton went to the outskirts of the village near Fourth and Columbia to look for a cow that had strayed away. It was a raw, rainy day. Seeing a fire burning under a big stump where someone was clearing land, he stopped to warm himself. Oliver Shorey and Gardner Kellogg, who were clearing the land, had been inspired to use an unexploded shell from the *Decatur*, which they had found, by placing it at the root of the tree to blow it up. They were not in sight when Mr. Horton unwittingly turned his back to the fire to enjoy the warmth. The shell went off with a terrific explosion. Fortunately he was not hurt, but he was humiliatingly disheveled. It was a long time before he could share in the hearty laughs of his fellow citizens over the picture of himself blown up with the stump.

Old Dutch Ned was the butt of many a pioneer joke. After Lakeview Cemetery was established, an idea formulated in Old Ned's mind. He was a canny little fellow and realized that when he was gone there would be no one to mourn him, no near or dear one to lay his body away. He plaintively said, "No one will care for Old Dutch Ned after he is gone." And, though he lived in a shack in life and scrimped along, he was determined not to lie in a shack at death. By the greatest economy he bought a lot in the cemetery and erected a mausoleum—his "house" as he called it.

When his "house" was finished and the grass was all fresh and green in the lot, he had his photograph taken standing at the door. He said when he gave his picture to his pioneer friends, "Old Ned is waiting for the door to open." Then one day he was carried out of the shack that life had given him to his "house" on the sun-lit hill—and the door opened.

Dr. Maynard furnished more tellable stories than any other pioneer. Even in his adversities there was usually a laugh to be found. After he traded his valuable town property to Charlie Terry for Alki his business was never good. For years the Alki property hung heavy on his hands.

Thinking to play a joke on David Stanley of Salmon Bay, the doctor told what a well-stocked farm he had at Alki and offered the old man half the fruit and farm stock for caring for it. Stanley was a man who did not like "crowds." He lived in the wilderness that he might keep himself "unspotted from the world." Dr. Maynard convinced him that his meditations would not be seriously interrupted at Alki; so the old man took his hens and household goods and rowed over. The stock he found, to use his own words, were "an old white horse, stiff in all his joints and blind in one eye; and a little runty, scrubby, ornery steer calf." The green pastures were interminable stumps. logs, and driftwood.

A few days later the recluse appeared at the doctor's office. Plummer was present and he and the doctor leaned back for a little fun when the old man should explode his wrath. Instead he expressed gratitude and enthusiasm and said that his visit at Alki had been a great triumph for religion, that it had inspired him to such heights that he was under obligations to the doctor.

It was not the scenery nor the view he explained in answer to the amazed doctor, but the miracle he had seen. "Nothing," he said, "short of the ingenuity and power of the Almighty could possibly have piled up so many logs and stumps to the acre as I found on your 'farm'."

The joke was on Doctor Maynard. He told the old hermit that he would doctor him the rest of his life for nothing if he would never mention Alki Point again.

At one time the doctor's love of fun nearly got the staid Daniel Bagley into trouble. A young couple who wished to get married sought the advice of Dr. Maynard, their difficulty being that the girl was not yet of the legal age of eighteen. That was a mere trifle to the versatile Maynard. who took two pieces of paper and wrote "18" on each and told the girl to put one of the papers in each of her shoes. He then went with the young people to the parson and assured Mr. Bagley that the girl was "over 18." Shortly after, when the irate parents descended upon Mr. Bagley. he went indignantly to Dr. Maynard, who laughed heartily and explained what he had done.

Seventy years later this young couple, Mr. and Mrs. Christopher Simmons of Olympia, recounted the details of their elopement, laughing heartily as they told them. Mr. Simmons, being a nephew of Mrs. Maynard, knew of the good fellowship of the doctor. When he spirited his sweetheart away, he took her across the waters of Puget Sound from Steilacoom to Alki in a canoe. They landed at two o'clock in the morning, expecting to find Dr. Maynard, but his house was deserted. Again they set out in their canoe and arrived at Seattle at four o'clock, where they found the Maynards then living in the former Felker house.

During his later years, especially between '68 and '72. Dr. Maynard was engaged in troublesome litigation over his right to a donation claim of three hundred and twenty acres. At the time he had taken up his claim in '52 he was not yet divorced from his wife in the East nor married to his second wife. This situation led to much confusion as to his right to claim one hundred and sixty acres in the name of his wife.

Dr. Maynard finally sent for his first wife, Lydia, to come to Seattle to help settle the matter, but in spite of his producing, not one, but two wives, the case went against the doctor and the courts allowed him only the one hundred and sixty acres he himself could claim. As he had already disposed of this amount of land, he was left with nothing.

Sickness was added to his business troubles, but as Prosch writes, "He bore up under them bravely, presented to the public as strong a front as possible, and was as light-hearted, or pretended to be, as ever."

The very last glimpse we have of him, just a year before he died, is characteristic. It was the morning when he expected his first wife, Lydia, to arrive. He stepped into the village barber shop and said, "Dixon, fix me up in your best style." When the barber inquired what was going on, the doctor replied, "I am going to give the people here a sight they never had before and may never have again. I'm going to show them a man walking up the street with a wife on each arm."

Sure enough; when the steamer came in, there was Maynard and his second wife, Catherine, there to greet the first wife, Lydia. The three walked together to his home, where they lived for several months to the surprise and amusement of the public.

On March 13, 1873, he died. One of Seattle's great pioneers —first physician, first realtor, first justice of the peace, founder of the first hospital—generous, romantic Dr. Maynard.

The whole community stopped to do him honor. The funeral was conducted in Yesler's Pavilion. The Brass Band led the way to the grave—the first one in the new Masonic cemetery.

CHAPTER XXII

THE BOOM

IT IS OFTEN said that Seattle has never been a boom city. This is quite true; but the city has had several accelerated periods. The growth that began in 1865 developed by 1869 into a miniature boom, which continued through the year until, according to the Federal Bureau of the Census, there were 1107 people in the town by 1870. To the city of 400,000 this does not seem like a boom, but when we consider that in 1860 there had been only one hundred and forty-eight adults in the town, we can see that it had grown amazingly.

But this growth was more than an increase in population. The early townsmen were like a vanguard preparing for a multitude. There was an expectancy about the town as if the pioneers were standing on tiptoe peeking over the Cascades in expectation of the railroad.

The impetus to sudden growth came when Jay Cooke & Company, then America's foremost bankers, agreed to finance the building of the Northern Pacific Railroad. In 1870, with the $5,000,000 furnished by Cooke, the building actually began.

The construction was to be carried west from Duluth to meet that being built from the Northwest. Until the road could be built through the Cascades, temporary headquarters were established at Kalama, on the Columbia. From this point a road was begun toward a terminus on Puget Sound not then decided upon.

There was not much doubt now of Seattle's being the western terminus. Strangers were in town; buildings were going up; every one was preparing for the railroad, talking of the railroad. Surveyors were working on the Snoqualmie Pass and were making Seattle their headquarters. Sam Coombs changed the name of his hotel to "The Western Terminus," and one place known as "The Connoisseur's Retreat" now called itself "The Railroad House."

In *Harper's Magazine* for September, 1870, there is a description of the Seattle boom in an article entitled "The Mediterranean of the Pacific," written by Thomas Somerville, who had accompanied William H. Seward on a tour of Puget Sound the previous summer. Mr. Seward was then on his way to visit his recent "ice purchase," as the acquisition of Alaska was referred to at the time.

Seattle is described as having gained vitality through the discovery of coal.

and still more during the last few months by the popular belief that it is *the* place—the great terminus. The lands for miles around have been bought by speculators, divided into lots, and auctioned off at Victoria, through the Willamette Valley and even in San Francisco. Nine months ago there were not more than 500 people in it, now there are 1000. . . . . . Seattle lots are offered for sale all the way to San Francisco at prices varying from $50 to $500.

The article goes on at some length to explain how the discovery of the "Snowqualmie" pass had done much to determine the proposed location of the terminus and how an enterprising band from Seattle had explored this pass and found it easier of access than the "Natchez." The writer adds:

Great interest has thus been attached to the Snowqualmie and the people of Seattle regard it as their hope and boast. There is an interesting waterfall 270 feet high on the river about sixty miles from town and with great enthusiasm they treat their friends with a trip to the Snowqualmie falls.

The *Intelligencer,* Seattle's second newspaper—excepting a few newspaper attempts between it and the old *Gazette* —founded in '67, had its beginning in this railroad excitement, and grew with it. Every issue carried headlines about the coming of the railroad.

Of this boom period Grant says:

The demand for houses brought rents up and created such a demand as to make a building boom. Yesler's mill was unable to furnish the supply and other mills were drawn upon. In 1870 the population had risen to 2000 and Seattle was the metropolis of the

Sound basin. The city seemed secure and only waited to have greatness thrust upon it.

Of that year of '69 in which this sudden growth began Bagley writes:

The year 1869 was notable in local annals. During the year the village became a town. Its business more than doubled and its population trebled.

In the *Intelligencer* in September, '69, we read:

Three large stores on First Avenue South which have been built expressly for mercantile firms are now nearly ready. A building on Yesler Way to be occupied by a wagon maker is also about finished.

After naming more buildings, the article continues:

All the above buildings have been rented for some time and many more would be, if they could be obtained. It is likewise the case with respect to dwelling houses, for although about forty have been erected within the past twelve weeks, and several others are in the course of construction, yet there is considerable complaint that none can be had by those who have lately arrived.

The second real estate office—Dr. Maynard's being first —was opened at this time by L. B. Andrews, who had an office on Horton's wharf. A Portland realty firm by the name of Russell & Ferry is given credit for naming Seattle "The Queen City," for in a circular in which they advertised for sale fifteen hundred acres of land near Seattle. they referred to the place as "the future Queen City of the Pacific." Gradually the name became a slogan.

The original pioneers now began to reap the benefits of their early hardships. Henry Yesler, William Bell, and Arthur and David Denny became very active in platting and selling their land. Those who care to consult the old records in the County-City Building will find these city plats of '69.

For Yesler almost more than for any of the other pioneers, this building period meant prosperity. From this time he began to make money, and became one of the richest men in town. In '68 he built a new sawmill. And as his property was in what was then the very choicest commercial section. he not only sold lots but furnished the lumber for the build-

ings. He owned the principal wharf in town and a number
of warehouses, and put up many buildings to rent. But he
still lived on in his first little white house at First and
James until 1883. He then cut down his big orchard on the
site of the present County-City Building, and built a fine
house that supplanted Terry's as "the finest home in Washington Territory."

When William Bell returned in 1870 to the place that
was just a bullet-ridden remnant of a settlement with the
inhabitants huddled in a blockhouse on the fringe of the
forest when he left, he found himself wealthy. As Bagley
says, "His holdings had been advanced in value as the town
was rapidly extending northward."

Mr. Bell gave to the city the street names: Broad Street.
Clay, Cedar, Vine, Wall, Battery, Virginia, Olive, Lenora.
and Stewart. Virginia and Olive were named for two of his
daughters; the married name of the latter was given to
Stewart; and Lenora was named for Virginia Bell's warm
friend, the younger of the two covered-wagon daughters of
Arthur Denny. Seattle is graciously honored by the names
of three little girls who landed with the Seattle Pilgrims.

Arthur Denny returned from his duties in Congress in
'66, free for the first time since 1853 to actually settle down
and live in the city he had helped found. In '66 he built his
permanent home on that part of his donation claim which is
bounded by Union and University Streets, and First and
Second Avenues—now known as the Arcade Block. Where
but a few years ago this house was surrounded by a garden.
orchard, and pasture, the heaviest of the city's traffic now
eddies and whirls. This was the home in which Mr. Denny
lived for the rest of his life; the home which became the
landmark remembered by many today. It remained there
even after the city crowded and jostled about it.

At this time David Denny filed his first plat of what
was called "North Seattle," which not only bore temper-

ance names, but names that reflect the political faith of his father who had fought under "Old Tippecanoe"—names such as "Harrison" and "Republican."

As the first step in the development of "North Seattle" in 1870, David and Louisa built a large, comfortable house on Lake Union, where they and their eight children were to spend many happy years. What is now a teeming factory district was then a home in the woods on the shore of a lovely lake. The acres which David had cleared with his own axe and muscle now began to bring returns. Today the busy thoroughfare of Denny Way runs through his claim, a memorial to this young huntsman and woodsman who wrested it from the wilderness. He continued a huntsman even as the town grew and is credited with killing the last elk in what is now the City of Seattle.

David's good neighbor, Thomas Mercer, also began to reap the reward of his stump hauling and clearing. The little woods trail between the two families now became cleared so that they could see each other's homes—the forest was giving way to the axe—the town was creeping north.

Another plat which we find recorded at that time, labeled "Union City," was filed by Harvey L. Pike, whose land lay between Lake Union and Lake Washington. He too, like Mercer before him, dreamed of the day when there would be a canal between the two lakes, and in his plat he reserved a strip of two hundred feet for that purpose. He actually began to dig and with pick and shovel and wheelbarrow excavated a ditch of considerable length, but soon realized that it was too big a task for one man's shovel and muscle.

That same year Edward Hanford filed the plat of his donation claim south of town, which reflected the Civil War and local Indian War influence, for we find in the old records the street names: Lander, McClellan, Stevens, Sheridan, Grant, Sherman, Sterrett, and Gansevoort.

Mr. Hanford was not only developing his acres, but was

weaving into the fabric of the town's civic growth that splendid and deeply religious influence that was to make the name of "Hanford" so honored ever after.

For nearly twenty years these pioneers had struggled on through indescribably hard years; they were not suddenly rich but were beginning to see signs of a harvest. Boren, less aggressive than the others, had parted with his land. Frye. who had not taken a claim, began to profit by building. He had worked hard, been sawyer in the mill, had owned cattle. started the first butcher shop, operated a bakery, been partner in the grist mill, been captain on the steamer *J. B. Libby*. and now he began building. Dexter Horton reaped his reward in his bank, his wharf, and similar enterprises. Terry. the largest land-holder of them all, was not here at the harvest time; nor was Dr. Maynard. Much of the important building of this rapidly moving period was going upon what had been Dr. Maynard's original claim.

Those who had seen Seattle grow from nothing in 1852 must have looked on in bewilderment to see two-story buildings going up, a few of them brick, some with brick fronts, and all of them with the familiar "front" of the frontier-West style. Pile drivers were driving piles for the erection of wharves and the water front was losing its green outline and gentle beach where canoes had so recently come sliding in. Seattle was rapidly becoming the metropolis of the little towns about the Sound. Several of her little steamers were visiting the logging and farming communities of the Snohomish, Skagit, and Duwamish Rivers.

Seattle was growing because of its expectancy of the railroad, and in doing so was developing itself into a shipping and commercial center of strength and stability. The *Intelligencer*, speaking with editorial pride, said that it was "doing a business equal to a city treble its size as it is a center of trade for a considerable agricultural population and for many of the logging and milling points on the Sound."

Out of this activity grew the need for a wholesale general mercantile business, and the first house of this nature was Schwabacher Bros. & Co., hardware, saddlery and ship chandlery, whose advertisement appeared in the boom year '69. In October they announced "To the Inhabitants" "An Immense Attraction" and "Monster Opening" and a line of merchandise which not only included groceries but dry goods. Bailey Gatzert became their resident manager and enters the Seattle story at this point.

By 1870 the town had grown "away up the hill" to Third Avenue and there was a demand that that street be made passable. A large force of men and work cattle was put to work pulling and burning enormous old stumps, and filling in the gully. With as much pride in their progress as we today watch steam shovels improving the city, the townspeople watched the cattle and heard the men "Haw" and "Gee" them about as Third Avenue was being opened up from Yesler Way to Pike Street.

In a short time the demand came for sidewalks on Second and Third Avenues which, when built, were the plank walks familiar to early settlers.

While the progress of this period is evidenced in buildings, in trade and in population, other community interests are indicated in an account of the King County agricultural fair given in the *Intelligencer* for October 4, 1873. The fair lasted four days and was held in the buildings and on the ground of the University, school being dismissed for the occasion.

Although the editor regrets that "The men of our country have fallen far behind the ladies in bringing forward articles for exhibition," we read on and find among the exhibits from Seattle that "Mr. McGilvra had a pony and small jackass."

The ladies, however, with the work of their "fair hands," certainly carried off the honors. Miss Lilly Settle won a premium for salt-rising bread, Mrs. Yesler for beautifully arranged flowers, and other ladies for knitted hoods and socks and mittens, for rag carpets and log-cabin quilts, both in silk and worsted.

It was the day of wreaths, which were constructed of forest moss, of feathers, of seeds, and of sea moss. Frames were also in style and these were made of leather, of nuts, of cones, and of sea shells.

There were "numberless mats and tidys," "3 beautiful center table covers and 20 pretty little cushions." Raised worsted work was also listed and wax-work, one item being "white wax crosses, very pretty."

In among the more frivolous entries was one which read that, "Grandma Russell of Seattle had a nice home-made shirt."

The boom which resulted in so many activities was not confined to Seattle, although it was more marked here than anywhere. Meany says of this period:

*Industrial growth was present everywhere. The rivers and harbors were furnished with little steamers. Shipbuilding was begun and lumber exports pointed the way toward future wealth. Coal found a ready market. Fish and oysters were in demand. California to the south, Alaska to the north, the Islands and the Orient on the highway of the sea — everyone knew that Washington had a magnificent future. To hurry the dawning of that great day was the ambition alike of the patient pioneer and the impulsive newcomer. The one surest way to hasten that day was the construction of a railroad from the Mississippi River to tidewater on Puget Sound.

Washington Territory was everywhere taking on shape, both figuratively and actually. In 1863 the extreme eastern part of the Territory, feeling itself too far away from Olympia, just as northern Oregon had once felt itself too far away from the seat of government, became a separate territory known as Idaho. The eastern boundary was thus determined. In '72 the San Juan dispute over the boundary between the United States and Canada was settled, and the northern

---

*From *History of the State of Washington* by Edmond S. Meany. By permission of Macmillan Company, publishers.

boundary became fixed. Elwood Evans says that when all foreign claims had been effaced, Washington Territory became in truth and in fact Washington Territory.

The Territory had a keen interest in and a vital share in bringing about the purchase of Alaska by Mr. Seward in '67. Meany tells how a memorial presented by the Washington territorial legislature to Congress, *"praying that there be obtained certain fishing privileges along the coasts of Russian America . . . played a prominent part in a great national event," and goes on to say that when this memorial came into Seward's hands *"he made it the reason for beginning negotiations with Russia."

The occasion of Seward's visit to Seattle in '69 which we have referred to was brought about by a well known pioneer of Seabeck, Marshall T. Blinn. Mr. Seward had stopped at Victoria on his way to visit Alaska when Mr. Blinn invited him to see Puget Sound and offered to charter the steamer *Wilson G. Hunt* for the purpose. Mr. Seward accepted and the steamer made a quick swing around the Sound, making short visits at principal points. Seattle knew nothing of the visit of the distinguished guest until he appeared at six in the evening, but the people quickly gathered in his honor. The narrator of the event estimates that nearly everyone in town must have been down to the wharf to greet the visitor for it took nearly an hour for Mr. Seward to shake hands with the citizens as they filed past. He remarks that the town had not recovered from the excitement of a visit from Northern Pacific dignitaries two days before.

In numbers Seattle was small; but in ideas it was as big as we are today. The pioneers were laying a foundation big enough and wide enough and broad enough to support a great superstructure. They were preparing to be a great railroad terminus; in fact, they were even then a great ter-

---

*From *History of the State of Washington* by Edmond S. Meany. By permission of Macmillan Company, publishers.

minus and seaport in their potentialities and in the caliber of men who were here.

Many young professional men, who were more interested in empire building than they would have been in a gold rush, migrated to the Northwest on hearing that the Northern Pacific was to actually begin construction in 1870. These men were the new apostles of pioneering who were to write their names large in the second phase of Seattle's history.

Among those who came about this time and who were to have a part in the next Seattle adventure were James Colman, Judge Orange Jacobs, John Leary, and that silver-tongued orator, Thomas Burke. John McGilvra and James McNaught had already arrived.

Youth found its opportunity here and later in the seventies there arrived Robert Moran, a lad of eighteen with an aptitude for mechanics, who was to become Seattle's master shipbuilder; young John McGraw, who began as a clerk in the Occidental Hotel and later became Governor of the State, and a red-haired newsboy, Edmond Meany, who was to become one of the State's eminent historians.

The list grows long. We cannot name them all. A bit sadly we realize we have lost our little village Seattle and all the old intimacy—instead we have a town waiting for a railroad to make her a city.

CHAPTER XXIII

THE MAY DAY PICNIC

SEATTLE HAD known many struggles. It had had a struggle from the first—a struggle for existence; a fight to keep body and soul alive; a fight for bread, a roof, safety. Its people had blazed trails, made roads, fought Indians, carried coal upon their backs, and torn a living from among the stumps; always they had been tugging, digging, pulling, fighting at something that tried their souls and strained their backs— but always with the thought that it would not be for long, that soon many boats would be in the harbor, that a stream of people would come over the mountains through the pass and then, *then* the railroad would come! After that some of their burdens would be lifted; life would become easier. their hopes realized. Especially did this hope that life would become easier burn within the hearts of the women. But the pioneers' greatest fight was before them with the odds against them.

We have seen how from the very first summer the coming of the railroad runs like a dominating theme through the pioneer chapters. How that first year of '52 Dr. Henry Smith came from Olympia because he thought that Seattle would be the terminus, and then took up his claim at Smith's Cove, believing that to be the point where the railroad would touch the Sound; how David Denny named one of his first streets, the present Denny Way, "Depot Street"; and how David Blaine, Seattle's first minister, wrote enthusiastic letters about the coming of the road.

Then, in '53, how the news came that the newly appointed governor would survey for the northern road as he came west, and when he arrived, his unqualified enthusiasm over the feasibility of terminating such a road at Puget Sound. And then how the Indian War, coming so soon after the governor's arrival, halted the plans, and the Civil War following cut off all governmental aid. How the Indian

War had hardly ended before the pioneers were forming a
"Northern Pacific" of their own.

We recall that in 1864 the people heard with joy the
news that the government had granted a charter to the
Northern Pacific Railroad, and that six years later Jay
Cooke & Company had taken over the selling of the railroad
bonds. And so we have followed through the twenty years
of the pioneers' expectancy and preparation.

We of this generation can hardly realize the confidence
inspired by the name "Jay Cooke." The enterprise was as
good as completed when he took it in hand, for he went at
it in a big way, advertising the Puget Sound country widely and glowingly, so enticingly in fact with its advantages
of climate and productivity that it came to be known in the
East as "the banana belt." There was much ridicule, and
there were many doubters who remained unconvinced that
such a northern region could be anything but a place of
Arctic snow and ice.

This advertising, however, gave rise to the migration
from the East and contributed to Seattle's boom, which has
been described. But Seattle needed no flowery advertising
to whet its enthusiasm. It had the Snoqualmie Pass, which
was the lowest in the Cascades. It also had King County
coal, which was considered an especial inducement for bringing the railroad to Seattle.

The boom itself was a preparation. When the train would
come roaring in, as for a decade the pioneers had dreamed
of it, there would be schools and churches and a university;
industry, lumber, and coal; the beginning of commerce;
stores—a bakery, millinery, a jewelry store, and a meat
market; blacksmiths, and a saddle and harness maker; doctors, lawyers, and dentists; boiler makers, carpenters, paint-
ers; hotels; wharves; a big shipment of open and top bug-
gies—well, there was a terminus waiting for its road.

In '72 the *Intelligencer* wrote of Seattle:

It has a large steam sawmill, a grist mill, a soap factory, two breweries, a tannery, two shipyards, a sash and door factory, machine shops, seven wharves and warehouses, thirty-three stores, and about one hundred other businesses.

And so the founders of Seattle planned and waited. Meanwhile the railroad had been constructed north from Kalama as far as Tenino where it hung suspended like a question mark until the terminus should be decided. Then in the summer of '72, a committee of directors of the Northern Pacific visited Puget Sound to look over the ground and at last decide on the terminus. The excitement in the little town was at fever heat, and in all the other settlements from Olympia to Bellingham Bay, as well, for each also claimed the advantages of situation.

On the committee's arrival in Seattle, they asked the citizens to make pledges of a subsidy to the railroad for the location of the terminus. Thinking that the final decision depended upon their liberality, the people strained every purse in a stupendous effort to raise the subsidy. After a large sum had been raised privately, the following contributions were secured at a public meeting: 7500 town lots, 3000 acres of land, $50,000 in cash, $200,000 in bonds, and the use of a portion of the water front for terminal and depot purposes—in all, amounting in value to over $700,000, an enormous pledge for a little town of 1500 people.

The committee cruised about the Sound and were entertained by all the settlements. Each community offered a subsidy far out of proportion to its size and wealth, striving to impress the directors with the importance and desirability of its location. The directors listened to the settlers' arguments and considered what each settlement had to offer in the way of land and money. At the end of the week they left for the East, the choice of terminus resting between Tacoma, Mukilteo, and Seattle. With the Snoqualmie Pass opened and a road pointing the way to Seattle, and the unparalleled subsidy offered, its citizens felt confident of the outcome.

Such a nationally noted historian as Snowden says that everything "seemed to indicate that the builders of the road had no other terminus than Seattle in contemplation." Grant says:

> Every popular description of the route spoke of Seattle as the western terminus. This seemed to be taken for granted. The one great point in arguing the utility of the northern route was that the distance to Asia was less by some two hundred miles than by the central. Distance was, therefore, regarded as the determining factor in the location of the terminus. It would certainly be unreasonable to build a road on the ground of saving distance and then so place the terminus as to greatly diminsh that advantage. Seattle, therefore, felt perfectly confident that here the terminus would be located.

The matter dragged along for a year, with the people of Seattle eagerly awaiting and expecting the confirmation of their hopes. At last Arthur Denny received this telegram:

> Kalama. July 14, 1873
>
> A. A. Denny, Seattle
> We have located the terminus on Commencement Bay [Tacoma]
>
> R. D. RICE
> J. C. AINSWORTH
> *Commissioners*

It was a staggering blow, a bolt from a clear sky. Sudden and cruel. Arthur Denny sat with bowed head, as one stunned. It seemed as if he could not go out and tell his friends. They had felt so sure. For years they had worked and planned on the coming of the railroad. Every improvement, every investment made revolved about its coming. Now the very foundation of all their hopes and plans was knocked out from under them. There was the little town huddled about the mill, confident one day that the prize would be theirs—and then with cruel unexpectedness hearing the next day that they had lost. That which had seemed so real was but a rainbow bubble, and it had burst! It meant financial ruin for many. It meant another stretch of years of poverty.

Silently, Mr. Denny showed the telegram to his wife. At last he pulled himself together, took his hat, went out of the house and slowly down the street—all life, all vim gone out of his steps.

This is what had happened. Perhaps Grant explains it as dispassionately and clearly as anyone:

Like all great corporations it [the Northern Pacific Railroad Company] had become divided into a number of distinct departments, and one of the most powerful of these was the townsite company, which went under the name of the Lake Superior and Puget Sound Land Co. . . . . . The road must be brought up quickly to pay interest on its bonds. To do this the company felt that it must follow the policy of building its own cities. The advantages of this were two. Fisrt, it enabled the road to get, without cost, all the land necessary for its own depots and round houses, shops and sidetracks; and second, it enabled it to acquire land at a minimum price, and then, through its own agents, to sell town lots at an immense advance. . . . . The company would most assuredly not rest without creating a city on Puget Sound. It would make one from the bedrock. If Seattle had been a wilderness its site would no doubt have been seized upon.

So Seattle found that its very preparation for being a terminus had prevented its being one. It took several days to recover from the disappointment. Business was paralyzed. Many thought that Seattle would never be more than a sawmill town and closed their shops and moved away. But there were a few of the old guard left who did not know defeat and who knew how to fight. Right here they made a determined stand that decided the fate of Seattle.

They called a town meeting. They were indignant, hurt; but not weakened. They spent no time in self-pity. In their sober senses they assembled themselves at Yesler's Pavilion and doggedly announced that if the railroad would not come to them they would build their own railroad. Grant says:

Probably no city showed more instantaneously than Seattle its pluck and daring and its willingness to appeal from the decision of a great corporation to its own advantages and enterprise. In less than a week a policy was formulated which has been the controlling principle of the city ever since. It was this: Let Seattle rely on itself, build and run its own railroads and by force of its position compel commerce to recognize it. The columns of the city papers were filled with bold declarations and the people showed the utmost courage in sustaining them.

Selucius Garfielde, fiery orator of the day, pointed out that a line through their beloved Snoqualmie Pass connecting Walla Walla with Seattle would open up that country and bring the produce from eastern Washington to Seattle cheaper than by the way of the Northern Pacific.

A few days after this meeting a company under the name of "Seattle and Walla Walla Railroad and Transportation Co." was organized, and stock quickly subscribed. The trustees of the company were: Arthur Denny, president; John Collins; Franklin Matthias; Angus Mackintosh; Henry Yesler; James McNaught; Judge J. J. McGilvra; Dexter Horton and James M. Colman.

An appeal for financial help was made to the legislature. Arthur Denny and Judge McGilvra were appointed to visit Walla Walla to obtain the cooperation of that territory. They were received with enthusiasm and the people were much interested. But by spring Walla Walla's enthusiasm had subsided, and the legislature failed to give the hoped-for aid. Seattle found itself where it had begun. It realized that if anything was to be done Seattle must do it alone.

A survey was made to estimate the cost of the road, and it was reported that it would cost between three and four millions. Not having such a fabulous sum, nor any way of getting it, the people decided to *build the road with their own hands.*

At what the *Intelligencer* called "a Mass Railroad Meeting," with A. A. Denny, chairman, and Roswell Scott, secretary, the citizens decided to begin the building of their railroad at a big community picnic on May 1st. Speeches were made by John Leary, Judge Orange Jacobs, Beriah

THE MAY DAY PICNIC

Brown, and Judge McGilvra. Port Madison, Port Gamble. and Port Blakely were invited to join them on the picnic day.

So, on May 1, 1874, there was a magnificent manifestation of that definite and tangible thing which has been referred to ever since as "the Seattle spirit." Early that May morning, the people of Seattle were awakened by the shrill mill whistle and by the boats in the harbor—but not for the daily work. The church bells rang—but not for worship. The university bell rang—but not for the loitering school children, but to summon the people to a great May Day party, epochal in the progress of Seattle. Cannons boomed and the brass band played.

That morning Seattle was deserted. All the teams in town were commandeered to take the food, the women and children. On that May morning in one great exodus—in wagons, in boats, on horseback, and on foot—preachers, gamblers, teachers, laborers, bankers, and saloon keepers moved out to the old mill at what is now Georgetown and began to build their railroad.

The grade was laid out along the country road from one hundred and fifty feet east of the intersection of Spokane and Grant Streets to a point a short distance south of where the old brewery at Georgetown now stands. Three hundred feet north of the brewery was a little, trickly stream where there was a half-completed grist mill—where the bridge is now at Lucile Street—and there in the mill the women laid out the noon dinner. It was a wonderful dinner, so Mr. Harry Whitworth, one of the pioneers who was a young engineer at that time and helped lay out the grade, told me. They had chicken and ham, pickles and jellies, pies and cakes, hot biscuit and coffee. One wonders how the biscuits were baked. Perhaps there was a stove in the old mill, or perhaps those pioneer women had not lost their old knack of baking bread over a camp fire.

Of course, after the bountiful dinner the picknickers had

to have speeches, and some of the leading citizens were called upon. John Denny was the first speaker; Judge Orange Jacobs the next. It amused the audience to see their dignified judge in mud-stained work clothes. Henry Yesler. that man of action and few words, who stood near by whittling, was then called upon. He threw down the stick and pocketed his knife, mounted the wagon, took one look at the sky, and said, "Quit your fooling and go to work"; and *they quit their fooling and went to work*. And what better proof have we than from one who remembers that the next day every one in town had blistered hands?

It was not a gay party with May pole and dancing; it was not a pretty party with spring flowers and song. It was a party of stubborn and determined men with their picks and shovels and axes, of helpful women with their baskets of food and words of cheer. That May Day was not blossom time to them. It was the day they sounded their battle cry and made known to the world that Seattle could not be crushed. At sundown they looked ahead and saw the great forest; they looked back and saw the little road; but that little road gave them courage. That night as they turned homeward every man pledged himself to work one day a week to finish the road over the pass.

The account of that May Day's accomplishment as it was told to me by those who remember the occasion is supplemented by an account of it as it appeared in the *Intelligencer* of May 2, 1874:

May day was celebrated by our citizens in all respects according to the prearranged programme viz: by all hands turning out and breaking ground on the Seattle and Walla Walla Railroad, and doing substantial work in aid of that enterprise.

Early in the morning the firing of cannon, the ringing of bells and the strains of the brass band, called the attention of our people to what was going forward. The business of the city was entirely suspended, and our citizens almost to a man proceeded to the appointed spot near the mouth of the Duwamish river, and the celebration commenced in good earnest. The only misfortune of the occasion happened to the steamer, *Comet*, which with the schooner *C. C. Perkins* in tow, got aground on the mud flats with a large number of ladies and gentlemen on board who experienced a good deal of difficulty in getting to the scene of action, while the vessels were obliged to remain on the flats until the returning of the tides which enabled them to reach their destinations. All the vehicles in town were kept running two and from the grounds, and carried all who had not taken passage in boats.

No time was spent in idle ceremonies, but able-bodied men to the number of near three hundred "hauled off their coats and rolled up their sleeves" knowing that "Jordan is a hard road to travel" but with a steadfast determination to travel nevertheless. The utmost enthusiasm prevailed, and we do not hesitate to say that as much labor was performed as would have been done by the same number of men at a high rate of wages.

At twelve o'clock the laborers proceeded to the place appointed for dinner, where a number of ladies were in waiting with what they had abundantly provided for before the arrival of the workers, who proceeded to convince the ladies that they fully appreciated their skill in the art of cookery. The number of persons present was truly surprising.

After dinner was over, the venerable old pioneer, Hon. John Denny was vociferously called for. He mounted a wagon and, with a force and vigor surprising in one of his years, made a short, but appropriate speech. Chief Justice Jacobs was then loudly called for. He presented himself to the assembled multitude in a suit of working garments which, together with certain previous maneuvers on his part with mattock and shovel, clearly demonstrated that he had not come there to play. However, with true American instincts he did not fail to respond in a brief, but eloquent speech, which was loudly applauded.

H. L. Yesler, Esq., was then called for. He responded in brief, but exceedingly appropriate terms. He said it was time to quit fooling and go to work.

The result of the day's operations were preeminently satisfactory; and the whole affair clearly demonstrates how thoroughly in earnest our people are in their determination to push forward this railroad enterprise. The banker, the merchant, the lawyer, the doctor, the laborer and all classes of our citizens were seen working side by side, while the enthusiasm of the ladies was fully equal to that of the gentlemen. There can be no doubt about the seriousness of our citizen in their determination that the Seattle and Walla Walla Railroad shall be a success.

Brave as the little town was, a struggle was to follow That May Day picnic had to be supplemented by many courage-testing years. Voluntary work was kept up for some time, and by October twelve miles had been graded. But even with all the citizens' help the directors had a hard task before them; money was hard to get and the enterprise lagged. It was never given up, however.

Three years passed after that fateful telegram reached Seattle. The town was surrounded by those who ridiculed and worked against it, but instead of being deserted as its rivals predicted, it increased its population at the rate of one or two hundred a year. The big railroad picnic had advertised the town and stories of its spirit and pluck had reached the outside world and attracted some of the great tide of immigration of those years. Of this period Grant says:

> It was a significant struggle. It would seem to be most unequal with everything in favor of the corporation with its millions of acres, its Eastern bankers, its European connections and its influence in Congress. Seattle was a mere pigmy in comparison, a simple village in the woods. It had no capitalistic or political connections and no representation in Congress. The only thing to command respect was its assertion of the right to exist.

By this time the directors of the Seattle and Walla Walla Railroad realized that voluntary labor was uncertain and inadequate, and that something had to be done to put the road on a more businesslike basis. Their immediate objective now was to build as far as the coal mines which Capt. William Renton had developed at Renton.

They needed money and they needed the right man. Looking about they found him in James M. Colman, one of their own members, a leader of outstanding ability, willing to give unstintingly of his time, energy, and money. Although Mr. Colman was not a rich man, he offered to give $20,000 of his savings if the community would add $40,000. The proposal was accepted. Mr. Colman went to work at once and, in March 1877, finished the road to Renton with a branch to the mines at Newcastle. This completed the first section of the Seattle and Walla Walla Railroad headed for the Snoqualmie Pass.

The railroad to the coal fields was immediately successful and the stockholders met and with mutual felicitations elected the following directors: A. A. Denny, Franklin Matthias, James Colman, Bailey Gatzert, William Renton. James McNaught, John Collins, Angus Mackintosh, Henry Yesler, William Bell, Jesse W. George, C. B. Shattuck and John Leary.

Hopeful as the directors were their railroad, as the Seattle and Walla Walla, was never to fulfill its destiny. Ahead of them were over twenty years of battling single-handed for recognition as a railroad terminal. Their struggle through those years is one of the plucky and stirring periods of Seattle history, but it belongs to a decade not included in this volume.

Of this struggle Grant writes, "To prove its divine right to live a city must endure opposition, both fair and foul and must show that it possesses the courage and strength to withstand it."

That they did prove their "divine right to live" we have abundant proof in the city of today. Since that memorable day in 1874 when Seattle was but a sawmill town clustered about Yesler's mill, four hundred thousand people have come and made their homes on its hills and on the shores of its lakes and Bay; great ships from the Orient and from all world ports enter its harbor; airplanes roar back and forth over its tall buildings to the landing fields; and four great railroads thunder into its big terminal stations: the Northern Pacific, the Great Northern, the Chicago, Milwaukee, St. Paul & Pacific and the Union Pacific.

The Northern Pacific came first and so became Seattle's first transcontinental railroad just as the pioneers had hoped it would; the Great Northern came as the result of the faith of James J. Hill in the future of Seattle; and the Milwaukee was the result of the recognition of the city's possibilities by E. H. Harriman; the Union Pacific ties the Northwest to the rich Southland.

And the little line which Seattle commenced to build is now a part of the Chicago, Milwaukee, St. Paul & Pacific and today carries the weight of great, modern trains upon its road bed.

And on through the Snoqualmie Pass where the pioneers grubbed and dug their way for a wagon road, the Milwaukee today passes easily, electrically, over the Cascades.

All that has been accomplished began in the resolute stand taken by the pioneers when the news of their loss of the terminal came to them. Had they been disheartened, given up the battle and accepted defeat the history of Seattle would have been written different, and the "little lumber camp at the mouth of the Duwamish" would not be today one of the leading cities of the nation.

There are few left now who remember that tremendous reaction, or that Seattle's first railroad was the result of a May Day picnic. That day—May 1, 1874—when the citizens took pick and shovel and as a community went out to build a railroad by hand, that day, they turned their backs upon pioneer days forever; they showed their stamina, demonstrated their ability to weather storm and stress, ridicule and opposition; they stood the test and earned the right of their beloved city to live and to grow to greatness. On that day they wrote the name of Seattle in the annals of history and in the list of great world cities.

Here closes the pioneer period of Seattle history.

CHAPTER XXIV

As I BEGAN this story of Seattle in an intimate way, so I shall conclude, by paying a tribute of tenderness to those who have inspired me by the way they have met life's challenge.

Of that band that landed at Alki on that November morning, there is only one left in this year of 1931—Rolland Denny, who was the little red-haired baby born in Portland twelve days after his mother's perilous journey across the plains. His life has spanned the years from the Indian cayuse to the automobile, from the Indian canoe to the airplane. He has seen Seattle grow and change from one roofless cabin in the wilderness to a city of towering buildings; he has seen the winding Indian trails give way to straight and paved streets; his ears have heard the cry of the cougar, the chanting of the medicine man—and the voice of the radio. Coming here on the sailing vessel *Exact*, he now travels far and wide on palatial boats that steam into the harbor, on trains that roll into the stations, and in airplanes that soar aloft.

All the others of that little band have answered the Master's call, their work well done. The world is richer for their having lived; their names, written in history, are an inspiration for those who follow; their memories, a blessed heritage.

Of those of the Seattle founders who started out from Cherry Grove in the four emigrant wagons eighty years ago, all lived to see the settlement take the form of a thriving little town. Some lived to see it a great city.

The little six-year-old girl, Louisa Catherine, whose memories of her trip across the plains, and the years that followed, inspired the writing of this book is remembered as Louisa C. Frye. Her life together with that of the young sawyer at Yesler's mill is of more than family interest, for these two were among the first builders of Seattle. She was always in every enterprise, by her husband's side and it was these two who visioned and then built Seattle's first opera house.

The other little covered-wagon girl, Lenora Denny, who trotted barefoot over the hot sands, became one of the most beloved women of Seattle, known for her beautiful character and many charities.

Mary and Arthur, and David and Louisa all lived to a beautiful old age, loved and cherished by their children and grandchildren.

The story of David and Louisa, the John Alden and Priscilla of the settlement, is a romance from beginning to end. The sweetbriar bride became the sweetbriar matron, for wherever she lived she continued to plant her garden. David will always be remembered as the youth who held the fort at Alki until the others came. He grew to be a rich man but he did not stop there. He was in every big city enterprise. He helped to install the water system, the electric lights, and the street railway. To all of these he pledged himself and his fortune, that he might do greater things for his beloved city.

And then the crash came, the financial panic of '93, and David lost everything that he had crossed the plains to win. In terms of money he died a poor man. Every penny of his hard-earned wealth, which more than paid his obligations, was exacted from him.

Then, broken and sick and old, he turned again to the forest. All that he had left was a place in the wilderness that he had given to his daughter, out where Washelli is now. When he left his city home for the last time, he said as he paused at the door, and sadly looked about, "I'll never look upon Seattle again." Then, like a sorrowing father turning his back upon an ungrateful child, he went out of the city to his humble home in the woods. The forest had given him shelter when he first came, the forest sheltered him and hid his wounded heart in the end.

Yet, with all this sadness, I cannot write David's life as having had an unhappy ending. A life so well spent, so tenderly cherished by loved ones, and a name written so generously into the history of Seattle, a name that has come down to the city of today as a synonym of all that is upright and honest, are greater than wealth.

David went first. Some years later in the last summer of Louisa's life, she asked to be taken where she could see the water and hear the waves on the beach. There in a little cottage, facing west, within sound of the lapping waters of Puget Sound, she passed on to meet David on that other shore.

I shall close, as I began, with Mary and Arthur, for it was their decision one winter evening in Illinois that started the four wagons on their westward journey.

Mary Denny, the loving helpmate of her husband throughout their long journey, will always be remembered in the hearts of Seattle as the typical pioneer mother and wife, one of those women who followed their men in the conquest of the West.

Arthur stands out as a leader, staunch and true. As he began, so he continued, a dominant figure in the Seattle drama. This leadership came to him all unsought. The little settlement turned to him as toward a father, and whatever demands were made upon him he answered, whether trivial or serious, large or small. His greatest service as a leader was that even as a young surveyor he saw the possibilities of Seattle as a great seaport and railroad terminus and all through the years helped to direct the little town to that end.

His donation claim in the center of the city made him wealthy, and there he lived until his death, a patriarchal figure. When, as the city grew up around him, it was suggested that he give up the old homestead with its simple, old-fashioned house, he would answer with his characteristic humor, "Yes, but what shall I do with my cow?" That cow pasture in the heart of the city has become a Seattle tradition. It parallels the famous Boston cow paths.

The gabled house, set high up on a terrace and reached by a flight of stone steps, was connected with a woodshed and apple house by a covered porch. The whole spread over a good portion of the First Avenue and Union Street lots. On Second Avenue was the barn, the chicken house, the famous cow pasture, and the orchard, where small boys "hooked" apples from green-apple time to picking time.

The terrace along the entire length of the block of First Avenue was a wonderful place for the whole town to dig heels into and perch like a flock of blackbirds when watching the procession go down "Front Street" on circus day or on the Fourth of July. Then was the house thrown open to old friends who made a day of it.

While Arthur Denny lived the people came in streams to that house for advice and help. As a child I remember both the old-fashioned parlor and the sitting room filled with people waiting their turn to enter his office.

I am not writing this as his grandchild. In this book he has not been my grandfather as much as the leader of the four wagons and one of the founders of a great American city; a city raised on the foundation built by the pioneers. What those pioneers have done cannot be counted or measured or weighed. They builded better than they knew.

As we who come afterward and find things so easy, drive around Alki Point and come to that modest monument with the twenty-four names of that little band inscribed thereon, let us pause a moment; let us replace the pavilion, the band-stand—and if it be summer—the crowded beach and the gay summer pageantry there with another scene: the forest, the Indians, the sullen, lowering clouds, the driving rain, the women and children seeking shelter under the dripping trees and warmth from a flickering fire; and the men struggling to get their goods beyond the incoming tide, then working desperately to build a roof before night.

Surely, we owe those pioneers—those pilgrims of ours— a debt of gratitude. Oh, speak not lightly the word "Pioneer," but gratefully, lovingly—reverently.

INDEX

Index

383

254; work in legislature, 267; plans university with Bagley, 273-276; gives land for university, 278; appointed to land office, 280; elected to Congress, 298-299; speech in Congress, 331; received telegram about terminus, 366; his home, 379; later years, 379-380; 6, 34, 40, 51, 52-53, 79, 81, 87, 105, 150, 188, 194, 196, 198, 207, 211, 222, 246, 265, 277, 281, 304, 347, 356.

Denny, David, starts for Puget Sound, 28; explores Duwamish, 29; historic first letter, 32; explores Elliott Bay, 64-66; discovers Salmon Bay, 84-85; marriage of, 89; discovers McCormick murder, 167; interest in temperance, 337; Indians spare house, 252; later years, 378-379; 15, 31, 32, 33, 36, 43, 190, 194, 226, 324.

Denny-Horton-Phillips, 138, 188.

Denny, Inez, 271, 276.

Denny, John, arrives, 264; friend of Lincoln, 264; lectures, 338; grief over Lincoln, 299; 285, 296, 297, 338, 372.

Denny, Mrs. John (Sarah Latimer Boren), 34, 73, 264.

Denny, Lenora, 77, 275, 356, 378.

Denny, Loretta, 34, 264, 275.

Denny, Louisa Boren (also sweetbriar bride), flower garden, 102; experience with Indians, 205; rushes to blockhouse, 238; child born in blockhouse, 247; later years, 279.

Denny, Louisa Catherine (also "Kate" Denny and Louisa C. Frye), before fire at Cherry Grove, 1; bidding playmate bood-bye, 12; crossing plains, 13-14; in Indian attack, 17; marriage of, 273; 3, 85, 100, 127, 263, 377.

Denny, Mary (Mrs. Arthur Denny), decides to come west, 1; leaving old home, 1; weeps at Alki, 40; with her baby at Alki, 44; cares for Mrs. Low, 96; last days, 378; 12, 41, 43, 49, 74, 85, 210.

Denny, Orion, 275.

Denny party, leave Illinois, 3; members of, 4; cross Missouri, 6; Illinois to Laramie, 5-12; on Snake River, 17; encounter with Indians, 17-18; cross Blue Mountains, 20; reach The Dalles, 22; on Columbia, 23; reach Portland, 26.

Denny, Rolland, 32, 273, 275, 377.

Devore, Rev. John F., 267.

District Court, second session, 173.

Doane, Rev. Nehemiah, 267, 311.

Douglas, Sir James, 221.

Dutch Ned, 349-350.

Duwamish Head, 30.

Duwamish settlement, 32.

Duwamish tribes, 28.

Duwamish Valley, 30.

Duwamps precinct, 79.

E

Eaton, Capt. Charles, in Indian War, 212.

Eaton, O. M., 116, 193.

Ebey, Col. Isaac, 82, 258.

Eliot, President Charles, of Harvard, 290.

Eliza Anderson, 270, 276, 288, 292, 322, 327.

Elliott Bay, shore explored by Bell, Boren and Denny, 64; origin of name, 65; first summer on, 72-73.

Evans, Elwood, 165, 339.

Exact, sailing of, 34; voyage to Puget Sound, 36.

F

Fairy, first American steamboat, 147, 200.

Fanjoy, Joseph, 116, 190, 198, 208.

Fay, Captain Robert C., 28, 29, 32, 35.

Fay, Grandma (see Mrs. Alexander), 35, 39, 62.

Felker House, 140, 239.

Felker, Capt. L. M., 70, 140.

Ferry, Elisha P., 339.

First: Christmas at Alki, 47; store, 68; sermon, 77; plat filed, 106, 108; minister, 122; church, 123; school teacher,

Low, Mrs. Lydia, spanks Indian, 49; alone at Alki, 96-97.
Low, Minerva, 42.
Lumber, shipment in 1852, 71; early logging methods, 115; industry, 190.

M

Mackintosh, Angus, 368, 375.
Maddocks, M. R., 335.
Mail service, 128-129; boats, 147, 148.
Maine liquor law, 196.
Major Tompkins, 148, 149, 200.
Maple, E. B., joins father on Duwamish, 73.
Maple, Jacob, took claim, 30, 31, 115, 324.
Maple, Jane, 262.
Maple Prairie, 29.
Maple, Samuel, 30, 31, 47, 190, 220.
Massachie Jim, 116.
Mason, Charles H., 210, 222.
Masonic Lodge, St. John's Lodge, 274, 345.
Matthias, Franklin, 113, 173, 198, 368, 375.
Maurer, David, 140, 175.
Maynard, Dr. David S., arrives and stakes claim, 66-67; packs salmon, 67; first store, 68; justice of peace, 79; obtains legislative divorce, 82; clears point, 105; city plat, 107; donates land, 124; first realtor, 138; first blacksmith, 139; clerk of court, 165; friendship with Chief Seattle, 206; moves Indians, 223; moves to Alki, 256; sells Alki, 269; first hospital, 326; trades Alki, 350; litigation, 351; two wives, 352; dies, 352.
Maynard, Catherine (the widow Broshears), marriage to Dr. Maynard, 82; plants dandelion, 103; tribute to, 250; "saves Seattle," 250-251; nurse in hospital, 326.
May Day Picnic, account of in *Intelligencer*, 372-373.
McAleer, Hugh, 263, 283, 293.
McCarty, A. W., 172.

McClellan, Capt. George B., 150-151, 298.
McConaha, Eugenia, 267, 275.
McConaha, George, arrives, 69; Monticello, 81; president of council, 158; 166, 168, 169.
McConaha, Mrs. Ursula, 231, 261.
McCormick murder, 116.
McGilvra, John J., 294, 305, 339, 362, 368.
McGraw, John, 362.
McMillan, Maria, 262; Rev. J. R., 262.
McNatt, Francis, 173; Mrs., 324.
McNaught, James, 338, 362, 368, 375.
McNeill Island, 171.
Meany, Edmond S., 360.
Medicine Creek treaty, 183.
Meeker, Ezra, marks Oregon Trail, 19; visits Seattle, 118-119; at McNeill Island, 150; goes back through Naches Pass, 152, 218, 219.
Meig's Mill, 190, 240.
Mercer, Asa, first instructor of university, 284; gets students for university, 288; conceives plan to bring girls, 209; brings first party, 310; elected to legislature, 313; second "Mercer girls" expedition, 313; motives attacked, 316-318; sells machinery in San Francisco, 320; 286, 287, 300, 320, 323.
Mercer, Alice, 275, 341.
Mercer, Eliza, 126, 134, 261.
Mercer, Mary Jane, 126, 134, 261.
Mercer, Susan, 126, 134, 220, 247, 263, 275.
Mercer, Thomas, locates claim, 75; returns with daughters, 134; brings first team, 135; first transfer, 136; names lakes, 137; warned of Indian uprising, 219; Indians spare house of, 252; second marriage of, 262; 190, 192.
Mercer Girls, first expedition, 308-313; reception for, 311; names of first party, 312; second expedition, 313-323; voyage to Seattle, 317; experience in San Francisco, 320.
Meydenbauer, William, 326, 342.
Monticello convention, 81.